The Fight for the White House

The Fight for the White House

The Story of 1912

by FRANK K. KELLY

Thomas Y. Crowell Company

NEW YORK, ESTABLISHED 1834

To My Mother and Father:
Mr. and Mrs. Francis M. Kelly

15803

Bibliography and Acknowledgments

Many scholars have labored industriously and brilliantly to bring together much information and understanding about the Progressive period, and there are a number of excellent full-length biographies of the three men who dominated the American scene in 1912. In entering this field, the author of the present volume has concentrated upon a single year in an era crowded with significant happenings, and he has focused upon Taft, Roosevelt, and Wilson in terms of that one year.

The author of this book has not attempted to extend the boundaries of original research in this period. He has relied upon the large mass of existing material, and has interpreted this material from his own viewpoint—with due recognition of the conflicting opinions of scholars in the field.

At the writer's request, Henry M. Christman of New York City went through the files of the New York *Times* and made notes on the wide variety of events that occurred in the crucial months of 1912. The writer wishes to express his thanks to Mr. Christman for this assistance.

For general information about what happened in that

year, the author consulted *The New International Year Book: 1912,* published by Dodd, Mead & Company, and *The World Almanac and Encyclopedia: 1913* (issued by the Press Publishing Company—the *New York World*), which covered events in 1912.

On the general atmosphere of the time and the social trends developing in the period, the author found the following books most useful:

> *The Age of Reform,* by Richard Hofstadter. (Knopf: 1955).
>
> *Rendezvous With Destiny,* by Eric Goldman. (Knopf: 1953).
>
> *Image of America,* by R. L. Bruckberger. (Viking: 1959).
>
> *A New History of the United States,* by William Miller. (Braziller: 1958).
>
> *Beveridge and the Progressive Era,* by Claude G. Bowers. (Houghton Mifflin: 1932).
>
> *History of the Progressive Party, 1912–1916,* by Amos R. E. Pinchot; edited by Helene Maxwell Hooker. (New York University Press: 1958).
>
> *The End of American Innocence,* by Henry F. May. (Knopf: 1959).
>
> *Woodrow Wilson and the Progressive Era,* by Arthur S. Link. (Harper: 1954).
>
> *Postscript to Yesterday* by Lloyd R. Morris (Harper: 1947).

For an understanding of Woodrow Wilson and for a detailed picture of his campaign methods, his campaign organization, and his political problems in 1912, the writer relied principally upon the eight-volume biography of Wilson written by Ray Stannard Baker, the memoirs of a New Jersey editor, James Kerney, and the comprehensive

study entitled *Wilson: The Road to the White House,* by
Arthur S. Link.

Baker had access to Wilson's letters and private papers.
Kerney was on close terms with Wilson all through 1912,
and yet saw him with the relatively objective eyes of a
newspaperman. Link has done a magnificent job of examin-
ing all the important newspapers of the period, and has
gathered all the pertinent information necessary for comprehension of Wilson's day-by-day behavior in 1912. As
he has indicated in the text of this book, the present writer
went to Link's work again and again to obtain authentic
material about the Wilson campaign.

The books most often consulted in the preparation of
this volume's analysis of Woodrow Wilson were:

> *The Political Education of Woodrow Wilson,* by James
> Kerney. (Century: 1926).
>
> *Woodrow Wilson's Own Story* (selections from Wilson's
> statements and speeches, edited by Donald Day).
> (Little, Brown: 1952).
>
> *Woodrow Wilson and the People,* by H. C. F. Bell.
> (Doubleday, Doran: 1945).
>
> *Woodrow Wilson: A Great Life in Brief,* by John A.
> Garraty. (Knopf: 1956).
>
> *The Woodrow Wilsons,* by Eleanor Wilson McAdoo,
> in collaboration with Margaret Y. Gaffey. (Mac-
> millan: 1937).
>
> *Woodrow Wilson,* by Ray Stannard Baker; eight vol-
> umes, including many of Wilson's letters. (Double-
> day, Doran: 1927–39).
>
> *Wilson: The Road to the White House,* by A. S. Link.
> (Princeton University Press: 1947).

The books which contained the most detailed and interesting information about William Howard Taft are these:

The Life and Times of William Howard Taft, by Henry
F. Pringle. Two volumes. (Farrar & Rinehart: 1939).
*Taft and Roosevelt: The Intimate Letters of Archie
Butt, Military Aide.* Two volumes (Doubleday:
1930).
William Howard Taft, by Herbert S. Duffy. (Minton,
Balch & Co.: 1927).
Recollections of Full Years, by Mrs. William Howard
Taft. (Dodd, Mead: 1914).

The two-volume study of Taft and his period by Pringle
is one of the finest biographies of our time. Pringle went
through the enormous collection of Taft's letters and papers,
and produced a work of art. The present writer—as he
has shown in the text of this volume—has used Pringle's
work as an authoritative source for a portrait of Taft's character in 1912.

Duffy's biography is friendly, almost adoring in tone.
Archie Butt's letters give delightfully informal and intimate
glimpses of the rotund President in times of pleasure and
sorrow. Mrs. Taft's memoirs have many revealing passages
about the life of the Taft family in the White House.

In the case of Theodore Roosevelt, of course, the writer
has consulted the Rough Rider's autobiography and published letters. In addition, the following books were very useful:

Theodore Roosevelt and His Time, by Joseph B. Bishop.
(Scribners: 1920).
Theodore Roosevelt, by Henry F. Pringle. (Harcourt,
Brace: 1931).
The Republican Roosevelt, by John M. Blum. (Har-
vard: 1954).
The Seven Worlds of Theodore Roosevelt, by Edward
Wagenknecht. (Longmans, Green: 1958).

The Roosevelt Family of Sagamore Hill by Herman
Hagedorn (Macmillan: 1954).

*The Free Citizen: Selections from Theodore Roosevelt's
Writings,* edited by Hermann Hagedorn. (Macmillan: 1956).

In search of a clearer understanding of two other notable
figures of the era—Bryan and La Follette—the writer examined the following volumes:

Memoirs of William Jennings Bryan, by himself and
his wife, Mary B. Bryan. (Winston: 1925).

Robert M. La Follette, by Belle Case La Follette.
(Macmillan: 1953).

Contents

Foreword

MR. EDISON SAID:

"We've got to start to make this world over"

In America it was the year of the automobile self-starter and the call of the Bull Moose, the year of the *Titanic's* sinking and the shooting of Teddy Roosevelt, the year when hundreds died in train wrecks and thousands of Model "T" Fords were rattling on the roads, the year when suffragettes marched on Fifth Avenue and the children of starving Massachusetts strikers sang the "Marseillaise" in a New York parade. Two new states—Arizona and New Mexico—joined the federal Union.

Women's skirts were long and hats were high. People were reading Zane Grey's *Riders of the Purple Sage,* Owen Johnson's *Stover at Yale,* Dorothy Canfield's *The Squirrel Cage,* and *The Financier* by Theodore Dreiser. Financiers were on the front pages of the newspapers—running the "beef trust," the "sugar trust," the "tobacco trust," "steel trust," and all

1

the other giant combinations that dominated America's economic life.

It was a year when the *World Almanac* gave page after page to lists of the kings and royal families then ruling the nations beyond America's shores—and after the foreign royalty came pages of "American Multi-Millionaires": the Vanderbilts, the Astors, the Goulds, the Rockefellers, the Morgans, the Whitneys, the Carnegies, the Armours. The benefactions of the rich were disclosed: endowments of colleges, gifts to hospitals, homes for the blind, donations to missions for the spread of Christianity in China.

In the course of the year J. Pierpont Morgan gave art treasures valued at fifty million dollars to the Metropolitan Museum of Art. A wealthy real estate man, D. M. Farson, gave one million to a religious sect known as the Holy Jumpers. John D. Rockefeller, Jr., put up a million to establish a psychological laboratory to save women from a life of crime, and formed a $50,000 fund to fight "white slavery."

George M. Cohan scored a smashing success in his own play, *Broadway Jones*, presented at his own theater with members of his own family in the cast. The critics welcomed a dramatization of Louisa M. Alcott's novel, *Little Women*, hailing it as "a lovely, fresh, wholesome play." Those who wanted something a bit naughty went to see *Never Say Die* or *Oh! Oh! Delphine!* at the Eltinge.

Millions of American women were members of social clubs and civic societies. Thirteen million American men belonged to fraternal organizations with such names as the Odd Fellows, the Sons of Temperance, the Tribe of Ben Hur, the Order of Owls, the United Ancient Druids, and the Order of the Blue Goose, which was headed by the Most Loyal Grand Gander and the Keeper of the Golden Goose Egg.

Six quarts of hard liquor could be purchased for one dollar from a mail-order house in Cincinnati. Regular customers could get a free booklet entitled "Secrets and History of

Making Liquors at Home." A competing company offered free tumblers and corkscrews. Meanwhile, a political party founded on the idea that intoxicating beverages should be prohibited in the United States—the Prohibition Party—was recruiting tens of thousands of new members.

The murder of a gambler, Herman Rosenthal, led to the exposure of pay-offs and bribery in the New York police force. Reporters around the country noted that similar corruption existed in other cities. The "muckraking" reporters and magazine writers turned up endless quantities of "muck," and reform movements rose and fell. Crime in America kept growing.

All the revelations of all the corruption did not dent the confident attitudes of most Americans. It was a year of fireworks and folly, of songs and fights, of confusion and passion and pain, and still a year of hope—of stubborn belief that in America, in spite of everything, the trend was upward. Somehow or other things were going to get better and better.

Of course, workingmen and housewives worried now and then about the High Cost of Living. According to the United States Commissioner of Labor, the average American family in 1912—consisting of 5.31 persons—had an average annual income of $827, or less than $2.50 a day. Out of this income, most families spent a third or more on food.

The price of sirloin steak had risen 17 per cent between June, 1911, and June, 1912, and round steak had risen even more. Pork chops, eggs, and butter also had become more expensive. Wages had not continued to climb as rapidly as living costs.

Yet there were consolations. There was no personal income tax, and other taxes were low. The federal debt amounted to $11 per person. Shoes, dresses, and men's suits were plentiful at fairly reasonable prices.

It was a year when millions of families began to think

about getting a motor car. Self-starters had been introduced on many models in January and February at the motor shows. Cars were running better, and seemed more trustworthy than the earlier machines with their intermittent banging and sudden explosions.

The Winton Six, for example, was advertised as "A Car for *All* the Family." The ad promoted the appeal of togetherness, of family unity. The Six was said to be "big enough, so that nobody need to be left behind—self-cranking—a car of distinction—the Winton Six solves the family problem."

But 1912 was really a year of triumph for the Model "T," Henry Ford's dream car, tossed together with a few nuts and bolts, and declared to be cheap enough for almost anybody to buy. In Ford's plants the first long assembly lines in America were operating: mechanics finished a new Ford every 93 minutes during the working day. The American carriage industry, which had been the largest in the world, was in a steep decline.

There were buggy shops and blacksmiths and livery stables in many places, but motor garages were opening in towns and cities from coast to coast. The states were launching large road-building programs, competing to attract the motorists who went dashing along, crouched behind the steering wheels, faces hidden by goggles and veils. California claimed to be "the motorist's paradise."

The building of highways, the outpouring of cars by the hundreds of thousands, renewed the people's thirst for the open spaces, for the possibilities of travel, for the chances of discovering new opportunities in the hills and valleys of the Far West. Bloody strikes might occur in the East, there might be misery in the slums and poverty on the eroded farms in the Alleghenies, but America was still on the move and could not be stopped. That was the theme song of the time.

Of the 94 million persons then living in the continental

United States, about 60 million were native-born—50 million whites, over 9½ million Negroes, nearly a half million American Indians. More than one-third of the population was composed of immigrants or the sons and daughters of immigrants—restless people from Ireland, Italy, France, Serbia, Germany, all the countries of Europe and other lands. Fourteen million of them were foreign-born, and many did not speak or understand the American language. But they hoped they had entered the Land of Progress; they shared the big American Dream.

Although 300,000 to 500,000 disillusioned or defeated immigrants gave up the struggle and left America each year to return to their old countries, a million newcomers arrived annually at American ports—driven by desperation or drawn by their hopes and ambitions. The gates stood open to people from almost every nation; only the yellow-skinned Chinese and Japanese were excluded—the Chinese by a federal law, the Japanese under a "gentleman's agreement" between the rulers of Japan and the government of the United States.

For the submerged millions around the globe America was a shining goal in 1912, a light upon the horizon. In America there remained free land for homesteaders. There were jobs to be gained, fortunes to be made. Corruption and evil did exist, but the doors of opportunity were unlocked.

To those who could read, advertisements promised a happy life and a full life—patent medicines to cure all diseases, teachers to help young men get fine jobs, ways to make all girls beautiful, tonics to make skinny folk robust, pills to take fat from those who had too much, potions to restore vigor to the old. For those who couldn't read, there were the encouragements of the salesmen with enticing products—and the salesmen were everywhere.

The salesmen and the advertisers asked rough questions and then gave smooth answers. "Why not make $200 a month?" demanded a well-fed man in one ad. "That's $50 a week, almost $10 a day. Sell Victor safes and fireproof boxes to merchants, lawyers, doctors, dentists, and well-to-do farmers, all of whom realize the need of a safe, but do not know how easy it is to own one." It was a time of cash buying, the use of currency; few people carried bank checks or relied on credit.

"Why don't you work for Uncle Sam?" asked another advertisement, reaching into the yearnings of second-generation Americans who saw security in a government position. "Civil Service courses. Thousands appointed every year. New books. Personal coaching."

"Are your lungs weak or painful? Do you have night sweats?" cried an advertiser in a nearby column. "Lung-Germine has cured advanced Consumption. Try a bottle."

Many were skeptical of the promises in the advertisements, but few were skeptical about the promises of the future in America. Everybody could rise, the people felt. Everybody could eat well, live well, and eventually ride in an automobile. Times were tough for some Americans, but golden days were coming—and coming fast.

Millions of Americans from the families of recent immigrants and from families long living in the rich land, shared the feeling voiced by the old inventor Thomas A. Edison, who growled to an interviewer: "We've stumbled along for a while, trying to run a new civilization in old ways. But we've got to start to make this world over." Edison wasn't a long-haired scientist, ignorant of the problems of men. He had developed his incandescent lamp, his talking machine, his carbon telephone transmitter, by facing practical puzzles and getting answers.

In America in 1912, millions were positive that Edison knew what he was talking about. When he spoke, they listened. They thought it was time to begin making the world over. If Edison said it could be done, they were sure it could be. They wanted a President who could show them how to do it.

And so above all it was a year that produced a Presidential campaign never matched in American history. The spectacle of 1912 is not likely to be seen in America again— a sitting President, a former President, and a future President fighting for the White House.

Theodore Roosevelt, rallying his followers to stand at Armageddon and battle for the Lord; William Howard Taft, seeing revolution just around the corner and crying that he would fight fiercely against "extremists"; and Woodrow Wilson, beating the backwoods and demanding for Americans "a new freedom" to let the people rule—these three antagonists waged a contest that aroused the nation and stirred the world. This book attempts to recapture the spirit of the struggle, to show the natures of the men, and to give a picture of the time—a time closely related to our own.

I. Thunder in January

With a long sigh that slipped heavily through his drooping mustaches, the twenty-seventh President of the United States awoke in a warm bed in a cold room on New Year's Day, 1912. The chill breeze blowing through open windows made William Howard Taft dig a little more deeply under his covers. He liked warmth and comfort, but he lay in a cold room because his wife Nellie needed plenty of fresh air to sustain her. Her health was delicate, and had been for a long time; his health was excellent, but he was willing to make any sacrifice necessary to keep Nellie happy.

Taft glanced over to the mahogany bed in which his wife slept. He was glad that she seemed to be resting well. He had slept soundly, as he always did. He could sleep in almost any weather, hot or cold; he had slept through a typhoon in the Philippines when he had been civil governor there. He had once slept through a storm at sea. He had even been able to get in his regular stretches of sleep when he had been campaigning for the Presidency in 1908—

a campaign into which he had plunged reluctantly, with many misgivings.

The bitter wind in the room reminded him that he would face another campaign this year, a campaign he hated to consider, an undignified rumpus in which he was likely to be forced into the mud of politics. The icy blast against his face also reminded him of the terrible day in March, 1909, when he had taken the oath as Chief Executive. His administration had not been given an auspicious beginning; that March 4th had brought the worst winter blizzard of the season, had blocked roads and paralyzed rail travel, so that many of the distinguished guests he had expected on that day were not able to arrive in time to see him take the reins of power from President Roosevelt.

Nellie and he had been guests of the Roosevelts in the White House on the night before the inauguration. When he had descended the long staircase to the great hall of the Executive Mansion on that morning in March, he had found Mr. Roosevelt twinkling with genial vitality. As usual, Mr. Roosevelt occupied the center of the scene.

"Well, Will, the storm will soon be over," Roosevelt assured him. "It isn't a regular storm. It is nature's echo of Senator Rainer's denunciations of me. As soon as I am out where I can do no further harm to the Constitution, it will cease."

Taft had laughed and answered: "You're wrong. It's my storm. I always said it would be a cold day when I got to be President of the United States."

Roosevelt had been joking and Taft had given a bantering reply, and yet there had been a serious undercurrent beneath their words. Taft had made it clear that he would take responsibility for what happened in his administration. Much as he admired Theodore, he had refused to submit to Mr. Roosevelt's domination.

Now he knew that he faced trouble from Theodore. Roosevelt felt that he had not run the country as Roosevelt would have run it in the last three years—and indeed he hadn't. He had more respect for the constitutional limitations on the Presidency than Theodore had ever shown. He wasn't Colonel Roosevelt of the Rough Riders; he was William Howard Taft from the solid city of Cincinnati, a man who had served his happiest years as a judge—and whose father and grandfather had been judges, devoted to the heritage of the law.

Nellie shifted a little in the bed near him, and Taft turned toward her. His mind moved to pleasanter thoughts. He always tried to get his mind free of unpleasant thoughts as quickly as possible. It didn't pay to worry; it didn't do anybody any good to fret and fume.

Lying there in the cold room, Will Taft remembered the winter's night in Ohio, long ago, when he had met Nellie at a coasting party on a steep hill in Mt. Auburn, the suburb on the edge of Cincinnati where he lived. He had taken her down the hill on his bobsled at the fastest speed he could manage, and she had bubbled with laughter. After that night they had gone sledding and dancing many times; they had taken parts in plays together; they had read poetry at the Literary Club; they had talked about the meaning of life— and suddenly they had realized they were in love.

She was eighteen then, and he was twenty-four, a big young man with too much weight and not many worries. She wasn't exactly beautiful, but she was attractive—a slim, quick, vivacious girl with a piquant pointed face, a sparkling wit, and dancing eyes. He hadn't been able to understand her interest in him; he wasn't a man about town or particularly active in social affairs; he wasn't especially ambitious. He liked his job as a law reporter on the Cincinnati *Commercial;* he was studying law, and hoped to get into legal practice, following in the steps of his father. Yet he hadn't expected to attract the attention of the delightful Nellie

Herron, whose mother and sisters were leaders of Cincinnati society.

Nellie had insisted that he had depths of energy and intelligence beyond his own awareness. Nellie had sparked him, teased him, and guided him all the way from Mt. Auburn to the White House. Nellie had encouraged him to take every hard or exciting job offered to him. Nellie had consented to go with him wherever he went, simply disregarding the state of her health. She suffered principally from nervousness and excitability, the doctors said. Despite her difficulties, she managed to be a good wife to him and a good mother to their three children.

She had helped him in his role as a judge by encouraging him to stand firmly on the principles of justice in which he believed. She had helped him in his career as solicitor general in Washington, through her skills as a hostess and her charm as a conversationalist. She had made herself respected and loved in the Philippines when he had been the American administrator of the islands acquired from Spain. She had been with him on many of his travels after he had been appointed secretary of war. She had urged him to climb higher and higher, until at last he had attained the pinnacle of the Presidency.

All along the way Taft had wondered about his own capacities. He felt at home on the bench as a federal judge, but his other jobs had not been of his own choosing. He did his best; he overcame his own indolence, his tendency to take things too easily; he labored in his office, he studied official reports, he went to endless numbers of tedious meetings. He tried to understand the people and the world around him; yet he often felt that the complexities of the problems he faced as President were too much for him—and perhaps too much for any man to handle.

His brother Charlie and his wife and Colonel Roosevelt

had insisted four years ago that he was the best-qualified man in the country to be President; they had finally convinced him that he was really the man who should be in the White House. Theodore had told him that he was "a blessed old trump" and predicted that he "would be the greatest President, bar only Washington and Lincoln. . . ." His brother had felt that Theodore was right; so had his wife.

Of course, Theodore had changed. But Nellie hadn't. His brother Charlie hadn't. His closest friends hadn't. And he wasn't willing to let Theodore smash him without a struggle. Consequently, he would have to run again.

Lifting his huge bulk from his bed, Taft arose and put on his slippers. Shivering, he left the chilly bedroom and went to the small dressing room a few steps away. It was warmer there, and he began to feel better, thinking of the good dinner he had enjoyed the night before and remembering the jovial conversation he had held with two men who had been his friends since his triumphant days at Yale—Otto Bannard of New York and John Kean of New Jersey. He hoped that Bannard might be the director of his 1912 campaign, if he could persuade Otto to do it.

By the time he had dressed in his formal clothes for the New Year's reception, he was feeling calm and benign again. At fifty-four, he still had the expectant and hopeful temperament with which he had been born in Cincinnati. When he thought of all the tests through which he had passed successfully, he felt that he had reasons to count on the blessings of Providence.

He had been fortunate in having a mother who loved him deeply, and a devout and kindly father who had been a brilliant lawyer and an able member of the cabinet under two Presidents. His father, Alphonso Taft, had been secretary of war under U. S. Grant and attorney general under Rutherford B. Hayes, and later had served with distinction as a federal judge. He had tried to model himself in the image of his father, who was a man of quiet dignity and high ethical standards.

The most popular member of the 1878 class at Yale, Will Taft made friends at every stage of his life—and many of them were powerful and influential men. Through his friends he became assistant prosecuting attorney of Hamilton County, Ohio, in 1881, leaving his job as a law reporter. The next year he was appointed collector of internal revenue for Cincinnati—but he quit that post a few months later because he could not go along with the demands of Republican Party bosses, who wanted him to use jobs in the internal revenue service for party patronage.

He returned to private law practice, distinguished himself by participating vigorously in disbarment proceedings against a Cincinnati criminal lawyer, married Helen (Nellie) Herron, and returned to public life at the age of twenty-nine as a judge of the superior court of Ohio—the youngest jurist ever appointed to that bench. When President Harrison asked him to become solicitor general in 1890, Nellie begged him to accept the offer. She had become bored with the social routine of a judge's wife.

So he left the bench. He traveled to Washington ahead of his family, to get settled in his job and look for a place for them to live. He arrived at six o'clock on a gloomy February morning at the ancient, dirt-encrusted Pennsylvania Railroad station. He had a heavy suitcase and couldn't find a porter to carry it. As he dragged his ponderous luggage over to the Ebbitt House, a hotel near the station, he asked himself why he had made the decision to come to this bleak and forbidding city.

After breakfast he had gone to the Department of Justice to take his oath of office. Following the ceremony, he went to see the solicitor general's quarters. He was astounded and shocked. His "quarters" were a single dismal room, which held a battered desk and a chair. He learned that his stenographer was a telegrapher in the chief clerk's office, and had to be summoned whenever the solicitor general required assistance.

That first day as an officer of the federal government was one of the low points in Taft's life. He was anxious about his father, who was ill and obviously not long for this world. His father's resources had been depleted by sickness and debilitation. His brother Charles had assumed the task of aiding the Taft family to meet financial obligations. He was grateful to Charles for such generosity, but worried about his family's security.

Yet his acceptance of the federal post lifted him to a different plane. Instead of being a bright young judge in Ohio, he became a national figure. And after he returned to the bench as a federal judge, he was known and admired by a new group of powerful people.

When President McKinley had searched for a man to head the United States Commission to the Philippines in 1900, Will Taft was the one most often recommended. He had protested to McKinley that he had opposed the acquisition of the islands, he knew nothing about colonial administration, and he had really had no experience in executive work of any kind. But McKinley and the secretary of war, Elihu Root, had insisted that he had the qualities they wanted— a fundamental friendliness to which the Filipinos would respond, and the judicial nature and experience necessary to establish and preserve order.

He had told Nellie: "The President wants me to go to the Philippine Islands." And then he had added: "Want to go?" Without a moment's hesitation, Nellie answered: "Yes, of course." After she had answered his invitation to go with him to a land ten thousand miles away, she had asked him what he would be doing there. "Oh, the President and Mr. Root want to form a civil government, and they want me to go out at the head of a commission to do it," he had replied.

Nellie had no doubts about his ability to do it. That was Nellie—perpetually prepared for any change at any time, perpetually ready to go anywhere with him, perpetually sure that he could do anything the country or the President wanted him to do. Basking in her confidence, as he had basked in the doting love of his mother and the admiration of his father, he jumped from job to job, doing the best he could.

His best efforts might not have made him as strong and impetuous as Colonel Roosevelt, but he believed that his record was good—in spite of his own inadequacies, in spite of his own feelings of being overwhelmed by the magnitude of the tasks imposed upon him. He had been stirred in his heart and his soul by the warmth and love the Filipinos had given him, after they had realized that he had worked effectively in their behalf. Through negotiations with Pope Leo XIII, he had purchased the acreage acquired by some of the religious orders in the islands and had enabled Filipino farmers to buy and use this productive land. He had launched sanitation projects, established medical centers and clinics for the health of the people, relieved unemployment, and restored their agriculture to a flourishing condition. Thousands of poor Filipinos had gathered at the dock to bid him hail and farewell when he had left the Isles in 1904 to become Colonel Roosevelt's secretary of war.

As secretary of war he had done well enough as an administrator and spokesman for the President to become Roosevelt's choice for the Republican nominee for the White House in 1908. He had been reluctant to run, but he had beaten William Jennings Bryan that year by a plurality of more than one million votes—after a rough and feverish campaign.

Now on New Year's Day, 1912, he dreaded the campaign he saw ahead of him. He walked slowly from his dressing room down to the family dining room in the White House.

At breakfast he glanced at the editorial in the New York *Times:* "The year will be, like all other years, what we make it. . . . If 1912 turns out to be a year of great social and moral improvement, of blessings well received and afflictions meekly and sanely borne, it will be because we have made it so. There is a great deal to be done in 1912. Let us all bravely set to work to do it."

It was more of a sermon than an editorial, Taft thought. He sighed. He wasn't at all certain that the year would be what he made of it. He had started in life with few ambitions. He had wanted good food, good company, pleasant surroundings, laughter and dancing, children to cherish, interesting things to do, and chances for travel. Well, he had obtained all of them in the course of his journeying from birth to maturity—and many things he had not expected, many things he had not wanted.

Judge Taft—that was what he had wanted to be and all he wanted to be. He hadn't wanted to be solicitor general or the civil governor of the Philippines or secretary of war. He hadn't wanted to be President. He had loved the comfort and dignity and power based upon principles that went with being a judge. His wife and his friends had drawn him into the arena, into the dust and turmoil of politics.

From his childhood days he had extended both hands to the world. And people had filled his hands with gifts—gifts of admiration, of support, of opportunities offered and appointments to offices he had not coveted. He had wished for acceptance and approval, he had found it difficult to say no to anybody, and so he had gone from step to step, from one height to a still higher place.

He had carried one handicap: the burden of his large body. He had been fat as a baby, he had been a placid and cherubic child, and there were many who thought he still looked cherubic as President, in spite of his mustaches and his imposing height. He was expected to be jolly by day and by night; he had to appear to be happy and beaming in public. He tried to live up to the expectations people had for him.

When he left the family dining room, Taft encountered his military aide, Archie Butt, in the corridor. Major Butt gave him a correct, quick greeting and a respectful, yet affectionate smile. Knowing that Major Butt had taken care of everything, the President asked: "We're ready for the reception, are we, Archie?"

"We certainly are, sir. I predict a very large crowd."

"I'm afraid I'm getting tired of these things. And Nellie always gets so weary."

"There's a chair for her, sir. She can sit down if she wishes. Everyone will understand."

Had Butt seen Colonel Roosevelt lately? Were there any signs of what Roosevelt was going to do about the Presidential race? Taft wanted to ask those questions, but he checked himself. He was sure that Major Butt was keeping a diary, and every Presidential word probably went into it.

Recent events had convinced Taft that Major Butt, although a friend of Roosevelt's, was more in sympathy with Taft than with the Colonel. Archie had made that plain on the night before New Year's Eve, when the partisans of Theodore had tried to embarrass Taft at a dinner in New York.

After participating in the formal opening of the new Gimbel's department store in Philadelphia—Taft had gone to the opening because he regarded the promotion of business as one of the President's primary tasks—Taft and his staff had taken a train to Manhattan. He had rushed from the train to the Waldorf with Archie in a hired automobile, and he'd gone into the room they had reserved for him to get a little rest, and then he just couldn't get any. Archie told him the hotel was in a state of siege: there might be an effort by the Roosevelt people to break up the dinner before he got a chance to speak.

How could the friends of Roosevelt have treated him so shabbily? He was President of the United States. He was the man Roosevelt had pushed into the White House. They owed him a decent recognition of his struggle to do a decent job. But they were blinded by their idolatry of Theodore.

Whether Roosevelt realized it or not, Taft had continued and extended Roosevelt's reforms. He had actually exceeded Roosevelt's achievements as a "trust buster." More anti-trust suits against giant corporations had been filed in his administration than in Roosevelt's. He had strengthened the Interstate Commerce Commission. He had broadened the federal conservation program to include control over oil lands and water-power sites. He had put through a reciprocity treaty with Canada, and arbitration treaties with England and France.

But Archie came in with a rumor that the hotel was packed with Roosevelt partisans ready to jeer Taft. The police and the secret service had forty men dressed as guests scattered through the banquet hall to protect him.

Taft had been in the depths of despondency and he had talked too much to the major: "It is very hard to take all the slaps Roosevelt is handing me at this time, Archie. Everybody wants me to answer his last attack. He practically calls me a hypocrite. If it were anyone else I would know just what to do, but I can't get into public rows with him. He knows that, and he has me at a disadvantage."

The trouble was that he had too much affection and awe for Theodore. Theodore had been Mr. President for nearly eight years while he had been Will Taft, serving at the President's pleasure.

"I don't understand Roosevelt," Taft said that night to the major. "I don't know what he is driving at, except to make my way more difficult. I could not ask his advice on all questions. I could not subordinate my administration to him and retain my self-respect, but it is hard, very hard, Archie, to see a devoted friendship going to pieces like a rope of sand."

Then the banquet had been an unexpected success. When he had entered the Waldorf ballroom, the band had played "Hail to the Chief" and the audience had risen with cheers. His calm bearing and his evident determination to uphold the dignity of the Presidential office had won the crowd.

Thinking of these things on New Year's morning, Taft walked along the White House corridor with Major Butt. He was very fatigued, from his activities of the previous week and his celebration of New Year's Eve, but he was going to carry through his duties.

Major Butt went down the stairs to the main hall, to make a last-minute inspection of the red-coated musicians from the Marine Band. President Taft went into the library, where he found Mrs. Taft waiting for him, wearing an American Beauty satin dress, veiled in black net. "You look lovely, my dear," he said, and kissed her cheek. She looked better than she had at the reception the year before; her precarious health had improved.

At eleven o'clock the bugler who had been installed in the Mansion during the rule of Colonel Roosevelt blew a shrill stream of musical notes, announcing the appearance of the President and the First Lady. As the Tafts descended the grand staircase toward the guests waiting below, the round face of the cherubic President beamed upon all. He gave no sign that the sharp blast of the bugle was painful to his ears.

Diplomats from other countries were the first dignitaries to be received. Lord Bryce, the ambassador from Great Britain, led the procession. Close behind Bryce came the Kaiser's envoy, Count Von Bernstorff, with his jeweled countess and Major Harwarth of the German Imperial Staff. Major Harwarth caused astonishment by wearing blue dress trousers striped in double rows of cerise.

The Admiral of the United States Navy, George Dewey, conqueror of the Spaniards at Manila, presented a group of sea heroes. After Dewey and the naval contingent came the leaders of the American army, and after the army streamed people of all kinds.

It was a gay reception. The hall was brightly decorated with red poinsettia and green wreaths. The red-coated Marine Band played briskly. As Mr. Taft shook the rows of hands passing by him, he wondered about the size of the crowd. Perhaps the cold weather would keep many people from coming, and Colonel Roosevelt would interpret that to mean another decline in his popularity.

He didn't know that Major Butt, afraid that the crowd might be very small, had asked one of the Secret Service men to take the counting-machine away from the usher who was tabulating the number of persons in the reception line. Butt had ordered the figures on the machine increased by a thousand; he wanted to buoy the President's spirits and lead the press to believe that the 1912 reception had drawn the largest crowd ever admitted to the White House on New Year's Day.

As the people kept pouring in, Butt realized that his padding of the number on the machine had not been necessary. More than 8,000 persons actually went through the receiving line. It was really a tremendous affair—greater than the first one held by President Roosevelt after the death of McKinley had brought the Colonel into power.

Then after the ceremonies of New Year's Day, Taft faced a month of work and worry. On January 4, he issued a proclamation recognizing the admission of New Mexico to the United States. Five days later he ordered American troops transferred from the Philippines to China, to protect American lives and property endangered by the spreading Chinese revolution. On January 16, angered by the oppressive acts of Cuban army officers against the civilian population there,

Taft warned the Cuban government that the United States would intervene if such actions continued.

All through that month of January, Taft felt the thunder in the air. He received reports of the collapse of the Manchu Emperor's government and the installation of Dr. Sun Yat-Sen as Provisional President of the Republic of China. He was disturbed, too, on the domestic front by the violent rioting around the textile mills in Massachusetts, where a bloody strike was under way. He knew there were rumblings of revolution in many lands—and much discontent existed in America, due to unemployment and the rising cost of living.

In addition to being President, he had to maintain his leadership in the Republican Party. His friends from Ohio and the Middle West came to reassure him, and he talked optimistically about the future of the country and his own future as Chief Executive. No one could quite believe that Colonel Roosevelt would rip the Grand Old Party apart, to force a showdown with Will Taft.

Senators and governors were going to Roosevelt's home in Oyster Bay, to the rambling house on Sagamore Hill, trying to get the Rough Rider to ride again. "T.R." showed his thick teeth and roared: "No one can smoke me out until I'm ready to be smoked out."

Yet Taft had the knowledge in his bones. Roosevelt was only fifty-three—a bit younger than he was. Roosevelt was bored with traveling, bored with killing animals, bored with advising the kings of Europe; Roosevelt wanted to be aboard a battleship with the President's pennant flying over it, Roosevelt wanted to hear the band playing "Hail to the Chief" for "T.R." again.

COLONEL ROOSEVELT PREPARES FOR BATTLE

In Theodore Roosevelt's time Long Island was a land of woods and streams and relatively few people. It was a place of large estates and broad farms and little villages, connected by a wandering railroad over which trains occasionally ran to the city of New York. It was a rural area, principally occupied by farmers and rich men.

Roosevelt's home at Sagamore Hill was a tall frame dwelling with twenty-three rooms, ample porches, high chimneys and plenty of fireplaces. The rugged, homely house was filled with solid, comfortable furniture and trophies of his hunting expeditions—fur rugs, stuffed animals, guns, heads of rhinos and wild boars. It often echoed with the noise of children, the voices of visitors, and the shouts of the Colonel.

The Colonel had selected the site of the house. It stood on the crest of a hill where Indian tribes had gathered for councils of war and peace hundreds of years ago. It looked out over the rippling waves of Oyster Bay, where the Colonel and his children went swimming and sailing in spring and summer. It was near a clump of tangled forest, where the Colonel went hiking and log-cutting in the winter.

Roosevelt was accustomed to living in spacious surroundings. He was a member of a wealthy family, a Dutch family that had crossed the ocean from Holland to America in 1644. His sturdy ancestors had been officers in George Washington's army, and some of them had served in the first Continental Congress. When he had leaped into public life, he had been acting in the family tradition.

During his childhood and early youth, there had been doubts about his ability to live with the vigor of a true Roosevelt. Stricken with asthma, he had literally fought for his breath when the illness seized him with strangling pain. He woke at night gasping for air, his father and mother trying to help him. He was so near-sighted that he often ran into things, or stumbled and fell down. He had to have tutors at home; he couldn't get to school because he was sick so often.

His parents had finally realized that his eyesight was poor. He got a pair of spectacles, and the world of books opened to him. He read every book he could find—books on birds, on history, on geography, on poetry, on science—and he had once resolved to be a scientist. He was told that real scientists stayed in laboratories with microscopes and he had no desire to be cooped up in a laboratory. He dropped his plan to be a researcher. He was a curious combination—a bookworm who loved the out-of-doors, who wanted to be doing things, seeing new sights, or affecting people.

When he was fourteen, one of life's great unfolding experiences came to him. He had suffered a severe attack of asthma; he was sent by stagecoach to a camp at Moosehead Lake in Maine. In the coach he fell into the hands of two boys who tormented him easily because he was unable to defend himself; he knew nothing of boxing or fighting. He realized the agony of a defenseless creature.

He made up his mind that he would learn whatever he needed to learn to keep from ever being trapped again, utterly helpless and subject to tortures. He got his father's approval for boxing lessons. He was slow and clumsy in the ring, but he persevered until he became fairly adept with the gloves. Then he tried horseback riding and became a competent rider, although he was never first-rate at riding—any more than he was in boxing.

By the time he entered Harvard in 1876, he was a good athlete. He had climbed mountains. He had tramped through the woods. He had learned to shoot a rifle and a pistol. He had driven himself. He had refused to quit even when he realized that he could not be as capable in every field as he wanted to be.

At Harvard he was an enthusiastic student of politics, history, and literature. He was an honor student, although not the top scholar in his class. He also found leisure to drive

a dogcart and to go to parties, wearing sideburns and fashion-
able clothes. He was a dashing young fellow, full of bounce,
quick to laugh and have fun.

In his last year at college, in 1880, Roosevelt had told his
close friends that he intended to plunge into politics. They
had warned him that it was a dirty business. He had bared
his teeth and snapped at them: "You can't govern yourselves
by sitting in your studies and thinking how good you are.
You've got to fight all you know how, and you'll find a lot
of able men willing to fight you."

He had fought all the way. As a state assemblyman in
Albany he had exposed abuses in his own party. He was a
Republican, but he had no loyalty for corrupt bosses. He was
threatened and derided; he persisted in his demands for
honesty in the legislature: he called for the impeachment of
a judge who did not measure up to his standards. He was
tireless and fearless.

Then on a bleak day in February, 1884, just as his political
star seemed to be rising, he suffered two blows that were
too much even for his strong heart. The girl-wife he adored,
his Alice Lee, died soon after giving birth to a daughter. On
that same day, his idolized mother expired. He lost his zest
for everything; he found the air of New York impossible to
breathe.

Roosevelt fled to the wilderness—to the Dakota Territory
above Nebraska, where he owned a cattle ranch. For two
years he stayed on the plains, living as a cowboy, camping
beneath the stars, learning to hurl a lasso and put his brand
on a steer. He fought the despair that choked him, and at
last he conquered it.

When he returned to politics in 1886, his name was still
bright. At twenty-eight, he had the temerity to run for mayor
of New York against the Tammany candidate, Abram Hewitt,
and Henry George, the single-tax prophet who thought that
all of America's economic ills would be solved by obtaining

all governmental revenues through a tax on land. Roosevelt finished last, but he had entered the race with a statement that he knew it was "a perfectly hopeless contest." He had felt an obligation to offer the people a chance to vote for an honest Republican.

After the election he had hurried to London, where he startled his friends by marrying Edith Carow, a girl he had known since his childhood in New York. In addition to the little daughter born of his first marriage, he soon had four sons and another daughter. With his new wife, he settled his family in the house he had built on Sagamore Hill—and that was to be home for him through the rest of his days, no matter how far he traveled from it.

Wherever he went he left his mark. As the crusading president of New York City's police commissioners in 1895, he revealed the evils of the city's slums, demanded better housing for the poor, and reformed the police. Two years later, as assistant secretary of the navy under President McKinley, he had prepared the fleet for the war with Spain that flamed in 1898.

In '98 he had become the Colonel of the Rough Riders, a volunteer cavalry regiment he led through the fighting in Cuba before the liberation of that island from the Spanish forces. With his men he had charged the enemy troops on San Juan Hill and helped to win one of the decisive battles there.

As a war hero he had been elected governor of New York. When he took office in 1899, his assaults on the Republican state machine quickly caused Thomas Platt, the New York political boss, to make strenuous efforts to get "T.R." on the Republican national ticket in 1900. Despite his feeling that he would sink into obscurity if he accepted the Vice-Presidency, he ran with McKinley heading the slate.

When an assassin's bullets terminated McKinley's life in September, 1901, a few months after McKinley's inauguration for a second term, Roosevelt took over as the youngest President in American history. He was six weeks short of being forty-three when he took the Presidential oath to defend and uphold the Constitution of the United States.

From the fall of 1901 until he left the White House in the spring of 1909, he had shown the country what it was like to have a bold President. There were senators and congressmen who had denounced him as a would-be dictator; there were very rich men—"malefactors of great wealth," he had called them—who thought he had stretched the Constitution to fit whatever he wanted to do. When he had upset their schemes, they had foamed with rage.

Mark Hanna, the Ohio boss who had been McKinley's mentor, had denounced Roosevelt as "that damned cowboy." Well, maybe he was a "damned cowboy," he was rather proud of that title—but he didn't take orders from anybody. As President, he had summed up his policy in a phrase that was quoted around the world: "Speak softly, and carry a big stick, you will go far."

He had tried to speak softly but he sometimes lost his temper—and when he did, he bellowed. Reporters were always circling around him, seeking his views, even goading him to make statements. And he responded, perhaps too often; he couldn't help saying what he thought.

In Cuba, after the victory over the Spanish forces had been assured, the army had wanted to hold American troops in the mosquito-infested jungle in spite of an epidemic of malaria. As Colonel of the Rough Riders, he had not hesitated to release a letter to the military commander, Major General Shafter, in which he said: "To keep us here, in the opinion of every officer commanding a division or a brigade, will simply involve the destruction of thousands." The press and the people hailed him, and the army pulled the troops from the jungle.

As President, he had not hesitated to tell the Kaiser that he would ask Admiral Dewey and the American fleet to keep the Imperial German Navy from occupying Venezuela. Although the German government had announced it would move into Venezuela to collect overdue debts, the Kaiser backed down. The dispute was settled by arbitration.

He had stepped into the war between Russia and Japan to bring about the Peace of Portsmouth in 1905, won a Nobel Peace Prize, and declared that the nations should organize a League for Peace to prevent future international conflicts. He had sent the entire American fleet of battleships around the globe to let the people of all nations see the sleek efficiency and immense power of the navy he had worked to build. He thought the strong nations had to maintain their strength to keep the peace, and show their strength from time to time.

To secure the Panama Canal Zone, Roosevelt had welcomed the insurrection against the Colombian government, enabling Panama to secede from Colombia—and he had promptly negotiated an agreement with the Panamanian authorities to get the area needed for the construction of the Canal. He had broadened the Monroe Doctrine to claim in "the Roosevelt Corollary" that the United States might intervene—"however reluctantly"—in other American republics "in flagrant cases of wrongdoing . . . or impotence." In his first application of this Corollary, he established United States control over the collection of customs in the Dominican Republic.

As Colonel of the Rough Riders, as governor of New York, and as President, he had demonstrated that he was ever ready to be everybody's Big Brother. Yet he shouted from the housetops that he was devoted to individual freedom, to the right of the people to control their rulers—and he really meant it. He saw no contradiction between his allegiance to every man's freedom and his assertions of authority to act at home and abroad to correct "flagrant cases of wrongdoing . . . or impotence."

He hated wrongdoing and he had nothing but contempt for "impotence." In one of his eloquent orations he had declared: "I wish to preach, not the doctrine of ignoble ease, but the doctrine of the strenuous life, the life of toil and effort, of labor and strife. . . ." As a rancher in the Badlands of the Dakota Territory, during his years of trial in the wilderness, he had written to a friend: "All daring and courage, all iron endurance of misfortune . . . make for a finer and nobler type of manhood."

In the savage cold of the January days of 1912, Theodore Roosevelt went into the woods near Sagamore Hill with his axe and slashed furiously at the trees, arguing with himself, debating whether he should try to destroy the President he had placed in the White House as his successor. He was a hunter in torment—drawn to the hunter's trail, yet knowing that he would be hunting down a man who still sought to be his friend.

Since he had turned the White House over to Will Taft on that windy day of snow in March, nearly three years in the past, he felt that he had given Taft every opportunity to come up to his expectations. His expectations, of course, had been too high. He had expected Will Taft to be another Theodore Roosevelt—and no man could be that.

Yet the world was changing rapidly, the rivers of revolution were beginning to roar in many places, and amiable Mr. Taft was not the man to be the head of a great democracy in a time of danger. Under Taft the United States was dangerously close to being "impotent." Under Taft, in Roosevelt's view, some of the "wrongdoers" were escaping without punishment.

Of course, he was much to blame for not heeding his own inner misgivings about the weaknesses of his genial protégé.

He had acknowledged his own mistakes in a letter to Henry Cabot Lodge, the Senate leader: "For a year after Taft took office, for a year and a quarter after he had been elected, I would not let myself think ill of anything he did. I finally had to admit that he had gone wrong on certain points; and then I also had to admit to myself that deep down underneath I had all along known he was wrong, on points as to which I had tried to deceive myself, by loudly proclaiming to myself that he was right." He had stifled his qualms; he had not exercised his best judgment.

With his son Kermit, the Colonel had gone to Africa in search of danger and the thrill of the chase. Something inside him would not permit him to live happily in a quiet routine. He had to be changing, from hour to hour. In the course of a day he read books for a while, then boxed and wrestled, then entered the hunt. He had to try himself, to match himself against lions and elephants and other mighty beasts with courage and strength.

After the experience of being President, after his enjoyment of all that power and all that glory, nothing in life was really satisfying to him. To face charging lions and the horned rhinoceros, as he had done on the Kapiti Plains, was nothing compared to the joy of dominating the Czar of Russia and the Emperor of Japan, nothing compared to the unparalleled pleasure of being the recognized peacemaker between two empires.

Whether he held office or not, he was the First Citizen of America in the eyes of his countrymen. There could be no doubt about that. He was also admired in other lands. In western Europe, especially in Sweden and Holland, thousands of people stood for hours, trying to see him; at railroad stations there were packed crowds, cheering his train when it appeared.

And when he had returned to the United States, he had been given a reception fit for a king or an emperor. Horns had sounded, bugles had blown, cannon had rumbled, hats had been thrown in the air, fireboats in the New York harbor had sent glittering streams of water skyward. In the gray days of poor old Taft, the people had missed his presence in the White House—the sense of excitement he gave them, the expectation of new adventures into which he would gallantly lead them.

It would be easy for him to ride roughshod over Taft in 1912. And yet it would be hard, too. It would be a hard thing to break with Taft, his dear old Will, his "blessed old trump." Fighting with Taft would not be very exciting sport for a hunter with his experience. It would not be hunting a lion. It would be using a rifle on an old St. Bernard.

His friends felt that he had to do it. They felt, as he felt, that Taft had behaved badly about a number of things—in the Ballinger-Pinchot case, in defending the outrageous Payne-Aldrich tariff bill, in permitting the reactionaries in the Senate to dominate the government. Taft had removed some of the very able men he had appointed to federal positions, and had filled the posts with weak and mediocre fellows.

The Ballinger-Pinchot controversy was bad because it showed how far Taft had departed from Roosevelt's policies. That was how the Colonel saw it. He had made Gifford Pinchot the chief of the United States Forest Service because he knew that Pinchot was devoted to conservation. Pinchot was constantly on guard against the attempts of private groups to get control of the forests and public lands. When Pinchot had gotten into a fight with the secretary of the interior, Richard Ballinger, Taft should have backed Pinchot—or so it seemed to the friends of Roosevelt.

Taft insisted that he had investigated Pinchot's charge that Ballinger was taking certain lands and resources from the public reserve for the use of private interests—and Taft declared that the charge had no sound basis. Taft had fired

Pinchot, ignoring Roosevelt's support for the chief forester who had been prominent in "T.R.'s" fight for a national conservation program.

And Taft had the gall to call the Payne-Aldrich bill "the best ever passed by the Republican Party." Why, that act had raised the tariff levels on many items to the highest rates in American history. Roosevelt demanded to know how the United States could build up its trade with the world when Payne and Aldrich were putting up such walls to protect the special interests of certain manufacturers?

Roosevelt felt that Taft knew such a policy was a jump into folly—but if Taft didn't realize it, Taft wasn't bright enough to be President. Or Taft didn't have the right qualities of leadership.

Taft had gone far from him—over to the side of the conservative Senator Nelson Aldrich and Aldrich's Senate crew. Taft was chumming with the millionaires, getting advice from J. P. Morgan, even playing golf with Henry Frick, who had been in charge of the Carnegie Steel Plant during that bloody Homestead strike in which men had been burned and killed. Taft had fallen into the wrong company.

The Ballinger-Pinchot case, the tariff bill, the removal of his friends from the government—these things would not have been enough to turn him against Taft. But they were signs that Taft did not have the qualities necessary to be a great President. And the times called for a great leader in the White House—a man who could deal with the rising power of imperial Germany, a man who could curb the "evil trusts" in America, a man who could answer labor's cry for justice, give help to the farmers, and protect the liberty of all who lived under the American flag.

While Roosevelt swung his axe in the Long Island woods, in the cold month of January, 1912, it became clear to him that there was only one man who had the qualifications to meet the crisis arising in America and the world. That was a man of iron endurance and tremendous achievement, a man who could quell emperors and overcome lions, a man who could "speak softly and carry a big stick."

On Friday, the 5th of January, Roosevelt rode to the Long Island Railroad station at Oyster Bay. He took a train to New York. At the Century Club on Forty-third Street he met James Garfield, who had served as secretary of the interior in the last two years of his second administration. Jim Garfield had been a member of his Tennis Cabinet—one of the stalwarts who played tennis or went riding with him or shared the rough cross-country walks he took to keep in trim.

The Colonel talked bluntly for half an hour with Garfield, who was the leader of the Ohio Progressives; he asked Garfield to tell him honestly how much strength he had in Ohio, Taft's home state. Garfield's answer pleased and startled him.

When he left the club, bundled in his huge fur coat, pulling his fur cap on his head, Roosevelt was engulfed by reporters who had been standing on the sidewalk, shivering in the wind that whistled through Forty-third Street. He joked and brushed them off.

"Are you going to run, Colonel?" one of them asked.

"Not a word," he said, laughing. "Not a word, not a word."

But the Colonel had the look of the hunter, preparing for the hunt. And the word went to Taft and to the leaders of the Democrats. And through the country, the politicians braced themselves for a battle.

"AND WHO IS THIS MAN, WOODROW WILSON?"

While Judge Taft faced the future with anxiety and Colonel Roosevelt prepared to stalk the big judge in the White House, a tall lean man in Princeton was at his desk in his library, writing and planning. Pale and scholarly in his appearance, gentle in his voice and manner, Woodrow Wilson felt that he was the man to take on Taft and Roosevelt and knock their heads together.

Professor Wilson had come a long distance since the summer of 1910, when he had been little known beyond the academic circles in which he had spent most of his life. Then a veteran New Jersey politician, approached to consider the thought of nominating Wilson for governor, had asked in astonishment: "And who is this man, Woodrow Wilson?"

In January, 1912, Wilson was one of the top three candidates for the Democratic nomination for President. He had kicked up enough dust and fury in New Jersey, where he had been the first Democrat to be elected governor in a good many years, to make him a man the people watched. He had jolted the corporations and awakened new hopes in New Jersey crusaders by pushing through a progressive program in a state believed to be securely under the thumbs of the holding companies, the railroads, and the gas and electric utilities.

What had happened to the cautious professor, who had written books regarded as safe and sane by the genteel members of school boards? What had touched off the explosive energies in the breast of Woodrow Wilson, who had served with such elegance as the president of Princeton and had once deplored the "demagoguery of William Jennings Bryan"? He had turned the cagey politicians of New Jersey on their heads, chastised the corporations, and captured the warm admiration of the voters.

His rise was no surprise to his friends and his family, who knew of his restless energies and his soaring ambitions. From his youth he had been preparing himself for the years when the people would call him to power. He had the confidence of a God-chosen man.

The Biblical vision of his preacher father had hovered over his boyhood. Born in Staunton, Virginia, he was the son of the Reverend Joseph Ruggles Wilson, an impressive Presbyterian patriarch with a God-haunted eloquence and a religious sense of man's mission in the world. The Reverend Mr.

Wilson brought Woodrow up with the belief that Providence had planned a mighty important role for him—and it was his urgent duty to fulfill it.

Soon after his birth, the Wilson family had moved to Georgia. Woodrow's father, Joseph Wilson, had been a strong supporter of the Confederate cause; he had considered it a cause of honor. Honor and taking quiet satisfaction in doing right as one saw the right—regardless of the consequences—were fiery elements in Joseph Wilson's character, and he communicated these qualities to Woodrow.

Joseph Wilson was an omnivorous reader, interested in everything, and subscribed to the *Edinburgh Review* and the New York *Nation* as well as other publications. The father also read aloud to the family—excerpts from the Bible, from Dickens, from Walter Scott and other romantic poets. Reading, writing, and thinking—as well as serious conversation—were the main preoccupations of the Wilson household.

The Reverend Mr. Wilson used most of his modest savings to see to it that Woodrow got through Princeton as an undergraduate. Woodrow was a debater, an articulate student full of arguments, and decided then that politics would be his career. He thought the road to politics led through the law, so he went to the University of Virginia Law School for two years of graduate study.

As a lawyer, Woodrow Wilson got nowhere. With an ebullient associate, Edward Ireland Renick, he had opened offices in Atlanta—hoping for dramatic cases, for public attention. His hopes were vain. Few clients appeared. The law firm of Wilson & Renick went under.

It took him quite a while to recover from that setback. Still he had his sense of destiny, his feeling that he had a big part to play somewhere in the world. And he met a girl, Ellen Louise Axson, who touched the springs of gaiety hidden in him.

With Ellen he discovered that he liked to sing and dance, to take long walks under the stars at night, to laugh at the absurdity of human folly, to tell funny stories. He didn't have to be a stiff and solemn scholar. He relaxed a little; he renewed his research in political science and he was awarded a fellowship at the Johns Hopkins University in Baltimore.

His love for Ellen overwhelmed him. He wrote to her: "It isn't pleasant or convenient to have strong passions. . . . I have the uncomfortable feeling that I am carrying a volcano about with me. My salvation is in being loved. There surely never lived a man with whom love was a more critical matter than it is with me!" She answered tenderly, and they were married on a glowing June day in 1885.

While at Johns Hopkins he had written his first successful book—*Congressional Government,* a dissertation which earned for him a Ph.D. degree—and its publication brought him some academic fame and a flood of teaching offers. That was the real start of his career.

He taught first at Bryn Mawr, then a new college for women. From there he moved to Wesleyan University in Connecticut, and from Wesleyan to the summit of his aspirations as a scholar—membership in the political science department at Princeton. His brilliance as a lecturer and his popularity with the faculty, students, and trustees led to his election as president of Princeton in June of 1902.

As the head of Princeton, Wilson had tried to transform the university from a placid, sports-dominated school for the sons of the wealthy into an institution really dedicated to the higher learning and open to students from all economic classes. He had firmly established the preceptorial system, which later became the model for honors courses and individual tutoring at other colleges. He was rebuffed, however, when he tried to democratize the life of students by having them live in houses built around quadrangles. Vigorous opposition from faculty members and alumni defeated his "quad plan."

At the time when a few politicians began to talk about Wilson as a possible candidate for governor of New Jersey, Wilson was engaged in a bitter struggle with Andrew Fleming West, Dean of the Graduate School, over the location and management of the new Graduate College. In Wilson's eyes, West was a symbol of the aristocratic groups seeking to control Princeton and to destroy his reforms.

Wilson asserted that he was striving to make Princeton a democratic institution and to break down the walls of snobbery erected by the exclusive "eating clubs" to which the richest students belonged. He pictured West as a man who wanted to foster "social cliques, stolid groups of wealth and fashion, devoted to non-essentials and the smatterings of culture."

By the summer of 1910 most of the trustees had made it clear that they were on West's side. Most of them were reactionary, tradition-bound, snobbish men who had been shocked to find that Wilson was really a rather stubborn reformer. When West obtained a bequest of more than two million dollars from the will of an alumnus, Isaac C. Wyman, to be used for a Graduate College along the lines proposed by West, the Wilson trustees succumbed to the lure of the gift. Wilson's position became untenable.

Consequently, Wilson listened with a glad and receptive ear when Colonel George Harvey, the editor of *Harper's Weekly,* and former Senator James Smith, the Democratic boss in New Jersey, asked him to try for the governorship on the Democratic ticket. Harvey had persuaded Smith that Wilson was a potential President—and Smith dreamed of being the power behind the next occupant of the White House.

Before he went to whip his ward-heelers into line—the men who asked: "Who is this man, Wilson?"—Smith sought

Wilson's assurance that no attempt would be launched by Wilson to break the Democratic organization. "The last thing I should think of would be building up a machine of my own," Wilson declared in a letter to Smith.

Then Wilson added: "So long as the existing Democratic organization was willing to work with thorough heartiness for such policies as would re-establish the reputation of the State and the credit of the Democratic Party in serving the State, I should deem myself inexcusable for antagonizing it, so long as I was left absolutely free in the matter of measures and men." Those elaborate phrases made some of Smith's henchmen uneasy, but Smith accepted the statement. Smith admired the decorative quality of the Wilson style.

In Smith's lexicon no politician was "absolutely free in the matter of measures and men" and no one could reasonably expect to be. Smith and his reluctant lieutenants suffered a rude shock when they realized—after Wilson had been nominated and elected with their indispensable support—that Wilson meant exactly what he said.

As governor, Wilson was uncontrollable. Worse than that, so far as Smith's men were concerned, he was rambunctious. He drew to his banner a group of young progressive Republicans as well as nearly all the Democrats in the legislature— and he exhorted them to battle for righteousness day and night. He cajoled them in his own office, he lectured them in the halls, he pursued them into the committee chambers.

He secured the passage of laws providing very stiff penalties for the corrupt political practices which had made politics a rewarding game in New Jersey. He staged a flank-attack on the utilities, outwitted their lobbyists, and established state control over the gas and electric companies. He increased the state's aid for schools. At his urging, the legislature approved a law giving workmen compensation for injuries.

Under Wilson's leadership the direct-primary system of

choosing candidates for public positions was extended to cover every elective office. Every city in New Jersey was also authorized to adopt the commission form of government and to use the initiative, referendum, and recall for the acceptance or repeal of city ordinances or the removal of city officials. This law gave the residents of the cities all the instruments needed to overcome corrupt political machines.

Statutes were adopted for strict inspection of food and storage places, stringent inspection of safety conditions in factories, and limitations on the hours and kinds of labor in which women and children could take part. Newspaper correspondents who had covered the legislature for many years were stunned by Wilson's ability to get this program enacted.

Wilson was immensely pleased, but not astonished. His father had taught him that the Almighty would call him to serve his fellow citizens. The call had come, and he was serving. He would do whatever he had to do, and go wherever he had to go.

Former Senator Smith, who had done more than any other person in the state to lift Wilson into power, was first welcomed on visits to the governor's office and then received coldly. When Smith indicated that he wanted to return to the United States Senate with Wilson's blessing, the governor issued an official statement: "I know that the people of New Jersey do not desire Mr. James Smith, Jr., to be sent again to the Senate. . . . The only means I have of knowing whom they do desire to represent them is the vote at the recent primaries, where 48,000 Democratic voters, a majority of the whole number who voted, declared their preference for Mr. Martine of Union City. For me that vote is conclusive."

The fires that burned in Woodrow Wilson blazed forth in a letter he sent to a friend: "Smith has defied me to defeat him: and defeated he must be if it takes every ounce of strength out of me. . . . A nasty enough fight is ahead, and I shall have to do some rather heartless things which I had hoped might be avoided. They are against all the instincts of kindliness in me."

In his bout with Smith, Wilson used the means he generally employed in politics—reliance on his friends, firmness in his principles, and candor in appealing to the people. To the voters of New Jersey, he had become an awe-inspiring figure. They had never seen or heard anyone like him in the political arena.

Slender and stately, wearing the invisible mantle of the scholar, passionate and forthright in his speeches, capable of swinging from a solemn invocation of the laws of God to unexpected bursts of humor, Wilson captivated the people as Franklin Delano Roosevelt did a generation later. And the politicians, thinking of their own security, deserted Smith in droves.

The election of United States senators at that time was done by the state legislatures. Backing Martine—despite his doubts about Martine's caliber—Wilson first isolated and then smashed Smith in the session of the New Jersey legislature at which Smith made his bid for the Senate seat. At the end, he felt sorry for the dapper politician who had helped him to become governor. He wrote to a friend: "I pitied Smith at the last."

In his years as governor—as in his later years in a higher post—Wilson placed the principles of righteousness above personal concern for the fate of any individual man. This revealed in him a steely strength far greater than that possessed by most men in American life—and yet it was a factor in his eventual downfall.

During the icy days of the first week in January, 1912, Wilson sat in his library in Princeton, preparing a speech for the national Jackson Day celebration to be held by the Democratic legions in Washington. Although he had an office in the state capitol at Trenton, he did much of his writing at the home he had retained in Princeton.

As he wrote, he was well aware of the fact that he was one of the three Democrats considered likely to be a Presidential nominee. The other two were the old warhorses—Champ Clark, speaker of the House of Representatives, and William Jennings Bryan, the unstoppable orator and perennial candidate.

Clark and Bryan were scarred wrestlers, marked by their tumblings in the political ring. Wilson had soared on a trapeze into the limelight in a little more than two years. He held his political life steadily in his own hands. He was the center of attention and the center of criticism.

The professional Democratic strategists, trying to find a Presidential winner, were drawn to Wilson and repelled by him at the same time. They admired him and they feared him. They thought he was a winner, but they felt he had turned upon the man who put him in the governor's chair— and he might turn on those who helped him to the Presidency.

Wilson knew what they thought, and didn't let it bother him. He had his own strategy, planned far ahead. He would deal with the Clark forces and the Bryan backers when the right time came.

Two days before the Jackson dinner, on the evening of January 6, the New York *Sun* carried the text of a letter Wilson had sent to Adrian H. Joline, a Princeton trustee who had shared Wilson's early distrust for Bryan. Written in 1907, the letter contained a damaging sentence: "Would that we could do something, at once dignified and effective, to knock Mr. Bryan once and for all into a cocked hat!" Joline, who had been angered by Wilson's attempt to abolish the eating clubs at Princeton, had released the letter to embarrass Wilson.

This was 1912, and Wilson felt sure that Bryan knew his views had changed. Wilson refused to comment on the newspaper headlines. On the train from Princeton to Washington on Sunday night, January 7, he would not let the panic of his advisers affect him. He believed profoundly in a ruling Providence and he remained serene.

When he reached Washington, his friends held a strategy conference at the Hotel Willard. All agreed that he should make a statement. Wilson went to a table, took some hotel stationery, and started to write. He was interrupted by the arrival of Josephus Daniels, a North Carolina newspaper editor and friend of Bryan's. Daniels reported that Bryan had been in his home in Raleigh when the news broke, and Bryan had not appeared to be seriously disturbed.

Actually, Bryan had been warmly received by Wilson on a visit to Princeton some months before the publication of the letter. And Bryan had voiced enough indiscreet opinions in his own career to refrain from condemning Wilson severely for one sentence—a sentence that might have been penned in a moment of emotion and quickly regretted.

After receiving assurance from Daniels, Wilson dropped the statement. Instead, he decided to express his feelings about Bryan in his address at the dinner. He could not be budged from this position.

That night, more than seven hundred powerful Democrats —congressmen, senators, governors, members of the Democratic National Committee, district leaders—gathered in a hotel for the climax of the celebration of the late President Andrew Jackson's birthday. It was the major political event of the year in Washington.

All the candidates for the Presidency were there—the three front-runners, Wilson and Clark and Bryan, and the other hopefuls: Representative Oscar Underwood of Alabama, Governor Thomas Marshall of Indiana, Governor Foss of Massachusetts. The guests milled around the room before they took their places—shaking hands with one another, exchanging greetings, and watching Wilson and Bryan.

Speaker Clark and Governor Wilson had the largest numbers of followers. Bryan had not committed himself to either man. And on this night Bryan was cordial to both, greeting Clark with a solid shake of the hand and putting a hand on Wilson's shoulder.

The diners settled down. The speakers roared into their oratory. Wilson's turn came after the other notable men, except for Bryan, had addressed the audience. Bryan swung around in his chair, gazing directly at the man from Princeton. Silence spread through the hall.

In a short and simple speech—the shortest one of the evening—Wilson declared that the country was in trouble and the people knew it, the world was in ferment and the crisis called for brave and bold men. As he finished, Wilson leaned toward Bryan.

"Let us apologize to each other that we ever suspected or antagonized one another," Wilson said. "Let us join hands once more, all around the great circle of community of counsel and of interest—which will show us at the last to have been indeed friends of our country and friends of mankind."

The diners boomed their approval. Bryan participated in the wave of applause, his pink face beaming. Wilson had discomfited his enemies, especially those who had printed and circulated the Joline letter.

After the applause for Wilson ended, Bryan spoke. He expressed agreement that the hour had come for new men, new leaders. He was willing to march in the ranks, he said, to obtain victory for the principles of progressive change.

Bryan did not endorse Wilson or Clark as the 1912 candidate. He did not take himself completely out of the running. Yet his speech suggested that he was bending toward Wilson's side.

The next day, at a meeting of the Democratic National Committee, 32 of the 52 members present there proclaimed Wilson the most likely candidate. The New York *World* had a shouting headline on January 9: WILSON LEADS IN CLASH OF BOOMS.

Woodrow Wilson knew that the path ahead was still hard and steep, but he also knew that he had taken some giant strides toward the gleaming doors of the White House.

II. February: The Angry Days

In February, while President Taft waited in sorrow and resentment for Colonel Roosevelt's expected announcement, while Roosevelt read with glee the letters of Republican leaders begging him to restore the party to life, while Wilson wrote speeches and sang old songs in the evenings with his wife and daughters at his home in Princeton, the tides of change swept over men and nations.

Taft, whose memories were filled with sumptuous dinners and happy days at Yale; Roosevelt, the silk-stocking cowboy who had spent four full years at Harvard; and Wilson, the Princeton scholar with the patrician face, lived in an open world which stretched in many directions and had few barriers. In their world, people differed sharply in their ideas and struggled with one another for power but had no need to murder one another for beer or bread.

There was another world, populated by another kind of people—those who saw their lives stretching in only one direction, from one hungry day to another; those who were surrounded by barriers they generally found too high to jump.

This was the world of the three million Chinese coolies who were dying of starvation in that month of February, while American troops stood guard over the railways to make sure that communications between Chinese cities were maintained despite the fighting between the forces of the Manchu dynasty and the rebel troops.

This was the world of the field hands in Cuba, who refused to harvest the sugar crop because they cried out that their wages were not enough for them to feed their families.

This was the world of the 30,000 strikers in Massachusetts, who demonstrated in the icy streets around the textile mills which had been closed when they had demanded more pay. The plants had opened again, and strikebreakers entered the mills under the protection of a battery of artillery unlimbered by the Massachusetts militia.

This was the world of the garment workers of New York, who held a mass meeting and threatened to strike against the sweat shops in the dress industries.

This was the world of the miners of West Virginia and Pennsylvania, who had stopped the production of coal to show their disgust with their miserable conditions of existence. Fathers were struggling to support families on wages of $7 to $8 a week in some of the depressed areas of the United States.

This was the world of the angry farmers, who had suffered under the Payne-Aldrich tariff bill, who had seen the prices of protected manufacturers' products rising, who had seen their own markets diminishing. The farmers felt that they were squeezed by everybody—the elevators, the warehouses, the railroads, the land speculators, the bankers, the storekeepers—and nobody seemed able or willing to help them.

This was the world of Eugene Debs, a railway fireman who had been sent to jail for his participation in the strike against the Pullman Company in 1894 and had emerged a Socialist. His Socialist Party now had more than half a mil-

lion members. Crowds screamed and whistled when Gene
Debs spoke for the working people of America: "The forces
of labor must unite. . . . Labor's hosts, marshalled under
one conquering banner, shall march together, vote together,
and fight together, until working men shall enjoy all the
fruits of their toil."

In Europe—where the Socialists gained in France and
elected sixty-four members of the German Reichstag, shock-
ing the Kaiser and frightening other kings—as well as in
America, the hungry millions were demanding a larger share
of the upper world's wealth and threatening violence if they
did not get it.

THE FRUSTRATIONS OF BOB LA FOLLETTE

To an American prophet from Wisconsin—the stern, rock-
jawed United States Senator named Robert La Follette—the
furious currents of the age proved that he had been right
about the radical reforms he had installed in his state. To
end the stagnation of the federal government under Taft
and to stave off the threat of Socialism, he felt that America
needed La Follette and the Wisconsin Idea.

Before Colonel Roosevelt indicated a desire to get back
into the political whirlpool, the natural leader of the insurgent forces against Taft had appeared to be the blunt crusader from Wisconsin. And there were many who flocked
to La Follette's banner.

With La Follette the urgency of progressive change did
not seem to wax and wane in terms of personal moods—as
it did in the case of Roosevelt. Roosevelt seemed to be a
radical one day, a conservative the next. La Follette was an
indefatigable explorer, slowly and patiently beating a path
through the jungle, striving toward a goal determined after
much meditation.

The Wisconsin Idea, as developed by La Follette, used the
best American brains to soften the rough edges of capitalism

and make it work for the general welfare, while preserving individual freedom. Through the state university, he had drawn around him the first "brain trust" in modern American politics. The skills of many experts—lawyers, economists, sociologists, psychologists—aided him in drafting effective laws to control the corporations and to create the state regulatory commissions designed to enforce such laws.

Convinced that this Idea or Plan could be applied to the whole country, La Folette had organized the National Progressive Republican League at a meeting in his Washington home in January of 1911. He had drafted its charter of principles. He had obtained the backing of nine other senators, six governors, sixteen representatives, and twenty notable private citizens, including a former senator and the famous Kansas editor, William Allen White. Colonel Roosevelt had been asked to join and had refused.

Those who participated in the meeting knew that one of their major problems was the choice of a Presidential candidate. The names of several senators and governors were discussed, but La Follette towered over them all. As governor of Wisconsin before he entered the Senate, La Follette had demonstrated the kind of executive capacity a President had to have. La Follette had a program, courage tested in many situations, and the stamina that seemed to be required.

In essential ways La Follette's background fitted him perfectly to be a popular candidate. He came of pioneer stock. He had actually been born in a log cabin. He had lived on a farm as a boy. He had made his own way to success as a lawyer and then had gained a series of high public positions.

A consistent idealist, La Follette was also a shrewd politician. He had been able to build a strong and efficient machine to support his administration in Wisconsin and to sustain his reforms after he had been sent to Washington. He had a phenomenal memory, endless enthusiasm for thorough investigation of every subject he tackled, a natural flair for oratory, and the physical resources of a man who worked night and day month after month with few outward signs of fatigue.

He saw himself as an American giant, struggling with lonely integrity against the octopus-tentacles of greed and corruption that trapped so many men. He believed that the principles of Abraham Lincoln—the great son of Illinois— were just as applicable to the twentieth century as they had been in 1865. Wisconsin and Illinois were sister states of the Middle West—and La Follette envisioned himself as a leader standing before the nation in the Lincoln tradition.

Lincoln had declared that the Republican Party had to be dedicated to government *of* the people, *by* the people, and *for* the people. In Wisconsin, La Follette had broken the grip of the railroads on the state legislature and had restored it to the people. He had taxed the real values of the properties owned by the rail companies, and relieved the tax burden on the people. He had extended the state civil service to give the people fair opportunities for jobs. He had provided for the conservation of natural resources—public lands, mineral deposits, parks—belonging to the people.

For these actions, La Follette had been depicted in many quarters as an enemy of free enterprise, very close to being a Socialist. Actually he was trying to stop Socialism. He wasn't against corporations as such. But corporations, he felt, had to be kept under strict supervision for the benefit of the public. Why, the railroads had behaved as if they owned Wisconsin and the other states, before he whipped them.

Roosevelt shared his views, La Follette was positive. In moments of true vision, "T.R." acknowledged that if Socialism came to America "the malefactors of great wealth" would be largely to blame—the bankers who thought only of money, the mill owners who kept their employees just above the starvation line, the men who wanted to have their cake and eat it, too. "T.R." knew that La Follette was correct in saying that Socialism couldn't expand if the people became really prosperous.

If there was a Progressive movement in the Republican Party—or out of it—La Follette considered himself the man to lead it. He had been a more consistent and thorough Progressive than Roosevelt. He had borne the heat of more battles than Roosevelt had endured in the Progressive cause. He had written the Progressive Manifesto of 1911.

La Follette felt that Roosevelt—because of the enemies "T.R." had made—could not win the G.O.P. nomination away from Taft. If "T.R." supported La Follette, however, the combined forces might triumph over the conservatives in the Republican camp. And so he hoped that Roosevelt would give him the backing he had earned.

The Wisconsin senator believed that the Colonel had practically pledged support to him on several occasions. Roosevelt had asserted, in a magazine article, that Wisconsin had gone "farther than any other State in securing both genuine popular rule and the wise use of the collective power of the people." And "T.R." had placed the credit on the shoulders of Bob La Follette.

Suspicious of Roosevelt's intentions to stay in retirement if the chances for a Progressive looked bright in 1912, La Follette had delayed the formal announcement of his own candidacy until he had been assured of the loyalty of several of "T.R.'s" ardent admirers, including James Garfield and Gifford Pinchot. He didn't want to be a stalking horse for Roosevelt or any other man. Once he got into the race he intended to stay in it, regardless of what any one else might do.

Progressivism, as he said later, had become his life work. He felt he had achieved results of a character too important and substantial to lend himself to any campaign schemes in which he would be a mere pawn. He declared that he did not want to be "cast upon the political scrap heap, my ability to serve the Progressive cause seriously damaged, and possibly the movement itself diverted and subordinated to mere personal ambition."

After he had opened his headquarters in Washington in August of 1911, his strength had grown with astonishing rapidity. In October of that year, three hundred Progressives from thirty states met for a three-day conference and passed a resolution endorsing La Follette for President. Large magazines like the *Saturday Evening Post* and the *American* published favorable articles about him.

For a time messages of support poured into his office. Financial contributions flowed in from the Pinchots and other faithful Progressives. Newspapermen became interested in his chances, and Mark Sullivan of the New York *Herald Tribune* regarded it as probable that Taft would be defeated for renomination and La Follette would be the G.O.P. standard-bearer.

Then everything seemed to go wrong for the dedicated man from Wisconsin. In January La Follette ate some tainted food at a dinner and collapsed from food poisoning. In February, the bitterest month of 1912 for him, he got definite reports that Roosevelt was not going to support him after all.

The size and scope of the Progressive movement, revealed by the number of people rallying to La Follette, had impressed Roosevelt. There seemed to be a clear chance of a Progressive victory at the Republican convention. If there was such a chance, "T.R." thought he was entitled to it himself.

Roosevelt declined to agree with La Follette's contention that "T.R." had given a firm pledge to him for the 1912 campaign. La Follette thought he had been betrayed—by Roosevelt and by Roosevelt's friends, particularly the Pinchots and James Garfield. He had been used as "a stalking horse" and he was expected to accept his role. He would not do so. He was in the fight to the finish.

The cold facts, as Roosevelt and most of the Progressive leaders saw them, were against La Follette. Fighting Bob was a fine man, with many adherents. But Fighting Bob had not made a dent in the industrial East—in the heavily populated states where most of the votes were. Nobody could win without those votes.

Certainly La Follette had created a surge of enthusiasm in some states, showing what a vigorous campaigner against Taft could arouse. But La Follette was tagged as a western insurgent, and did not have a national appeal. The Colonel was certain that La Follette could not mobilize the hard-bitten professionals in New York, Pennsylvania, and New Jersey. In spite of some superb qualities, Fighting Bob just wouldn't do.

Until the black hours of February, when he realized that his forebodings about Roosevelt were coming true, La Follette had clung to the idea that 1912 was going to be his year —the year when he would march into the White House at the head of the Progressives he had guided and inspired for so many years. Even after he had faced the truth, he would not withdraw.

Hampered by the confusion of his disintegrating campaign, La Follette wrote and rewrote the speech he had been invited to give at the annual banquet of the Periodical Publishers Association in Philadelphia. Woodrow Wilson was also scheduled to be on the program. La Follette felt that if he could make a stronger impression than Wilson, his drive might revive.

On the evening of the banquet, misfortune plagued him again. His daughter became ill and he rushed to the hospital with her. He arrived very late at the hotel where the publishers, editors, and writers had gathered.

Just before midnight La Follette rose before them with a thick manuscript. His frustrations were evident in the scorching words he shouted there—in his attacks on the press, "the money trust," Colonel Roosevelt, the rotten state of American society. Scores of men walked from the room. Others yelled: "Stop it! Stop it!" Half blinded by his rage and his despair, La Follette roared grimly on until 1:30 in the morning of the next day.

As the crowd straggled wearily from the banquet room, it was apparent that La Follette had damaged his cause. Instead of presenting himself as a strong, defiant candidate, he had simply seemed desperate. By contrast, Wilson's poise had been impressive and his short speech seemed a brilliant performance.

Thus Wilson and Roosevelt, between them, and La Follette's own inability to cope with his rivals, had eliminated the old Progressive as a dangerous contender even though he told everybody he was continuing in the race. And one week after the Philadelphia dinner, seven Republican governors met in Chicago and signed a pleading petition, requesting Colonel Roosevelt to run.

To Roosevelt, the list of governors on the petition—J. M. Carey of Wyoming, Will Stubbs of Kansas, Charles Osborne of Michigan, Herbert S. Hadley of Missouri, Chester Aldrich of Nebraska, Robert Bass of New Hampshire, and W. E. Glasscock of West Virginia—represented the Far West, the Middle West, and the Northeast. Their support made it seem possible that he could dislodge Taft and get the Republican nomination.

The Colonel told the governors that he would accept the nomination if it came within his reach. The hunter on Sagamore Hill had been smoked out.

WILSON HITS THE ROAD

Buoyed by the heady excitement of his victory over La Follette in Philadelphia, Wilson beat the bushes in search of delegates to the Democratic convention slated to be held in Baltimore in June. This was the first Presidential year in which many delegates were being chosen through direct primaries in the states, and he knew he didn't have much time. His most active opponent for the Democratic crown, Speaker Champ Clark, had been a member of the House for decades and was closely connected with the organization men around the country; Clark would be hard to defeat.

Wilson trusted in Providence, but he also believed that God helped men who helped themselves. He absorbed strength of spirit from audiences of many kinds, composed of people who listened to him and applauded. He asked them to think, to take the path of reason, and they liked that, they liked his straight talk, and they liked him, too.

He spent so much time away from his office in Trenton that the Republican New York *Sun* referred to the New Jersey governorship as "Wilson's travelling scholarship." A few of his friends thought he was too eager in his chase for the nomination. He went to Michigan, New Hampshire, Virginia, Kentucky, Illinois, Iowa, Pennsylvania, Kansas, Tennessee, Georgia, Maryland. He wrote to his wife: "Every fibre of me is tired out every day."

His scholarly reserve gradually gave way to the easy fraternal manner of the campaigner. He told funny stories about Scotsmen, and the crowds cheered and laughed. He felt warm waves of response coming to him when he spoke of high and noble things without talking over anybody's head. He used simple, plain sentences without being condescending. He did not feel superior to his audiences; as citizens, they were as much concerned with the future of the country as he was.

He brought the flag into his speeches, but he did so without using the pat phrases of Fourth of July spellbinders. In Richmond, Virginia, he was invited to speak before both houses of the legislature on February 3. That evening he appeared before 4,000 persons in a large auditorium. Among them were three hundred men from the town of his birth,

Staunton. When he asked them to consider the meaning of the flag, they made the rafters ring with the echoes of their applause.

"I have heard men say that it was un-American to criticize the institutions we are living under," Wilson said. "I wonder if they remember the significance of the American flag—the first insurgent flag that was flung to the breeze—the flag that represented the most colossal 'kick' that was ever taken in political transactions; a flag that I cannot look at without imagining that it consists of alternate strips of parchment upon which are written the fundamental rights of man, alternating with the streams of blood by which those rights had been vindicated and validated."

No one asked Wilson whether "the fundamental rights of man" were involved in the rioting around the textile mills in Massachusetts, where American strikers seeking better wages were being clubbed and fired upon by American soldiers. No one seemed to know what to do or say about that strike, except to express horror and fear that the Socialists or the anarchists were at the bottom of it. The mill owners and the strike leaders, hardened by hatred, had refused to compromise with one another.

Wilson, who had had some harsh things to say about unions in his academic years, now declared that "America's economic supremacy depends upon the moral character and the resilient hopefulness of our workmen." If he were a manufacturer, he vowed that he would "create such conditions of sanitation, such conditions of life and comfort and health as would keep my employees in the best physical condition." He would go farther: "I would establish such a relationship with them as would make them believe that I was a fellow human being, with a heart under my jacket, and that they were not my tools, but my partners."

Such a policy did not immediately endear him to union

chieftains, who regarded it as a flowering of paternalism. Still his advocacy of a labor program "with a heart" won him admiration among the millions of American working people who did not belong to unions. They were skeptical about their chances of being "partners"—and they weren't sure they wanted to be—but they did feel that they should not be treated as "tools."

In the middle of February a gust of antagonism shook Wilson and his lieutenants. Nearly a thousand Hungarians met in New York to protest against some passages in Wilson's *History of the American People*. One section which had aroused their ire contained these statements: "But now there came multitudes of men of the lowest class from the south of Italy and men of the meaner sort out of Hungary and Poland, men out of the ranks where there was neither skill nor energy nor any initiative of quick intelligence; and they came in numbers which increased from year to year, as if the countries of the South of Europe were disburdening themselves of the most sordid and hapless elements of their population. . . ." Wilson had gone on to describe these immigrants as "a coarse crew" and people "less desirable than the excluded Chinese."

At the New York meeting a letter from Wilson was read to the crowd. In this communication Wilson said he was "not speaking of a nation but of certain elements." Catcalls and boos came from the Hungarians; his letter was scorned and denounced.

Reporters from the Hearst newspapers, spurred by William Randolph Hearst, scanned all Wilson's writings for prejudicial remarks against minorities or signs which indicated that the Princeton scholar had been very conservative before running for public offices. Hearst, who liked to think of himself in those days as a liberal Democrat, had served as a congressman from New York, had tried twice to be elected mayor of New York City, had run for the governorship of the Empire State, and nursed Presidential ambitions of his own.

Woodrow Wilson had incurred Hearst's wrath by refusing to meet him or have dinner with him privately. Hearst publicly painted Wilson as "a perfect jackrabbit of politics, perched upon his little hillock of expediency, with ears erect and nostrils distended, keenly alert to every scent or sound and ready to run and double in any direction."

Wilson did not let the publisher's personal diatribes disturb him. But his advisers were worried by the antagonisms of the Poles, Hungarians, and Italians, who voted in large numbers in the eastern states. Under the prodding of his friends, Wilson wrote letters to notable citizens from these lands, giving praise for their contributions to American progress. Pursued by the Poles, he rewrote parts of his *History* referring to them.

Feeling that the nomination for the Presidency was worth whatever efforts he had to make, driven by his own compulsions to seek power in order to "help the people" to fulfill the will of Providence, Wilson was able to rationalize his compromises. He was quite convinced that he was not seeking power for his own personal advancement; he was availing himself of the opportunity to be a servant of the Lord and to put his abilities in harness for his nation.

His goals, he thought, were the goals of all men of good will. He attacked "privilege" and "the great combinations" that dominated American business, but he did not indict business as such. "No man indicts natural history," he said. "No man undertakes to say that the things that have happened by the operation of irresistible forces are immoral things, though some men may have made deeply immoral use of them."

He demanded the elimination of political corruption, reduction of unfair tariffs, conservation of the huge natural resources of the United States, and reforms in the banking system to make credit available to the millions who needed it. He felt that his fellow Americans shared his belief that these demands were "eminently just" and "intensely practical."

He had to speak to the people morning, noon, and night because the odds were against any man who did not have the support of the political machines in the heavily populated states. He had to get headlines, he had to make the people aware of him, he had to be in as many places as he could, he had to make splashes and stir excitement to have any chance of overcoming those odds.

Champ Clark was the man the politicians wanted to nominate. The party leaders told Wilson that, the newspaper correspondents explained it, his foes and his friends repeatedly reminded him of it. His body grew wearier and wearier, his voice grew hoarse, his brain groped for more ideas; he could not stop, he must not stop, he had an appointment with destiny and he had to keep it.

Aside from the Hearst chain, most of the newspapers treated him with increasing approval. After one of his appearances in Chicago, the *Evening Post* there commented: "It cannot be denied that the governor of New Jersey made an excellent impression here. Democrats of all kinds came to hear him, and he performed the heretofore unknown miracle of accepting them all as Democrats, instead of separating them into Sullivanites, Harrisonites, Hearstites, and so on. . . . The effect was astonishingly invigorating." (The Sullivanites were henchmen of Roger Sullivan, one of Chicago's powerful bosses. The Harrisonites followed another Democratic leader, and the Hearstites were, of course, the minions of W. R. Hearst.)

Such editorials refreshed Wilson, and persuaded him that his journeys were not wasted. He informed his friends that he felt like "a man living on strong stimulants." The letters he received, from people who had heard him in halls and hotels in half a dozen states, encouraged him to forget his fatigue.

Although he proclaimed himself a progressive, Wilson had a gift for convincing conservatives as well as progressives that he was a man to be trusted. He was obviously far from being a radical. He was "forward-looking," they concluded, but still "sound" and "sane." He did not frighten anyone.

Colonel Roosevelt, on the other hand, did frighten people who recalled the unpredictable adventures of "T.R." as President. Robert La Follette also frightened people: he glared at audiences, he waved his arms, and sometimes he clenched his fists. William Jennings Bryan frightened other people: they feared that he might flood the country with "printinghouse money."

Woodrow Wilson, although eloquent and evidently determined to be a powerful leader, was somehow reassuring. His statements were clear and easily understandable, and yet had a touch of the learned phraseology that was pleasing to many. He had a penetrating voice, which he did not raise too often.

And while he did not seem to evade any fundamental issues, he was a master of generalities. He declared that "the government must be restored to the people"; he said "the gates of opportunity are wide open and he may enter who is fit"; he was confident that "out of a mass of uncatalogued men you can always count on genius asserting itself, genius suited to mankind, genius suited to the task." These were things people liked to hear; and he said them with obvious sincerity.

Yet the ward bosses, the precinct captains, the clubhouse regulars, kept aloof from him. The politicians felt that he was unpredictable. In their eyes he could not be counted upon to perform steadily in the stresses and strains of a national campaign. They didn't like the way Wilson had broken with Colonel Harvey, one of his early backers, after it became evident that Harvey's Wall Street connections might become a severe handicap.

The crowds flocked to hear Wilson as the days of February flew by. But there were few men in the crowds with the political positions necessary to be delegates at the Democratic National Convention. Wilson was reaping a harvest of cheers, but not the votes he really needed.

THE EXPLOSION OF MR. TAFT

For the huge man who occupied the White House, the situation was reversed. William Howard Taft had a comparatively small amount of popular acclaim, and still he moved with ponderous certainty toward another nomination for the Presidency. He didn't have Wilson's troubles; he had others, which seemed to him much worse.

The professionals in the Republican Party kept slipping into the White House to tell him they were going to stand by him. They loved him dearly, and they distrusted Colonel Roosevelt, who had ridden over them just too often.

He had to seem grateful, and of course he actually did appreciate their loyalty. However tired of the Presidency he might be, however saddened with politics he had grown, he didn't wish to be humiliated and deprived of the nomination by Roosevelt. His wife had told him that he must not stand for such treatment, and he did not intend to stand for it.

It was difficult to maintain his jovial front when he had to miss delicious dinners and marvelous parties, when he had to give up some of his poker games and go around making speeches. Major Butt, who was a good fellow and honestly concerned about him, informed him that he looked awful.

"Archie, you go to hell!" he said to Major Butt, and whacked the major on the back to take the sting from his words. Butt had begged him to see a medical specialist. "I will not be hauled and pulled about by specialists."

He did not like to be hauled and pulled about by anybody. But he allowed himself to be pulled and hauled, because he was fed to the teeth with the rudeness of Roosevelt. He was President, and he wasn't going to lie down and let any lion-hunter walk over him.

On Lincoln's Birthday he called for an open car and drove through New Jersey, laying wreaths on every statue of Lincoln he could find. Major Butt wrote his sister about that trip:

"The President hates hypocrisy. He always feels like a fool when he is forced to undergo such farcical programs. . . . He always looks foolish when forced to go about hanging wreaths on bronze people's feet and tying them around their chests, but it is a part of the game. He hardly ever makes any complaint, but once yesterday he said: 'Archie, how well McKinley did this sort of thing! He was a born undertaker.' "

The ceremonial side of the Presidency gave him agony, although he well realized there was no escape from it. Apparently Theodore enjoyed it; Theodore appeared to enjoy everything.

Still he was going to do everything in his power to see to it that Theodore didn't get a chance to enjoy the Presidency again. He drove that point home to Major Butt in a long conversation on February 14 while they were walking through the streets of Washington.

"He could not get Roosevelt off his mind," Butt reported. "He kept saying that if Roosevelt succeeded in defeating him for the nomination Roosevelt would be the most bitterly discredited statesman ever in American politics. . . . The clash which must follow between these two men is tragic. It is moving now from day to day with the irresistible force of the Greek drama. . . ."

A few days later Major Butt was with Mr. Taft when the news came that Colonel Roosevelt had advocated the recall of judges from the bench by popular votes and had told a reporter that he intended to try for the Presidency. Taft was depressed by both developments.

As a former judge, Taft viewed with disgust and horror Roosevelt's proposal for the removal of men from the bench through the people's votes. As a President who felt entitled to Roosevelt's enthusiastic aid rather than Roosevelt's rivalry, he was equally horrified by the Colonel's last statement.

Taft saw a dire future ahead for the Colonel: "He will either be a hopeless failure if elected or else destroy his own reputation by becoming a socialist, being swept there by force of circumstances just as the leaders of the French Revolution were swept on and on, all their individual efforts failing to stem the tide until it had run itself out."

The formal announcement that Roosevelt would accept the nomination "if offered" came over the Associated Press wires on the night of February 25. The Tafts, Major Butt, and two guests at the White House sat down to dinner in silence. Finally Mrs. Taft said to her husband: "I told you so, four years ago, and you would not believe me."

The President laughed good-naturedly and replied: "I know you did, my dear, and I think you are perfectly happy now. You would have preferred the Colonel to come out against me than to have been wrong yourself."

Under Taft's laughter there was the pain of a man caught in a trap from which there could be no easy escape. In the remaining days of February the President's gloom grew darker and Major Butt suffered with him.

Major Butt, torn between Roosevelt and Taft, had asked and received the President's permission to take a vacation trip to Italy. Seeing the President in torment, the major lay awake nights worrying and at last told Judge Taft that he had decided not to go.

The President insisted that he deserved a rest. Taft would not let the major cancel his sailing plans. Taft assured Butt that he could return in plenty of time for the campaign.

Neither the President nor the military aide had the gift of foreknowledge, although Major Butt had a curious presentiment that he might never see Mr. Taft again. He wrote to his sister: "Don't forget that all my papers are in the storage warehouse. If the old ship goes down you will find my affairs in shipshape condition." (On the return voyage from Europe, he was one of the passengers on the doomed *Titanic*.)

Meanwhile Taft wavered between depression and rage. Members of his cabinet kept pleading with him to make onslaughts directly against Roosevelt, and he kept refusing. He considered "T.R." a neurotic, and he detested the quarrel into which Roosevelt had plunged him, he knew he had a right to swing savagely at Theodore. And yet he felt that fulminations did no good.

At times he even regretted the smashing speech he had delivered at the Lincoln's Birthday dinner of the Republican Club in New York. On that occasion he had let himself go. He had not been judicial and detached that night. He had said: "There are those who look upon the present situation as one full of evil and corruption and as a tyranny of concentrated wealth, and who in apparent despair at any ordinary remedy are seeking to pull down those things which have been regarded as the pillars of the temple of freedom and representative government, and to reconstruct our whole society on some new principle, not definitely formulated, and with no intelligent or intelligible forecast of the exact constitutional or statutory results to be attained."

Such extremists, he warned the gentlemen in evening clothes at the club, "would hurry us into a condition which could find no parallel except in the French Revolution, or in that bubbling anarchy that once characterized the South American Republics."

Lifting his hands in solemn gestures, Taft declaimed: "Such extremists are not progressives—they are political emotionalists or neurotics—who have lost that sense of proportion, that clear and candid consideration of their own weaknesses as a whole, and that clear perception of the necessity for checks upon hasty popular action which made our people, who fought the Revolution and drafted the Constitution, the greatest self-governing people that the world ever knew."

That was Mr. Taft's explosion. Some of his friends thought it was the finest thing he had ever done—and others thought it was a disaster. Some wrote to him, asking him to keep it up, to "pour it on Theodore." Others beseeched him to retain his judicial composure, saying that he could not compete with Roosevelt in a contest of invectives.

As February dwindled and vanished, Taft could not decide what his course should be. He paced through the rooms of the Executive Mansion, sighing and brooding. He ate more and more, he grew more and more depressed, and he felt more and more repelled by the requirements of politics.

THE TURMOIL BEYOND THE WHITE HOUSE GATES

While the President worried about the extremists who might pull down "the pillars of the temple of freedom," and gained weight by eating too much in moods of sheer despair, the world outside the White House descended deeper into turmoil.

Pale and scrawny children, sent to New York for food and shelter by the desperate Massachusetts textile strikers, paraded singing up Fifth Avenue while a band played the "Marseillaise." They did not seem to know any American revolutionary songs.

Taft hated to think of people going hungry, and Taft hated to think of the bloodshed in the Massachusetts strike, but he did not believe the President could play any role in such events. The President could only hope that charity would feed the children, and that the strike would somehow be settled.

The President was alarmed about many things. He was concerned about the chaos in China. His peace-loving nature was harrowed by the Italian bombardment of Beirut and the sinking of two Turkish vessels by Italian shells. He was distressed by the civil war in Mexico, where American rights and American property were being threatened.

He labored conscientiously at his functions. He proclaimed the admission of Arizona as the forty-eighth state in the Union. He appointed a new member of the Supreme Court. He held cabinet meetings with regularity.

It was a bad time to be President, Taft felt, although his countrymen did not seem to realize it. He had always been interested in what went on beyond American shores, but it was extremely hard to get the American people interested.

Germany was planning an attempt to break the grip of Standard Oil on international petroleum supplies, and some American businessmen were troubled about that.

Supremacy in the air was declared to be the aim of France, and some Americans demanded action in the United States to build more airplanes. These citizens did not want to see France or any other foreign country get ahead of America in any field.

Alphonse G. Koelbie, a New York lawyer, and his associates organized the American Truth Society to oppose a proposed 1914 celebration of a century of peace with Britain. The Society included German-Americans, Austro-Americans, Hungarian-Americans, and others suspicious of the British.

The American consul at Johannesburg sent an urgent message to the U.S. asking Americans not to rush to the South African diamond fields. Too many prospectors were there already.

Japan's Minister of the Interior, Mr. Tokonami, proposed

a comprehensive scheme for uniting Shintoism, Buddhism, and Christianity in one great religion. American leaders did not show any enthusiasm for Mr. Tokonami's idea.

Percival Roberts, Jr., a director of the United States Steel Corporation, said that men in the steel mills liked to work long hours. (The Bermuda season was at its height, and society reporters declared that the beautiful wives and daughters of corporation executives were enjoying the sun and the surf.)

Rome was having a mild winter, and some people thought it was a sign of the blessing of Providence on the Italian conquest of Tripoli.

Efforts to obtain home rule were rising in Puerto Rico, with rebellious elements seething.

There was a drive in England to revive dueling, on the grounds that it would improve manners and discourage divorce.

In New York home seekers were looking to the suburbs for living comforts at moderate costs, according to the *Times*. Police Commissioner Dougherty threatened to arrest all idlers on sight, to end a wave of holdups. Crime grew worse.

That was the way the world went in the cold days of February, in the bloody leap year, 1912.

THE SOUND OF GUNS IN SPRING

Explosive eruptions in other nations and the evident alarm of their ordinarily placid President compelled Americans to turn for a time in March from their domestic arguments to what was happening abroad.

Thomas Edison had urged them to realize that the Chinese revolution might change their lives and their children's lives. So they rushed to buy newspapers that carried the hard headlines heralding the sound of guns in China: YUAN'S TROOPS KILL, BURN AND LOOT PEKING, CHRISTIAN CONVERTS SLAIN.

American soldiers stood guard along the rail lines, and the American missionaries in China were not believed to be in personal danger except in a few places. But the savagery of the Chinese revolt made millions of Americans wonder what effect their gifts of sons and dollars to the missions had brought into that vast, mysterious land.

The provisional administration of Dr. Sun Yat-Sen, a

British-educated physician, had not lasted long. Sun Yat-Sen's place at the head of the Chinese Republic was taken in March by Yuan Shi-kai, who had the support of insurgent generals. Yuan promised a general amnesty for all the factions fighting in the Chinese valleys, but the raping and rioting continued in some cities.

Meanwhile in Mexico, President Francisco Madero was confronted with a growing rebellion. Elected as the leader of the Constitutional Progressive Party in 1911, Madero was menaced by the ragged troops of Victoriano Huerto, a roving soldier from the hills.

Early in March, President Taft issued a proclamation warning Americans to be strictly neutral in the affairs of Mexico. Later he put United States units on the alert to protect the long American border facing Mexico across the Rio Grande.

Violence spread with pulsing fury through Latin America. Outbreaks were occurring in Ecuador, where a mob had lynched five generals soon after the beginning of the year. Strife flared intermittently in Honduras, where General Bomila had assumed the presidency in February, and in the Dominican Republic, where Senator Eladio Victoria had become the chief of state.

In the third week of March revolutionists overthrew the government in Paraguay. Rumblings of discontent rolled through Colombia and Panama. With President Taft's approval, Secretary of State Philander Knox left the United States on a hurried tour through the Central American countries.

During the month nearly a million coal miners in Europe —mainly in Prussia and France, after a walkout by miners in Britain—were on strike in protest against their working conditions.

Italy prepared to shell the Dardanelles, to extend the Italian war against Turkey. Peace proposals were rejected. An anarchist tried to kill the King of Italy: his bullets struck an army major, who shielded Victor Emmanuel with his own body.

Within the United States the major events of the month were the ratification by the Senate of arbitration treaties with Britain and France—and the initiation by Mr. Taft's administration of two new anti-trust suits. Under Taft's orders, the Department of Justice took legal action against sugar refiners, claiming that they controlled the sugar trade, and demanded the dissolution of the merger between the Southern Pacific and Union Pacific railroads.

Throughout the month President Taft was condemned and denounced by Colonel Roosevelt—for acting too soon, for acting too late, for delaying action, for failing to act as vigorously as the Colonel would have acted to deal with all the problems America had encountered.

The prices of meat and eggs in American cities edged higher. The prices of farm products were not high enough to satisfy American farmers. Crime grew worse. The number of alcoholics increased.

As the month wore on the attention of the people shifted again from Mr. Taft and foreign affairs to the antics of Theodore Roosevelt and the wrestling between Woodrow Wilson and Champ Clark for Democratic delegates.

COLONEL ROOSEVELT RAISES A RADICAL BANNER

The more Theodore Roosevelt had hobnobbed with millionaires and kings, the more convinced he had become that the troubles of America and the rest of mankind were largely due to the misbehavior of the ruling classes. He was a patrician landowner, the descendant of a family with the virtues of landowners. He owed nothing to businessmen or those who put on the airs of royalty.

Men who had made their money in ordinary commerce were often inclined to be greedy and irresponsible. Kings and other gaudy fellows, who lived by pomp and circumstance, had no rooted knowledge of the realities of existence. Yet the people needed leadership—the people needed someone to assert their dignity and protect them from the exploiters, the swarms of parasites existing in every society.

As President, he had done that. He had shown the world that a free man, with both feet firmly planted on American ground, could do whatever had to be done to make progress. He wasn't afraid of labels. He wasn't a creature of "the wealthy class" or "the middle class" or any other "class." He was a unique human being, as all Americans were. He could be conservative when he thought it was right to be so. He could be radical when he felt it was time to be radical.

Perhaps that was why he had puzzled people now and then. He felt they were often much more puzzled by him than they needed to be. He was simply a man who had refused to be pinned down. If they understood that, they understood him.

In Roosevelt's view the lives of men and nations were not laid out by an invisible Planner. God reigned, of course, in the skies above and beyond the stars and planets—he acknowledged the Divine Hand in the universe, but he did not believe in the strict Presbyterian Providence of Woodrow Wilson. He woke every day with a tremendous surge of energy, with a sense of wonder at what he had accomplished the day before, with eager expectations that the best was yet to come.

When he had been elected Vice-President on the ticket headed by McKinley, he thought he had been sidetracked. But he began immediately to do what he could to make his job more interesting, although he often felt like throwing the Vice-President's gavel at the dull senators over whom he presided. He said to his friends: "If I have been put on the shelf, my enemies will find that I can make it a cheerful place of abode."

After McKinley's tragic death and his own accession to

power, he told the nation: "Much has been given us, and much will rightfully be expected from us. . . . We have become a great nation, forced by the fact of its greatness into relations with the other nations of the earth, and we must behave as beseems a people with such responsibilities." During his years in the White House, he never allowed the people to forget that they were part of an enormous world. They kept slipping back into their dreams of isolation, and he kept blasting them to their feet with bold actions and resounding statements.

As Police Commissioner of New York, he had seen the sullen misery of the dwellers in the slums. He had seen the immigrant families packed into rat-ridden tenements smelling of garbage and filth. He had seen the burned bodies of children caught in tenement fires. Such things should not happen in America. If it took drastic reforms to keep such things from happening, he was one who would fight for such reforms.

The America in which Roosevelt had grown to manhood was rich and spacious. America had an abundance of everything—fertile land, coal and iron, plenty of water, a temperate climate, missions to perform and millions of people with talents to be cultivated. Bryan had been a wrong-headed demagogue, but Bryan had almost beaten McKinley by crying to the people: "Look! Look around you! Look at the riches you could have!" Roosevelt realized the appeal of that cry.

The Colonel had read many books, and he had been fascinated by the French Revolution. Why had the French nation gone through such a bath of blood? Why had the mobs torn French aristocrats to pieces in the streets? Why had the guillotine sliced so many noble heads from so many noble necks? The king and the nobles had not possessed the vision necessary to share their wealth with the people. That might have been the reason for the fury that destroyed them.

On his trips to his ranch in the Dakota territory Roosevelt talked with the bitter farmers in the Middle West. He realized the evil effects of low farm prices. He understood the resentment of factory workers in cities such as New York and Chicago, where men sweated sixty hours a week in dark and dangerous manufacturing plants for little wages. In 1900 Andrew Carnegie had made $23,000,000 from steel—free of taxes—and the average American had an income of less than five hundred dollars. Carnegie had a conscience, and resolved to give most of the money away; yet the factory workers and the work-worn farmers did not feel that they shared in Mr. Carnegie's gifts.

Roosevelt had called for "a Square Deal" for every American. He had said: "No man can be a good citizen unless he has a wage more than sufficient to cover the bare cost of living, and hours of labor short enough . . . to bear his share in the management of the community." The Morgans and the Carnegies, the Vanderbilts and the Harrimans, had the leisure as well as the money to take part in governing the states and the federal government. The people had to be brought into the picture.

The clock could not be turned back. At an accelerating pace America was becoming an industrial society. Larger and larger corporations were inevitable because industrialism demanded efficiency and the big corporations, combining into "trusts," were more efficient than small companies. But the government, the instrument of the people, could make the changes in society orderly and beneficial to all. The government could eliminate the "bad trusts" and preserve the "good trusts." That was the set of principles Roosevelt had slowly developed.

During his Presidency his domestic program was designed to adjust the political progressivism of his age to the realities of the enormous industrial system which had transformed American life since the Civil War. Passionately devoted to individual freedom, Roosevelt had tried to interpret that freedom in terms of social obligations. Men were free to help one another, not to hurt one another.

He was high-handed in foreign affairs, because he felt that the Constitution empowered him to act as the representative of the entire nation. In the Panama Canal controversy, he said: "I took the Isthmus, started the Canal, and then left Congress—not to debate the Canal, but to debate me. . . ." He intervened in the Japanese-Russian war of 1905 on his own initiative. He checkmated the Kaiser and halted German intervention in Venezuela as the self-appointed spokesman for the Western Hemisphere.

In domestic affairs he was much more cautious, although he talked just as boldly. He had revived the Sherman Anti-Trust Act, but prosecutions under it were not very numerous. He threatened "the malefactors of great wealth," but their wealth kept expanding. He aided the coal miners in the great strike of 1902 by refusing to swing the power of the government behind the mine owners, but he offered no positive help to the struggling unions. While he deplored the harsh contrast between the wealth of the few and the poverty of many, he seemed half-hearted in his attempts to correct the situation.

As a President he had zig-zagged from the progressive line to the conservative line. He had been defeated often by the Old Guard in the Senate—the "elder statesmen" such as Aldrich of Rhode Island, Orville Platt of Connecticut, William Allison of Iowa, John Spooner of Wisconsin—and he had been swayed by their counsels of reaction.

Yet in the field of conservation he had done magnificent things with the sweeping authority he had gained from Congress to preserve the public lands from the groups he called "plunder gangs." He had withdrawn from private exploitation 148,000,000 acres of forests, 80,000,000 acres of coal lands, 4,700,000 acres of phosphate areas, and 1,500,000 acres of waterpower sites. All these resources were set aside for the future needs of the people.

Under his prodding Congress had ended the tax rebates to the railroads, given more scope to the Interstate Commerce Commission, passed a meat-inspection act and a pure food and drug law, and put the federal government into the enforcement of workmen's compensation rules. He had backed the federal income-tax amendment and the proposal for federal taxes on inherited wealth.

So he had reasons for claiming that no one should have been astounded when he seized the radical banner of the Progressives from La Follette in the spring of 1912. But he rushed across the country like a blazing comet. He soared higher and his gyrations were wilder than La Follette's had ever been.

Consequently, quite a few of his old associates—the bearded senators and the gentlemen in top hats—expostulated with him. He was a true American with a long line of respectable ancestors. He had been a club man, a believer in a Big Navy, a patrician who was gallant with ladies and loved children. He could not really be a radical.

He pounded his chest and insisted that he was. He roared at the New Haven Chamber of Commerce: "The criticism has been made of me that I am a radical. So I am. I couldn't be anything else, feeling as I do."

Then there were members of the Chamber of Commerce who remembered that he had made a rip-roaring speech in August of 1910, in a town with the odd Indian name of Osawatomie, Kansas. He had rocked the country with a war-whoop: "We must drive the special interests out of politics. . . . Exactly as the special interests of cotton and slavery threatened our political integrity before the Civil War, so now the great special business interests too often control and corrupt men and the methods of government for their own profit."

In March of 1912 he took a similar line. He insisted this time that he was in earnest, although his previous war cries had not been taken too seriously—especially by the executives of J. P. Morgan & Co. and United States Steel: the intelligent bankers and corporation executives who raised campaign money. They thought he was just putting on a show and regarded him as actually more likely to cherish the interests of big business than that stubborn judge, William Howard Taft.

After all, he had written an amusing letter to old Chauncey Depew, long ago when Depew had left the Vanderbilts' railroad to take a seat in the Senate. Roosevelt was then governor of New York. He confessed to his witty friend Depew: "How I wish I *wasn't* a reformer, oh, Senator! But I suppose I must live up to my part, like the Negro minstrel who blacked himself all over!"

In 1912, however, Roosevelt thought of himself as much more than a minstrel. He felt that he was to sacrifice himself, to awaken the nation to the creeping perils of Socialism, to combat the blind complacency of Mr. Taft, and to overcome the plotting of the Democrats, who were obviously not fit to govern. He might be destroyed—he had a premonition that he might be killed—but he had a task before him that he could not shirk.

Some of his wealthy friends stood with him. Frank Munsey, the magazine publisher, and George Perkins, a Morgan partner and an organizer of the International Harvester and United States Steel trusts, knew that the thinking in the Chambers of Commerce had been outmoded. The day of competition was over: Munsey and Perkins shared Roosevelt's conviction of that fact. Munsey advised the Colonel that the United States should base its future on "good trusts" and federal regulation of the country's economic life. Perkins, a public-spirited man, had provided recreational parks for the employees of his companies and had developed a large-scale profit-sharing plan which enabled them to swim in the golden tide of profits. If the government encouraged profit-sharing and the "good companies," Perkins felt that what he regarded as the foolish war between the people and the corporations could be ended.

Roosevelt had been profoundly impressed by a book written by a young editor, Herbert Croly, under the title of *The Promise of American Life.* Croly advocated the establishment of a tremendously powerful national state to regulate corporations, unions, small businesses, and agriculture in "the national interest." He described his program as the New Nationalism. The New Nation-State would represent "the nation of yesterday and tomorrow, organized for its national historical mission."

That was what America needed, Roosevelt declared. The country had to have a sense of National Purpose, of its mission in the world of the future. The general good of all the people had to be placed above the selfish desires of individuals and groups. He admired men like the Pinchots— Gifford, who had helped him carry through his conservation program, and Amos, a wealthy young man dedicated to progressive legislation—because such men put the general welfare above everything else.

Mr. Taft might brand the Pinchots, the Roosevelts, and all far-seeing men as "extremists" or "neurotics," but the Colonel was not daunted by such smears. On March 20, in Carnegie Hall, he dealt with Mr. Taft's fears. Since Mr. Taft had dwelt upon the bloody Terror of Revolutionary France, the Colonel presented the history of France as he saw it.

Roosevelt shuddered at what had happened to France because of the refusal of the French reactionaries to face reality: "They gained twenty years' freedom from all restraint and reform, at the cost of the whirlwind of the red terror; and in their turn the unbridled extremists of the terror induced a blind reaction; and so, with convulsion and oscillation from one extreme to another, with alternations of violent radicalism and violent Bourbonism, the French people went through misery toward a shattered goal."

The same thing could happen to the United States, he feared, unless the Republicans rejected Taft and nominated Roosevelt. Taft had been given every opportunity to rise to the heights, and Taft had failed.

Roosevelt was ruthless about Taft's fate: "The leader for the time being, whoever he may be, is but an instrument to be used until broken and then to be cast aside; and if he is worth his salt he will care no more when he is broken than a soldier cares when he is sent where his life is forfeit in order that the victory may be won. In the long fight for righteousness the watchword for all of us is spend and be spent. It is of little matter whether any one man fails or succeeds; but the cause shall not fail, for it is the cause of mankind."

The crowd in Carnegie Hall thundered approval. The people there were ready to cast William Howard Taft aside as a broken instrument, no longer useful. To the crowd that night, Roosevelt was the Shining Crusader, mounted to slay the Dragon of Greed.

Roosevelt stirred them with a description of their own role: "We, here in America, hold in our hands the hope of the world, the fate of the coming years; and shame and disgrace will be ours if in our eyes the light of high resolve is dimmed, if we trail in the dust the golden hopes of men. . . . To turn this government either into government by a plutocracy or government by a mob would be to repeat on a larger scale the lamentable failures of the world that is dead. We stand against all tyranny, by the few or by the many."

Few of those in the hall knew Roosevelt. Few of them knew what his phrases meant in terms of economics or politics; and Roosevelt wasn't sure of his own meaning, his own understanding. He was carried on the currents of his inner needs and his consuming ambitions.

Throughout his public life Roosevelt had been haunted by nightmares of revolution in America. He had been frightened by the violence of labor in the desperate strikes of the 1880's and the 1890's; he had forebodings of a class war between the poor and the rich; he saw the pillars of American society collapsing in the wreckage.

In 1912 the Socialist Eugene Debs was in the field with proposals far more radical than Theodore Roosevelt's. And Debs seemed to be making headway, especially in the rat-ridden slums. The shots fired by troops at the textile strikers in Massachusetts, the clubs wielded by policemen, were making votes for Debs and the Socialist program of public ownership of all major industries, all the means of production.

With a surge of self-awareness, Roosevelt decided that he had to move at the head of the people marching toward a new America. The part he had been playing gradually had become true for him. He was really a radical then: much to his own astonishment and much to the horror of his friends, his comfortable companions on the tennis courts and in the Union League Clubs.

Perhaps George Perkins and Frank Munsey fooled themselves into thinking that Roosevelt was playing their game. Perhaps the Pinchots deluded themselves into thinking that Roosevelt was a White Knight, riding in their direction. He was more complex than any of the people who surrounded him: he continued to surprise them. They felt that they could use him for their own aims, their own power. Yet they could not control him, any more than he could control himself.

Some of his old associates thought he had gone overboard —that he was tramping shoulder to shoulder with Debs. Nicholas Murray Butler, the president of Columbia University and one of "T.R.'s" admirers for many years, savagely

denounced him. Philander Knox, who had become secretary
of state under Taft, contended that Roosevelt was driven by
"imperious, ambitious vanities and mysterious antipathies."
Henry L. Stimson, who had been raised to political prominence by Roosevelt, came out for Taft, calling the judge in
the White House "the true Progressive."

There were other observers who felt that the Colonel had
galloped beyond the borders of eccentricity into the realms
of madness. Dr. Morton Prince, a solemn disciple of the
Freudian school of psychology and a professor of neurology
at the Harvard Medical School, published an analysis of
Roosevelt's personality in which he indicated that a sub-
conscious desire to be President again had utterly poisoned
Roosevelt's system. Dr. Prince was quoted by the *Times* as
saying that Roosevelt would "go down in history as one of
the most illustrious psychological examples of the distortion
of conscious mental processes through the forces of subcon-
scious wishes."

Where he kicked over the traces—as he did in Carnegie
Hall, throwing away his prepared notes—Roosevelt roused
the people with an evangelical fervor. Whether he was conscious or unconscious of what he was doing, whether he was
an egomaniac or selfless crusader sacrificing his own career,
did not seem to matter. The citizens hailed him; many followed him through the streets, and many others jammed the
halls in which he spoke.

"We the people cannot turn back," cried the hunter from
Sagamore Hill, the democratic aristocrat who had awed the
kings of Europe. "In order to succeed we need leaders of
inspired idealism, leaders to whom are granted great visions,
who dream greatly and strive to make their dreams come
true; who can kindle the people with the fire from their own
burning souls."

His audiences felt that he had great visions, and he was
kindling them as they yearned to be kindled.

TROUBLES FOR PROFESSOR WILSON

While Colonel Roosevelt was soaring upon the wings of his dreams and Judge Taft was wearing the hair shirt of the Presidency, Woodrow Wilson tossed upon a sea of troubles in his home state of New Jersey. He had made too many trips to other states; he had neglected his own bailiwick, and he had to pay the price.

In his first year as governor he had mesmerized the state legislature, Republicans succumbing to his spell as readily as Democrats. The legislators had rolled over and fawned upon him. He had magic in his voice and in his lean, long-jawed face. Whatever he touched then seemed to go well.

Things were very different in the spring of 1912. Wilson's mind was concentrated upon winning the White House. His energies were spent in drafting statements on national issues, in meeting leaders from all parts of the nation, in building an organization of loyal Wilson men in every state.

The higher his stock went in the nation, the more persistent were the Republican leaders striving to knock him down in Trenton. With the aid of insurgent Democrats guided by ex-Senator Smith—who was determined to get even with Wilson for the humiliation he had suffered—they passed measure after measure which Wilson publicly opposed. Wilson threatened to veto the bills, and they defied him to do whatever he wished.

Wilson also awakened antagonisms by his patronage appointments. He rewarded his friends, added strength to his Presidential movement in New Jersey by giving plums to men who would be delegates at the Democratic convention, and ignored others who had not hurried to his Presidential headquarters to offer their assistance. The Princeton professor who had lambasted professional politicians now played a hard political game.

Wilson's aides were so lavish with promises that a feud

almost flamed between two of his devoted followers: David Crater, state committeeman from Monmouth County, and State Senator George Silzer of Middlesex. Each declared that Wilson had promised to make him New Jersey's secretary of state.

Crater was finally appointed to the job, after Wilson had been informed that Crater would apparently carry more weight than Silzer at the national convention. Silzer's friends in the state senate were then outraged. Wilson soothed them by naming Silzer as county prosecutor of Middlesex.

While the echoes of that row were dying away, another broke out when Wilson put a Princeton professor—Henry Jones Ford—into office as commissioner of banking and insurance. Precinct captains pointed out that Ford had lived in New Jersey for only three years; Ford was also known to be a conservative who had been against Bryan. Ford's appointment was delayed until an investigating committee of the state senate had inquired into his qualifications.

Wilson came under fire for other appointments, and some of his academic friends felt that he went much too far in his efforts to quell the revolt against him. But he was aware of the incessant back-alley maneuvers of Smith and Smith's ward-heelers, who were trying to grab control of the New Jersey delegation to the coming national Democratic convention.

Some thought he was too adroit for his own cause—too willing to compromise, too eager to deal with slippery characters. These New Jerseyites preferred the Wilson of 1911, who had brought a new breath of integrity into the state's politics. Wilson apparently believed that he could keep his integrity and operate adeptly at the same time.

While he labored to regain the ground he had lost at home, Wilson's candidacy in other states suffered from his inability to devote his full energies to it. William McCombs, who was in charge of his headquarters, was a sick man—

jealous and quick-tempered. Wilson had to settle a series of quarrels and squabbles.

Devoted to Wilson, McCombs was a crotchety, nervous, suspicious man who felt that he had more practical experience than Wilson and tried to keep everything in his own hands. McCombs had been on crutches when he had entered college as one of Wilson's students; he had been crippled as a boy. Wilson had befriended him, invited him to the Wilson home in Princeton. McCombs had become a lawyer, had made a fortune, and had volunteered to devote his time and financial resources to the cause of making Wilson the next President.

To keep a national organization in operation required a steady flow of money. This was a nagging source of anxiety for McCombs. Wilson's friends and Princeton classmates sent in checks, McCombs used part of his personal fortune, Edward A. Filene of Boston helped generously, but the campaign treasury had to be replenished at a rate which staggered everybody.

On March 21 a supporter of Champ Clark, the aggressive Senator James A. Reed of Missouri, raised some angry questions: "Where is all this money coming from for the Wilson campaign? . . . Where is all this money coming from to open up headquarters in almost every state?"

William Jennings Bryan swiftly sent a letter to Wilson: "Letters are pouring in here reiterating the charge that you have a large campaign fund. . . ."

Reed's charges were answered by Walker W. Vick of Wilson's organization in a sharp statement: "All contributions to Governor Wilson's campaign fund have been spontaneous and voluntary from his personal and political friends, mainly in small amounts. A contribution of $2 from a textile worker in Massachusetts was received today.

"It is true that there is a Wilson organization in practically every state throughout the Union, organized and being maintained by the friends, both personal and political, of Governor Wilson throughout these states, who see in his election the embodiment of clean government and progressive Democracy, and the hope of the Democratic Party in resuming popular government."

Ray Stannard Baker, Wilson's biographer, later acknowledged that Wilson's supporters used as much money, probably, as any other group in the Democratic race that spring. This was not surprising, because Wilson's managers had to build committees in every state: they had no old organization behind them. They could not call upon the political bosses who were tied in with Speaker Clark.

Although the evidence mounted during March that the speaker's cool pulling of political strings was tugging more and more delegates to the Clark camp, Wilson continued to rely on the power of newspaper editorials and the eloquence of his own voice to sway the people. In the end, he thought, the people would somehow have a decisive role. He wasn't sure of the way in which they could exercise their strength, but they would do it.

When the New Jersey legislature stumbled to the end of its regular session in 1912 in the closing days of March, the miserable record was plain for all citizens to see. Writing to a friend, Wilson said: "This has been a petty and barren legislature. It has done nothing worth mentioning except try to amend and mar the wonderful things we accomplished last year. . . ." He refused to accept any of the blame: "Small men have ignorantly striven to put me in a hole by discrediting themselves! It is a merry world—for a cynic to live in. . . ."

Still he was not downhearted.

"Now I must rush out again in search of delegates—shy birds more difficult to find in genuine species than the snark itself," he wrote to Mary Hulbert. "I keep singularly well, and some of my adventures I enjoy thoroughly. Last night, for example, I spoke at a chamber of commerce dinner in Plainfield and then came the twenty-seven miles back through the midnight in a motor, speeding amidst misty moonlight full of ghosts and mysteries—everything still and asleep except the creeping chilly vapors. It does not sound very wholesome, does it? but it was good for a weary, jaded mind within the thinking box of a tired governor!"

Wilson was not completely weary or jaded. He had a peaceful, pleasant family life with his wife and daughters. He could relax with his family, read poetry, and listen to music. He was surrounded by friends who were perpetually dazzled by his brilliance.

Yet to some of the newspapermen who admired him and wished him well, his campaign definitely seemed to be dropping into low gear. The Charlotte *News and Courier* reported: "While it is plainly a case of the field against Wilson, the fact remains that the field seems to be winning nearly all the instructed delegates. . . ." The paper added in a mournful editorial: "Almost every day now is marked by some development which emphasizes Woodrow Wilson's need of a campaign manager with large experience in practical politics. Until recently it has seemed virtually certain that Governor Wilson would go to Baltimore with more delegates than anyone else, but, while his popularity has not declined, the other candidates are out-generalling him. . . ."

Through his fellow members of the Congress, Speaker Clark had access to the ward bosses, the county officials, the precinct captains who were likely to be delegates or to name the delegates to the June convention. Clark's representatives dickered with these men, made bargains with them, offered promises of future favors.

Wilson, wary of local bosses after his bruising battle with Smith in New Jersey, cultivated the younger leaders in the states—the men who were independent of the political clubs. There were relatively few of these, and they did not carry the weight of the "regulars," the old wheelhorses who were linked to Champ Clark. Wilson's strategy did not seem effective to the political reporters closely following the struggle.

With his firm faith in Providence, Wilson went right on speaking and working sixteen hours a day. Thousands of copies of his speeches were printed and circulated. Letters of support streamed in. Yet some of the amateur strategists around him were beginning to wonder whether the barriers before him would not prove to be too high for him to leap over.

JUDGE TAFT IN TORMENT

The month of March was a bad one for William Howard Taft. He received three damaging blows that hurt him deeply—blows that hurt him almost as much as the entry of Roosevelt into the Presidential contest.

The first blow came when Dr. Frank Taussig, the Harvard economic expert, delivered a slashing attack on the report of the Tariff Board, which Taft had hailed as "a monument of the thoroughness, industry, impartiality, and accuracy of the men engaged in its making." In its four-volume report the Board—composed of economists—had attempted to lay down fair principles for revisions of the rates on wool and woolen products.

The Board's principles were based on estimates of the costs of producing wool in various parts of the country. Dr. Taussig declared that it was impossible to determine such costs in the United States or in any other land. The noted economist asserted that the report strengthened his conviction that there was no sensible excuse for maintaining an import duty on wool at all. "The strength of the wool duty lies not in economic reasoning but in the inevitable wish of every industry in every part of the country to get its share of what seems to be the benefits of protection," Taussig snapped.

In other words, Dr. Taussig indicated that the sheep producers and the woolen manufacturers had made dupes of President Taft and his Tariff Board. Taft felt the wool industry, along with other industries, deserved protection against foreign competition. He took his stand for protective tariffs, and he couldn't be swayed against them.

Yet there were many men in America who didn't agree with him—and Taft knew it. Theodore Roosevelt hadn't met tariff issues head-on; McKinley had ducked such questions whenever it was possible to duck. Taft showed more political courage by taking a firm stand, but he got little credit for doing so.

Another unhappy experience for Taft arose from the row between James Wilson, his secretary of agriculture, and Dr. Harvey W. Wiley, the chemist who had done so much to push through the Pure Food and Drug Acts. Dr. Wiley was a stubborn man; he had aroused the antagonism of some food producers who felt that he was being unnecessarily strict in enforcing the acts.

Charges had been brought against Dr. Wiley. He was accused of employing Dr. H. H. Rusby, a pharmacologist, at a daily rate of $20—more than twice the amount fixed as a maximum by Congress. Dr. Wiley admitted that he had got around the low compensation-rate prescribed by the legislators; he had employed Dr. Rusby at a substantial annual salary and then had required the pharmacologist to work only a certain number of days. Wiley said he couldn't get the man he needed at the low rate fixed by Congress.

The case was considered by President Taft, after Secretary Wilson had permitted the charges to be filed against Dr. Wiley. Taft was irritated with Wilson for getting Dr. Wiley into trouble. The President told his wife: "The Wiley business is a mess, and I am inclined to think I may have to get a new secretary of agriculture. Uncle Jimmy is not strong enough to manage. But he stands well with the farmers and it might be difficult to get rid of him."

Taft dismissed the charges against Wiley, saying that bureau chiefs had to use their discretion in employing experts. Yet Taft did not publicly praise Dr. Wiley's record of devotion to the pure food and drug laws. Thus the President alienated both the supporters of Dr. Wiley and the followers of Secretary Wilson at the same time.

When Dr. Wiley resigned in March of 1912, he asserted that conditions in the Department of Agriculture were "intolerable." Dr. Wiley added: "Secretary Wilson, approaching his dotage, was alertly antagonistic." Taft, striving to be just to all, was caught between the two camps.

But the departure of Dr. Wiley and the attacks on his Tariff Board were small disappointments to President Taft, compared with the third defeat he suffered that month. His third defeat was the emasculation by the Senate of the arbitration treaties with Britain and France.

From the beginning of his administration, Taft had sought ways to promote peace. As a lawyer and a jurist, he placed his hopes in carefully drawn treaties. He labored over the documents with the French and British leaders; he had joyfully hailed their official signing in August of 1911, and he had tried valiantly to induce the Senate to ratify the treaties. He had voiced a deep desire to reach similar pacts with Germany, Russia, the Netherlands, Norway, and Sweden—and thought that Japan, too, might join the movement for international arbitration of all disputes.

He had refused to abandon the struggle when a majority of the Senate Foreign Relations Committee voted against them. In a letter to his son, Robert A. Taft (who was later to assert the authority of the Senate in many conflicts with other Presidents) he displayed his determination: "I am going . . . to see if I cannot arouse the country. . . . Carnegie and all the peace cranks are interested in this, as well as the church, and I am hopeful that we may set a fire under the senators which may change their views."

He had no help from Colonel Roosevelt. In fact, the Colonel laid down a barrage against the treaties, declaring that he preferred "righteousness before peace." Roosevelt had expressed his own ideas in May of 1910, when he had accepted the Nobel Peace Prize; he had then called for the creation of a League of Peace with enough military power to keep the nations from engaging in wars.

When Congress, excited by Roosevelt's plan and pushed by the people to take action, had adopted a joint resolution later that year authorizing the establishment of a Peace Commission, Mr. Taft had promptly offered the chairmanship to Mr. Roosevelt and he had turned it down. Perhaps Roosevelt felt that Congress had gone too far; the resolution had been rather sweeping in its terms, empowering the Commission to "consider the expediency of utilizing existing international agencies for the purpose of limiting the armaments of the nations of the world by international agreement, and of constituting the combined navies of the world an international force for the preservation of universal peace. . . ." It was a daring declaration. Some senators were horrified by it—and the idea was speedily abandoned.

The admirals of the American navy were not quite ready to have their battleships taken into an international fleet. Neither were the admirals of Great Britain, Germany, and Japan.

Mr. Taft's modest proposals for international arbitration, to be carried out by Joint High Commissions with representatives from the nations involved in international disputes, seemed much more practical to most officials—except for many members of the United States Senate. When Mr. Taft went over the heads of the senators to the voters, he got nowhere. The people did not come to his rescue.

When the Senate gave its verdict, in March of 1912, Taft suffered a humiliating defeat. Before giving a formal agreement to the treaties with England and France, the Senate removed everything that gave the pacts effective force. The ambassadors from Paris and London protested, saying that the treaties had become utterly useless—and Taft agreed with them.

After that, Taft did not know what to do. The Senate had removed the provision that gave a Joint High Commission the power to decide whether an issue between nations was "justiciable" and could be submitted to the Permanent Court of Arbitration at The Hague or to another international tribunal. This was the heart of the matter, Taft believed.

The President did not drop his efforts for new treaties, but his confidence had ebbed. The people had at first appeared to respond to his appeals, and then popular interest had abruptly declined. He was saddened by the public's failure to see what was involved. The principle of arbitration seemed to Taft so simple and so just—he could not understand why the treaties had been torn apart.

His will to fight for such international agreements was depleted by the demands of an election year. He was becoming absorbed, almost against his will, in the duel with Roosevelt for the Republican Presidential nomination. As the spring days of 1912 approached, the see-saw struggle grew more agonizing for all who were in it.

Teeth bared, claws extended, Roosevelt was like a prowling lion. Taft ruefully observed: "The truth is he [Roosevelt] believes in war and wishes to be a Napoleon and to die on the battlefield. He has the spirit of the old berserkers. . . . It is curious how unfitted he is for courteous debate. I don't wonder he prefers the battle-axe."

The Colonel, of course, insisted that he did not seek war, did not wish to be a Napoleon, and certainly did not wish to die on a battlefield. But he was quite willing to swing a political battle-axe at Taft; he believed that Taft must be demolished politically before the country could march on to the New Nationalism.

Taft put on his helmet and his armor and met the crashing charges of the old hunter from Sagamore Hill, but hated every minute of the sweaty combat. He was alarmed by Theodore's ferocity; he was convinced that Roosevelt was smashing the Republican Party as well as William Howard Taft.

In the last week in March, Taft scored a triumph in New York—the Colonel's former stronghold. He got 83 of the state's 90 delegates to the Republican convention. And yet this triumph brought him no pleasure, because he knew it would only make Roosevelt fight harder.

Taft stayed in the fight because he felt that he had to do so—to protect "constitutional government" from the extremists led by Theodore. Yet he restrained his friends from denouncing Roosevelt. He wrote to one of them: "Personal abuse is not likely to control ultimately in this campaign; and I certainly don't want to be responsible for it if it does. . . ."

In a conversation with the Kansas editor, William Allen White, President Taft insisted that nothing would induce him to attack Roosevelt personally. And he said that he hoped once the campaign was over the two of them could get together again "and be as of old."

However, there was much turmoil ahead, and Taft knew it. The days of personal attacks and recriminations were coming.

Conditions in America would never again be like the halcyon days when Roosevelt reigned in the White House and Taft had been his favorite. William Howard Taft often harked back to the past; nevertheless, he plunged ahead now in preparation for the stormy future.

IV. The Shocks of April

DISASTER AT SEA, AND A LANDSLIDE IN ILLINOIS

For many people in the United States, the month of April, 1912, produced two severe shocks—the sinking of the magnificent liner *Titanic* in the North Atlantic, and the overwhelming defeat suffered by Woodrow Wilson in the Illinois Presidential primary.

The catastrophe for Woodrow Wilson came a few days before the *Titanic* disaster. In the Illinois primary Wilson fell beneath an avalanche of votes cast for his opponent, Champ Clark of Missouri. Despite all the efforts of his followers and despite his desperate tour of the state in the final days before the balloting, Wilson lost by a landslide.

Clark received better than 218,000 votes, Wilson a little more than 75,000. The Wilson magic seemed to have vanished. How could a country politician from Missouri, a rambling old gentleman in a slouch hat, totally lacking in Wilson's magnetism and Wilson's eloquence, put the glamorous governor of New Jersey so far into the shade?

From the beginning Clark had enjoyed the backing of fellow members of Congress, the endorsement of the Hearst newspapers, and connections with professional politicians. But Wilson had the encouragement of the most respected magazines and newspapers, and fervent support from church publications and Presbyterian, Methodist, Episcopalian, and Baptist leaders. Wilson had been called "the Christian in politics," and ministers in the Middle West and elsewhere believed that he might be selected by God to guide America in a time of crisis. This faith in Wilson's destiny had been bolstered by his superb showing on the second day of April in the Wisconsin primary. There he had captured twenty of the state's twenty-four delegates.

So Wilson had entered the Illinois primary, armed by the enthusiasm of his energetic supporters, and certain that his attacks on the Illinois bosses would arouse the citizens, just as his assaults on New Jersey corruption had rallied voters to him in his home state. To be sure, William McCombs, his campaign manager, warned him that he had little organized strength in Illinois and insufficient funds to make a fully effective fight there. But Wilson counted on a ground swell of popular approval.

Just before he boarded the train for Chicago, Wilson received a message from McCombs which contained a blunt warning: "The great difficulty with your campaign is the aloofness of a great many of the men in the various districts who do things. These are the men the people follow and are the men who in the main select the delegates. They have an impression of you in a large degree that you are austere and dictatorial and that you will not have a due appreciation of what is to be done for you. It is hard to convince the hundreds of men who really control things that this is not so. . . ."

Before Wilson went to Illinois for his last-minute effort, his advisers told him he was making a blunder to stake so much in a single primary. McCombs and others thought it would take a miracle to enable him to beat Clark there. And an overwhelming defeat, in such a key state, was bound to dampen the spirits of his lieutenants in other places.

But Wilson would not heed such advice. As he proved later in his fight for the League of Nations, he believed he could arouse the people when no one else could. And he would not withdraw from a conflict if he felt it had to be endured to the end—no matter what the end might be.

McCombs raised thousands of dollars—he did not refuse a contribution from any source—and tried to form a Wilson organization in Illinois. Unfortunately for Wilson, the Democrats in the state were divided into warring factions—and Wilson's men could not line up any of the major groups for him.

Mayor Carter H. Harrison of Chicago, head of one faction, was close to William Randolph Hearst and consequently opposed to Wilson. Another faction, led by Edward F. Dunne, was firmly roped to Champ Clark. That left only the conservative machine, headed by the hard-boiled Roger Sullivan, who didn't give a damn about Wilson's principles but did want to control the Democratic Party

While Wilson was denouncing the bosses, McCombs and others in the Wilson headquarters tried furiously to swing Sullivan over to the New Jersey governor's side. Sullivan wouldn't swing. Harrison and Hearst, aided by Senator William J. Stone of Missouri, slammed Wilson day and night, getting him on the defensive and keeping him there.

Senator Stone, a snorting, frock-coated orator known to reporters as "Gumshoe Bill," accused Wilson of voting against Bryan in 1896 and declared that Wilson had not become a progressive until the tide of popular feeling seemed to be moving in that direction. Wilson was labeled "the Wall Street candidate," the aristocratic Princetonian who had shown contempt for "unwashed" immigrants from southern and eastern European countries. Chicago was crowded with such immigrants.

From the beginning of his trip to Illinois, Wilson's nerves had been stretched taut. Soon after his arrival in Chicago, someone went into his hotel room, searched through his baggage, and removed a suitcase full of letters. He was positive that this was the work of people who sought to destroy him.

Then goaded by the daily attacks of his opponents, Wilson changed his temperate tone. At Joliet, answering charges that he was financed by Wall Street, he cried: "If I knew the money for the expenses of my campaign were coming from such sources I'd be ashamed to show my face." (By this statement he admitted that he did not check carefully into the origins of campaign gifts.)

In Springfield a reporter for the Chicago *Daily Tribune* heard him attack Senator Stone and publisher Hearst in these terms: "I have heard within the last thirty minutes that in Springfield I am to be considered a dangerous man. I am told that since the announcement of my coming it has been deemed necessary to telegraph a United States Senator from Missouri to come here tonight to furnish an antidote for the poison I will spread. The one who has compounded this happens to own newspapers in several sections of the country. It has been his particular pleasure to seek to destroy every man who speaks for the Democratic party. I am sorry a United States Senator will distribute his wares."

Wilson disliked being considered "a dangerous man." He regarded himself as a man of solid substance who had ventured into politics to give the people the kind of leadership they needed. He was astonished when he found that some citizens believed the charges hurled against him.

Going from town to town, he realized that he was encircled at every turn by members of the Harrison-Hearst-Clark combination. He began to feel alone and besieged.

The end in Illinois was worse than anyone had expected it to be. Far from working a political miracle, Wilson was slaughtered at the polls. After that, his stock sank close to political bankruptcy even in the eyes of editors and civic leaders who had previously predicted his nomination.

Wilson was sorely hurt, but he did not act like a man whose back had been broken. The day after the Illinois disaster, he addressed a large audience in Pennsylvania and wrote to A. M. Palmer, one of his friends: "I spoke in Pittsburgh last night and had a very gratifying reception from a splendid audience." He kept his faith in Providence, and went on toward his goal.

But the politicians in the House of Representatives felt that the Illinois voters had pointed the way for the Democratic convention. When Speaker Clark entered the House, the day after the Illinois verdict, the Democratic members rose and greeted him with cheers, saluting him as "the next President." Clark took the cheers with the delighted expression of a man who expected to win easily.

After that Wilson showed new strength on April 13, when the Pennsylvania primaries gave him a majority of the 76 delegates from the coal and steel state. But from then on he suffered one setback after another.

In the middle of April Wilson traveled to Georgia with his wife and William Gibbs McAdoo, a lawyer and railroad president who had been born in Georgia and had many friends there. They expected acclaim in Georgia. Wilson, in his early years, had practiced law in Atlanta and Mrs. Wilson came from an old Georgia family. The Wilsons were welcomed by waving crowds, but the Georgia politicians remained loyal to Oscar W. Underwood, the Alabama congressman with followers throughout the South.

Underwood, chairman of the House Ways and Means Committee, was an able speaker and an aggressive champion of tariff reforms. He presented himself as a southerner among southerners. Wilson, though born in Virginia, was not sufficiently a southerner to overcome Underwood in Georgia, Florida, and other conservative southern states.

In Nebraska, the home of William Jennings Bryan, Clark triumphed in spite of covert assistance to Wilson from Mr. Bryan. Publicly Bryan was neutral, blessing both Clark and Wilson as "progressives." Yet apparently he tried quietly to swing votes to Wilson. If so, Bryan failed—because Clark won by a wide margin.

After the fall of Nebraska, other states moved into the Clark column. On April 29, Colorado Democrats instructed their delegates to vote for the speaker; on April 30 Massachusetts and Maryland also endorsed him.

At the end of April Clark was driving steadily ahead— and the Wilson movement seemed to be falling rapidly to pieces. The voters seemed determined to send the professor from Princeton back to old Nassau.

ROOSEVELT RIDES THE RANGE

The struggle between Roosevelt and Taft offered a curious contrast to the clash between Wilson and Clark. In the Democratic ranks the professional politicians favored Clark and demonstrated that they were able to get their allies to the polls. The Republican professionals, on the other hand, were for Taft but could not pile up popular victories for him.

While Colonel Roosevelt was riding the range, gathering the Republican voters into his corral, the Taft herders seemed to be virtually helpless. When Roosevelt lost in a primary— as he had lost in New York—he did not hesitate to raise the cry of corruption and "ballot stealing."

In the first three months of 1912 Taft's friends had assured the President they had corralled 274 delegates. With 540 necessary for the Republican nomination, he was more than half way to a majority. Then Roosevelt increased the pace of the campaign, rushing from city to city, rousing people's emotions, calling Taft a tool of the corporations, throwing one epithet of scorn and anger after another.

"The conduct of the Colonel is certainly that of a desperate man who stops at nothing," President Taft wrote to a friend on April 10. A few days earlier, he had said in a note to his brother Charles: "He has become so violent that some people feel he is losing his reason; others say he is drinking but I do not think so." Taft had long considered the possibility that Theodore was "temperamentally irresponsible."

Roosevelt had convinced himself that he was acting in a most responsible manner: he was sure that he was saving the Republican Party and perhaps the nation itself from a feeble man enslaved by the forces of evil. His old friend Taft was a pitiful puppet, or if not a puppet a man indictable for "the grossest hypocrisy."

The Colonel named bosses who were dominating Judge Taft. He cited Boies Penrose of Pennsylvania, Richard Ballinger of Washington, Samuel S. Koenig of New York, Nelson Aldrich of Rhode Island, and others. It was vain for Taft to protest that these same people had supported Roosevelt in the past. Why, he asked, if it was all right for Roosevelt to take their aid, why wasn't it all right for William Howard Taft?

It wasn't all right, Roosevelt insisted. *He* had controlled *them* because he had been a strong President; *Taft* was controlled *by them* because Taft did not have the qualities of a Theodore Roosevelt.

In 1905 Roosevelt had penned high praise of Taft in a letter to George Otto Trevelyan, the British historian: "He has no more fear in dealing with the interests of great corporate wealth than he has in dealing with the leaders of the most powerful labor unions; and if either go wrong he has not the slightest hesitation in antagonizing them. To strength and courage, clear insight, and practical common sense, he adds a very noble and disinterested character." At that time Roosevelt had known Taft for some years; Taft was nearly fifty years old and had been in public life for a long while:

his character and habits were certainly well known to the Colonel.

But in April of 1912 Roosevelt flailed his old friend with accusations of many kinds. The Colonel went to endless lengths in attempting to prove to the voters that he had been utterly wrong in praising Taft on so many occasions. He now said he had been utterly wrong in appointing Taft secretary of war, and utterly wrong in picking Taft to succeed him as President. It was a painful performance—the spectacle of a former President, a notable public figure, a man whose words carried much weight, trying to tear down the image of Taft as a wise and judicious leader, an image that he himself had done so much to create.

Yet the oddity, even the absurdity, of Roosevelt's position did not keep many Republican voters from following him. In the same Illinois primary which brought disaster to Wilson, Roosevelt administered a heavy thrashing to Judge Taft, winning by two to one.

Two days later the New York *Times* reported that Washington Republican leaders were talking of Governor Charles Evans Hughes of New York as a "compromise candidate." These leaders hoped to get Roosevelt and Taft to withdraw from the race and to pledge their mutual support for Hughes.

Roosevelt quickly scotched that talk. In an exultant mood he said that no one dared to suggest a compromise to him. He was in the fight to the finish, and he was prepared to make it even hotter for Taft.

REPUBLICAN RIOT SPLITS MICHIGAN, said the *Times* headline in an adjoining column the same day. Fights with fists and intemperate words were features of the G.O.P. state convention. Police and militia were called, and the convention finally picked two sets of delegates, one for Taft and one for Roosevelt.

On April 14 the Sunday *Times* carried another headline:

ROOSEVELT WINS IN PENNSYLVANIA PRIMARY. The Colonel carried the coal-mining districts by huge majorities over Taft. With two large states in his camp, he began to believe that he had an excellent chance to take the Republican nomination away from the incumbent President.

Tempers rose to such heights at the Missouri Republican convention that riots broke out there, too. The Taft chairman of the convention received a beating from a Roosevelt man, and three men involved in violence at the meeting were held on assault charges.

The *Times* on that April Sunday, after reporting the riots and the rough behavior of some of Roosevelt's lieutenants, summed up one of the Colonel's speeches with an ironical headline: ROOSEVELT LAUDS HIS FIGHT FOR PEACE—ALWAYS FOR IT, HE SAYS, WHEN THERE WAS NO DISHONOR TO THE NATION.

A few days later the Colonel's cockiness was somewhat diminished by the Connecticut primary, where Taft voters elected all twelve delegates to the Republican national convention. Roosevelt recovered his aplomb, however, when he learned of his sweeping endorsement by the voters in Nebraska and Oregon.

His drive for the nomination continued to gain momentum on April 20, when he carried the West Virginia primary. The Taft forces were suddenly showing signs of panic, and White House reporters began to ask if Mr. Taft had decided to abandon the contest.

Roosevelt made it impossible for the President to make such a decision, even if Taft had wanted to. The Colonel's accusations grew more and more stinging. He charged that the President was using government patronage "shamelessly" to "secure Taft's renomination." He asserted that fraud and violence had been "systematically used to defeat the will of the people" and to gain delegates for Taft.

Roosevelt's statements undoubtedly contained a grain of truth. The Colonel knew the political ropes: he knew that he had encouraged the federal office holders to vote for Taft in 1908. The Colonel knew that some frauds and some violence had been committed by factions in both camps.

But a fever of righteousness had heated Roosevelt's blood now. Methods which had seemed acceptable in 1904 and 1908 were not acceptable to a man who believed that America needed a cleansing crusade. He felt that he was locked in "the most momentous struggle since the close of the Civil War"—he was the Knight leading the people to the heights of "true democracy."

The Democratic Party was hopeless, in Roosevelt's view. And the only way to revive the spirit of the Republican Party was by showing its captains that the members wanted Theodore Roosevelt, the man who had cast away all compromises with evil.

So Roosevelt raged in the valleys and across the plains, summoning the voters to rise or fall with him.

TAFT REFUSES TO BE "A STRAW MAN" ANY LONGER

At long last William Howard Taft emerged from the White House. At long last the President decided "to nail the lies, to tell the truth, and let the people judge."

In the last week of April a train carrying the President and his staff rolled through the cold towns of New England. At each stop along the line he stepped to the back platform and sorrowfully attacked his old friend, the Rough Rider. Taft had been driven to the limit of his endurance.

He said that Mr. Roosevelt had been careless with the truth. He said that Mr. Roosevelt was not "a true sportsman" or "a good loser." He said that the fundamental issue between Roosevelt and himself was an issue of national policy, not a personal quarrel. If the bitterness between them had been purely personal, Taft said, he would not have broken his silence.

"This wrenches my soul," he told the quiet crowds. "I am

here to reply to an old and true friend of mine, Theodore Roosevelt, who has made many charges against me. I deny those charges, I deny all of them. I do not want to fight Theodore Roosevelt, but sometimes a man in à corner fights. I am going to fight."

Then he went on: "When the time came for this campaign to begin, I let the people know I would like to have my administration approved by their giving me another term. At that time Theodore Roosevelt said that he was not a candidate and that it would be a calamity if he were nominated. Since then he has changed his mind."

Soon after this Taft delivered two major speeches in Boston—a long one at the Arena, in which he took up every charge Roosevelt had made against him, and a shorter one at Symphony Hall, where he was received by a sympathetic audience.

Taft summed up Roosevelt's indictment of him in these words: "By excerpts from my speeches he has sought to show and has charged that I am one who has publicly announced that I am in favor of an aristocracy of political bosses, and that I am linked with political bosses in seeking my renomination. He charges that the patronage of the government is being shamelessly used to secure my renomination, and that in the conventions and primaries which have been held, fraud and violence have been systematically used to defeat the will of the people and to secure delegates for me."

Taft went on. "He says that I am not a progressive, but a reactionary; that I was nominated by progressives, and after election joined the ranks of those who opposed me for nomination; and he intimates that I have not the spirit of the progressive, or the imagination or the clear-headed purpose essential to the make-up of such a person. In short, he intimates pretty broadly that I am puzzle-witted. . . . He minimizes and flouts the importance of the laws enacted and the executive action taken during my administration."

By twisting one of his statements, Taft claimed, Roosevelt had depicted him as an advocate of oligarchy. Roosevelt had quoted a speech made by Taft in Toledo, in which Taft had pointed out that only about one-fourth of the people voted in elections and consequently the United States had a government by "a representative part of the people."

"Does Mr. Roosevelt deny this fact?" Taft demanded in Boston. "Can he or any fair man maintain that in stating such a palpable truth . . . I was advocating a government by an oligarchy? . . . Was it honest, was it fair for Theodore Roosevelt to seize one sentence from a speech, to garble it and then to give it a meaning which he knew from the context it could not bear?"

The question of the President's relationship with Senator Lorimer of Illinois had been raised by Roosevelt in the Illinois primary. Taft declared that it was indecent for Roosevelt to "give the impression to his auditors that a vote for me was a vote for Mr. Lorimer. I have not seen Mr. Lorimer for two years, and have had no communication with, or from, him." Taft then described his own part in the attempt to remove Lorimer from the Senate, and he read to the Boston crowd a letter he had sent to Roosevelt in 1911 saying that Lorimer's election had been accompanied by "a mess and mass of corruption."

Then he discussed Roosevelt's attitude toward the lowering of tariff walls between the United States and Canada. "T.R." had first been in favor of the reciprocity agreement, calling it "admirable from every standpoint." Taft said the Colonel's sudden switch was easily explained: "In the exigency of his contest for the nomination, and with the purpose of accentuating the supposed feeling of the farmers against me, he recants his approval. . . . I submit that Mr. Roosevelt's course on reciprocity is not in accord with the square deal."

Obviously controlling himself with difficulty, the President then answered the charge that machine politicians were stealing delegates and that he was "receiving stolen goods" and gaining by "the use of dirty instruments." Taft said he did not know what was going on in all the states, he could not be certain that his followers were not perpetrating frauds in some cases, but he felt that the courts were the proper places to settle such matters.

Why didn't Roosevelt go to the courts if evidence of such thefts really existed? Taft asked whether it was fair "to run away from the opportunity provided by law to establish fraud and injustice and only claim it in the newspapers and in charges against one's opponent." He added: "In Indianapolis, I am informed, the complaint of the Roosevelt committee that fraud had been committed in the primaries appeared in an afternoon paper sold on the streets before the primaries were opened. . . . The truth is that it has been perfectly plain from the first that the deliberate plan . . . has been to claim everything exultingly and with the utmost confidence, and to meet the reports of the election of adverse delegates by directing in advance the bringing of trumped-up contests."

Taft then discussed Roosevelt's assertion that "never before has patronage been so shamelessly used in politics as . . . to secure my nomination." Taft frankly acknowledged that officeholders supported "those to whose appointment they attribute their preferment." But most of the men holding important federal jobs had been appointed by Roosevelt, not by Taft, and many of them were now favoring the Colonel. Taft insisted that he had not fired "a single man" for supporting Mr. Roosevelt.

What about the charge that he was a "reactionary"—a traitor to the "progressives" who had put him in the White House? Taft said he was proud of his record—his assaults on the trusts, his protection of the public lands, his successful advocacy of the amendments to the railroad-regulation act, and laws enacted for the protection of working people.

"This was all progressive legislation," Taft said. "But I am not to have any credit for it because it was accomplished through regular Republicans."

In the closing section of his Boston Arena speech, Taft brought the third-term issue into the open. Roosevelt had already served nearly two full terms as President, and had repeatedly promised that he would never seek the White House again. Now Roosevelt had broken these promises.

Taft warned the people: "There is not the slightest reason why, if he secures a third term, and the limitation of the Washington, Jefferson, and Jackson tradition is broken down, he should not have as many terms as his natural life will permit. If he is necessary now to the government, why not later?

"One who so lightly regards constitutional principles, and especially the independence of the judiciary, one who is so naturally impatient of legal restraints, and of due legal procedure, and who has so misunderstood what liberty regulated by law is, could not safely be intrusted with successive presidential terms. I say this sorrowfully, but I say it with the full conviction of truth."

Taft did more than hit hard at Roosevelt in his speeches. He also revealed the background of Roosevelt's failure to prosecute the International Harvester Company in 1907 under the Sherman Anti-Trust Act. These documents showed that Roosevelt had failed to push the case, after Herbert Knox Smith, commissioner of corporations, had written to Mr. Roosevelt: ". . . It is a very practical question whether it is well to throw away now the great influence of the so-called Morgan interests, which up to this time have supported the advanced policy of the administration."

The emotional strain of questioning the honesty, the decency, the fundamental qualities of his old friend Roosevelt proved to be almost more than President Taft could bear. He was stricken with grief on board the Presidential train after delivering the harsh New England speeches. One of the newspapermen traveling with the President found Taft seated in a lounge-chair with his head between his hands. As the reporter entered, Taft raised his heavy head. "Roosevelt was my closest friend," Taft said brokenly. Then he started to weep uncontrollably.

Taft's tears had given way to a cold rage a few days later when he spoke in Massachusetts, on the eve of the Presidential primary there: "Condemn me if you will, but condemn me by other witnesses than Theodore Roosevelt. I was a man of straw, but I have been a man of straw long enough. Every man who has blood in his body, and who has been misrepresented as I have, is forced to fight."

His audience was astonished and shocked by his admission that he had ever been "a man of straw." Such a statement, coming from the President of the United States, created a sensation throughout the country. Taft's willingness to fight was obscured by the national revulsion against a Chief Executive who said: "I have been a man of straw long enough."

Roosevelt's barrage of accusations hurt Taft far less than the President's own handling of the situation. His pleas for sympathy, his image of himself as a rather helpless fellow kicked and cuffed by the Colonel, lost him the admiration of many people who expected their Chief Executive to be strong and undaunted by any attacks.

The issues of national policy were blurred and overshadowed by the intensely personal nature of the conflict between the two men. The contest seemed more like a tragedy by Shakespeare than a political debate.

As April ended, the curtain came down on the first act of the Taft-Roosevelt tragedy, with each man crying out that he had been stabbed and betrayed.

And on the other side of the national stage, Woodrow Wilson found himself thrown to the very edge of despair by the Clark avalanche.

V. May: What Did the People Say?

In 1912 Wilson and Roosevelt strove to take advantage of the fact that millions of voters had their first opportunity in American history to express preferences for Presidential candidates in primary elections held in many states.

The preferential primaries were authorized in some areas by the state legislatures, and approved in other states by the local committees of the two national parties. There was a general belief among many Republicans and Democrats as well as insurgents that the government had grown too far away from the people. The primaries were designed to give the citizens a chance to speak out directly.

Everyone recognized the fact that the national conventions would pick the nominees. But it was hoped that the primaries would help to determine the composition of the conventions, and give guidance to the politicians in their choice of candidates. Much to the amazement of many cynics, several million citizens did go to the polls and register their preferences for Taft or Roosevelt, Clark or Wilson. In some places the tides seemed running heavily for Clark and Roosevelt; in other states Wilson and Taft had the edge.

Yet the primaries were hurried performances, impromptu affairs, conducted in a helter-skelter style. The candidates panted frantically from town to town, denouncing one another, shouting their own wares, sometimes alarming and confusing the voters with all the skills at their command.

Then, too, local skirmishes affected the outcome. In New York the chiefs of Tammany Hall were more interested in city and county jobs than in choosing a possible President. The attitudes of other satraps in cities and villages, the moods of ward heelers, the amounts of money flowing for one man or another, greatly influenced the primary results. In Virginia, to take another example, the whims of Thomas Fortune Ryan counted for more than the votes of thousands of obscure citizens. The merits of the candidates were often lost in the dust of inter-party battles.

Yet in 1912 none of the contenders dared to say that the primaries were more misleading than valuable. Roosevelt called the people his sovereign judges; and so did Wilson, Taft, and Clark. Only President Taft was realistic enough to cite some of the glaring defects in the primaries, and some of the newspaper editors acknowledged the truth of what he said.

Taft declared that he favored Presidential primaries whenever full and fair notice of the elections could be given and wherever there were guards to prevent the stuffing of ballot boxes. He added that a "voluntary primary outside the law —known from its informal character as a 'soap-box' primary —is worse than none." Some states permitted informal primaries, managed by volunteers. Such elections, he thought, made a mockery of popular suffrage.

Despite his realism about the political juggling that went on, Mr. Taft was optimistic: "We all concede that the operations of government and the operations of election are not perfect. . . . Now in spite of all the corruption, in spite of all the machine politics, in spite of every defect in the operation of our government that can be pointed out, I do not hesitate to say that the history of the last 135 years shows that the people have ruled."

Woodrow Wilson, wearily accepting blow after blow from the hands of Champ Clark, bowed his head and agreed.

DEFEATED AND DESERTED, WILSON FALLS ILL

The bright and beautiful days of May were darkening days for Wilson. The year had begun so auspiciously, the Democratic nomination had seemed within his hands, but as the weeks of spring went by his efforts seemed futile—the states under Clark's banner formed a lengthening column.

William McCombs came to tell him that the Wilson headquarters at 42 Broadway in New York were empty and gloomy. The torrent of letters and callers had dropped to a slow trickle.

Wilson's dear friend, Colonel Edward M. House of Texas, who had been pushing Wilson for President since 1911, began to show signs of pessimism. Always sensitive to the prevailing winds, House felt that the nominees of the two major conventions might be William Jennings Bryan and Theodore Roosevelt. He wrote to Mrs. Bryan, offering his aid to her husband if Bryan should be chosen. He even wondered whether Senator Charles Culberson of Texas, another old friend, might be available as a compromise choice.

The money needed to carry on the Wilson campaign could not be obtained as the Clark bandwagon rumbled on. Some contributors were still faithful, but many seemed to believe that the contest was finished and the triumph of Clark was certain. There didn't seem to be much point in putting money into Woodrow Wilson's organization.

Early in May the *Jersey Journal* reported that Wilson had taken to his bed, suffering from fatigue and despondency.

There were rumors that he had undergone a nervous collapse. Denials were greeted with skepticism by some of his friends as well as his foes.

Republican newspapers and Republican campaigners, apparently believing that Clark would be easier to beat than Wilson, spread the word that the New Jersey governor was in a condition more to be pitied than condemned. The brilliant educator, the governor who had flashed to national prominence in two years, was described as a man whose career was ended.

Wilson was pale and drawn, and marks of anxiety emerged in his face; but he returned to the arena with a statement to his friends: "I am all right again and the reports about my 'breakdown' were absurd. I simply had to go to bed to cure a severe cold. . . ."

He professed an optimism few of his followers shared: "I think that, politically, things are in a fairly satisfactory shape. As a matter of fact most of the support of Clark and Underwood [of Alabama] is perfunctory and on the surface, and underneath, if I am correctly informed, the purpose to nominate me is as strong as it ever was. These things cannot be depended upon, of course, but this is what is reported to me by men who ought to know."

He expressed these views in a letter to R. H. Dabney, a friend, on May 13. In the same letter he tried to discount the effects of Clark's victories in the primaries: "The combination against me has certainly done wonders, and yet my chief disappointment in the primaries of the various states is not that they did not result in my favor, but that they were so small in respect to the numbers who voted. The people did not take any interest in them. They were about equivalent to caucuses held through the polling places. Possibly the people will wake up later to the significance of the whole thing, but for the present there seems to be extraordinary lethargy and indifference."

In this interpretation of the primaries he ignored the size of the vote in Illinois—where 300,000 people participated—and the consistent trend in favor of Clark in the Middle West. His letter revealed an obvious desire to comfort himself as well as his friends.

On the day he wrote the letter to Dabney, Wyoming's primary showed a majority for Clark. One day later Clark overwhelmed Wilson by nearly three to one in the California primary and captured the Democratic delegation in New Hampshire.

Wilson's supporters staged an active drive in Iowa, without encouraging responses. Clark took the state, and went on to more triumphs in Kentucky, Rhode Island, West Virginia, Vermont, Louisiana, Arkansas, Idaho, Montana, Nevada, New Mexico, Arizona, and Washington. Two states indicated their backing for "favorite sons"—Connecticut going for Governor Simeon E. Baldwin and Indiana for Governor Thomas Marshall.

Could Clark be stopped before the Baltimore convention began in June? The speaker was rapidly assembling a majority of the delegates, and Wilson's strength was dwindling, no matter what the New Jersey governor tried to believe.

The evidence of Clark's runaway gains in the primaries inspired Wilson's backers to unite in a desperate effort to halt the speaker. Newspaper editors and publishers, as well as the intellectuals in the Democratic Party, began to predict that Clark's nomination would make the Democrats a laughingstock and might damage the Democratic chance for victory or lead to the election of a man even weaker than Taft.

Conservative papers like the New York *Times* and the Springfield *Republican* joined liberal papers like the New York *World* and the Cleveland *Plain Dealer* in lambasting Clark and his backers. They contended that he was a tool of Tammany and a slavish friend of the flamboyant Hearst. They made fun of the backwoods tune his followers sang at rallies—the old "houn' dawg" song with its mournful chorus and homespun humor:

"I doan' keer if he *is* a houn',
You gotta quit kickin' my dawg aroun'."

On paper Clark had a commendable record. He was a graduate of Bethany College, and had been president of Marshall College, the first normal school in West Virginia. He had taken courses at the Cincinnati Law School before he moved to Louisiana, Missouri, where he became city attorney, edited the *Daily News,* and was owner and editor of the *Riverside Press.* He had been elected to Congress in 1892 and had been re-elected for term after term. He had become the Democratic minority leader in 1907, and had led the House revolt that broke the dictatorial rule of the former speaker, "Uncle Joe" Cannon. He was a member of the two most important Committees of the House—the Committee on Ways and Means, where domestic legislation was shaped, and the Committee on Foreign Affairs.

Yet he had an old-fashioned, almost antiquated appearance. He was a wheeler and dealer—a man who made deals in conference rooms, and relied on bargains and compromises to get what he wanted. He was a shrewd legislator, wary and foxy, but he lacked the stature, the commanding presence needed by a potential President. He had an air of the nineteenth-century rural atmosphere about him.

Although he had been in Congress for nearly twenty years, he had not been primarily responsible for any notable legislation. He had not stirred the country by enunciating any great principles. He had not displayed far-ranging vision or cast a glowing light upon the vital issues of his age.

Some Republican newspapers and magazines foresaw that the Democratic nominee in 1912 was likely to get elected. Roosevelt and Taft, in their personal feud, were wrecking the Republican Party. Accepting a Democratic triumph as almost inevitable, these publications wanted the Democrats to choose a man of the highest possible caliber—and Wilson seemed to be that man.

With Wilson ill or unable to speak effectively in his own behalf, some writers and newspapermen brandished cudgels for him. Ray Stannard Baker, in the *American Magazine,* said Clark appealed to many voters who could not quite decide to face the needs for drastic changes in America. The liquor interests were financing Clark, according to a correspondent for the New York *Times.* The *Nation* gave a shrill warning: "The menace of Champ Clark as the Democratic candidate for the Presidency daily grows greater. . . . Plainly, the man to beat Clark is Wilson. It is high time to check the drift to Speaker Clark—a drift due chiefly to popular ignorance of his complete unfitness for the Presidency."

Many of the reformers and intellectuals, then as now, had little faith in the wisdom of the people. The people needed guidance, these spokesmen felt; the people's untutored minds were incapable of choosing the right man for the White House. Democracy was splendid in theory, but likely to be dangerous in practice.

Norman Hapgood, editor of *Collier's Weekly,* described Clark as a "patent medicine salesman" because Clark had once endorsed a popular tonic, and he charged that Clark was "the candidate of the reactionaries." Actually Clark had a generally progressive record in Congress, although he was not a deep-thinking reformer. Clark had, however, made the mistake of signing a testimonial for a patent medicine named "Electric Bitters," saying: "It seemed that all the organs in my body were out of order, but three bottles of Electric Bitters made me all right. It's the best all-round medicine ever sold over a druggist's counter."

Most of the people who voted in the Presidential primaries, however, had no prejudices against patent medicine. Most of them used home remedies of one kind or another, and did not regard Clark's glowing testimonial for "Electric Bitters" as proof that the speaker was foolish.

Clark continued to pile up the popular votes—and Wilson continued to win the endorsements of editors. A statement by the New York *World,* made late in April, was quoted around the country during the dreary days in May when the Wilson campaign was grinding to a halt. The *World* article said: "We had hoped that it would not be necessary to treat Mr. Clark's candidacy seriously. That was a compliment we had paid to the intelligence of Western and Southern Democrats, but it was a compliment which we now find was undeserved. The sooner, then, that the plain, blunt truth is stated in the frankest possible fashion the better. . . . *Champ Clark's nomination would be Democratic suicide!"*

In spite of the *World's* angry prediction, some Democratic leaders seemed bent on suicide. In New Jersey former Senator James Smith and his able lieutenant, James Nugent, continued to seek vengeance for Wilson's earlier assaults on the Smith machine. They found an ally in a tough Hudson County man named Frank Hague, who managed to get five of the county's assembly members—Thomas F. Martin, Charles M. Egan, Thomas Donnelly, Thomas Griffin, and William Davidson—to attend an anti-Wilson rally in Jersey City on May 17.

Hague, Smith, and Nugent, aided by a Jersey City banker, George A. Young, financed the distribution of thousands of pamphlets quoting statements Wilson had made about immigrants. Some of the Hungarians and Poles were already down on Wilson. Through these pamphlets, Hague tried to turn the Italian-American voters against him, too.

During the first three weeks in May, Wilson did not help his supporters fight the Hague-Smith forces. He was not in good health; he was trying to maintain his dignity as governor, and he did not want his foes to think that he was desperate.

Wilson did speak at one meeting on May 20. He slashed at Smith, Nugent, and Hague: "The chief purveyor of office in this state was a man who was the chief conspirator in the party's ruin in the Democratic councils. I am not here to mince words; I have found some of these gentlemen out. They have handed me the credentials of their characters."

On May 25, three days before the voting in New Jersey, Wilson made it clear that his leadership and his work as governor were the major issues at stake. He declared that a vote for his delegates to the Democratic convention was a vote for "principle and honor and free government" and a vote for the Smith slate was a vote for "the special interests."

His pleas were evidently effective. On May 28 he received huge majorities in twenty out of the twenty-one counties of the state. Twenty-four of New Jersey's twenty-eight delegates were instructed to vote for him at the Baltimore convention.

On the same day the Democratic convention in Texas told its forty delegates to support Wilson. These two triumphs restored the morale of some of Wilson's followers. But those who studied the tabulations of the primaries still foresaw an uphill struggle.

Clark was perilously near to a majority—545—of the convention delegates. Wilson, with a few more than 200, was lagging far behind the "patent-medicine man" from Missouri.

On May 30, however, the editors of the *World* thundered again. Previously they had concentrated on blasting Clark but had not unlimbered their heavy guns for Wilson. Now they called for Wilson as the man who could overcome Theodore Roosevelt. They considered Theodore Roosevelt "the most cunning and adroit demagogue that modern civilization had produced since Napoleon III."

After giving their reservations about Wilson, the editors went on to endorse the man from Princeton: "Governor Wilson's elements of weakness are vastly overbalanced by his elements of strength. He has proved his political courage and his fearlessness. He has proved himself sound on the Sherman law. He has proved himself sound on corporation control. He has proved himself sound on trust prosecutions and personal guilt. He has proved himself sound against government by Wall Street plutocracy.

"He has proved himself sound on the independence of the judiciary. He has proved himself sound on the fundamental principles of constitutional government. He has proved that he is instinctively and temperamentally a Democrat. He has proved himself a free man who cannot be bull-dozed by bosses or influenced against his convictions even by his personal friends. That is the sort of man who ought to be President."

It is worth noting how many times the editors of the *World*—a "liberal" newspaper—used the word "sound" when referring to Wilson. What did the term "sound" mean in an era when every public leader, when nearly every newspaper and magazine, when nearly every minister and educator wanted to be regarded as "progressive"?

Judging by the writings of those times, a "sound" man was one who stood for the maintenance of certain moral values—for "clean government" as opposed to corruption, for "the people's rights" as against "the bosses," for small business against "big business," for "independent thinking" against "the machine," for "reform" against "the stand-patters," for a benevolent, paternal attitude toward working-men and immigrants from countries with "lower standards" than the British Isles. A "sound" man felt that judges on the bench deserved the respect, almost the reverence, of citizens who accepted the rule of law as the highest sign of civilization.

A "sound" man was one who felt that all the principles

of the good life were known, and had been eloquently enunciated by the Founding Fathers of America. A "sound" man saw plenty of room for improvements in American civilization, but did not want to tamper with any of the foundations of the pillars of society. A "sound" man appealed to "sound people"—middle-class people, mostly of Anglo-Saxon origin, who were anxious to throw out the "muckers" and the "dirty dealers" and get ahead on the basis of hard but decent competition under the rules of fair play.

Perhaps Wilson found it impossible to set the prairies on fire because he was such a "sound" man. He had fervor, he had stern convictions, but he lacked the frenzy of a William Jennings Bryan. He could not pull the mass of ordinary men from the moorings of their traditional political organizations.

He approached the end of the pre-convention drive for delegates with a mixture of confidence and detachment which mystified many of the people around him. He had done his best. If he could not defeat Clark, it was the will of Providence—and everything was intended for the best.

TAFT FIGHTS TO HOLD OHIO

While Wilson's men were striving to keep Clark from collecting an overwhelming majority of Democratic convention delegates, Taft was fighting grimly to keep Roosevelt from winning the Ohio Republican delegation.

On May 12, the day when he left Washington for the eight-day battle in Ohio, Taft wrote to his brother, Horace: "I don't expect to be successful. I think the American people are not quite alive to the dangers of Roosevelt's success and that there is too short a time to teach them in the preliminaries of a primary."

Nevertheless, Taft told Horace: "From a sense of duty I am going through this fight, distasteful and undignified as it is. . . . The trend is toward Roosevelt. I have thought he would be certain to be defeated if nominated, but I am not sure now, though I still think so. He can't keep up a campaign of bluff and pretense for four months. . . ."

There were some observers, normally sympathetic with Taft, who felt that the bewildered President had shown bad judgment when he declared in Hyattsville, Maryland, on May 4: "I am a man of peace, and I don't want to fight. But when I do fight I want to hit hard. Even a rat in a corner will fight." The reference to the "rat in a corner" did not appear in the official transcript of his remarks, but the phrase was printed in newspapers from coast to coast. The reporters declared he had used those words, and he was labeled by them.

A President who admittedly had called himself "a man of straw" and then, in the eyes of the press at least, had compared himself with a cornered rat, found it difficult to arouse the enthusiasm of the voters, even in his home state of Ohio. Probably the Ohioans were puzzled about Will Taft. He had seemed benign and sure of himself on the federal bench; he seemed a pathetic, flabby figure now as a Chief Executive. He was a fat, perspiring, embittered "rat in a corner."

He himself was downcast by the attitudes of the people. These were his own people. They had showered their affections on him—when he had been a judge, when he had triumphantly returned from the Philippines, when he had been secretary of war, when he had mounted the hustings for Theodore Roosevelt, when he had been a candidate for President in 1908.

Everything had changed now. The crowds gathered around his train and filled the halls where he spoke—for he was, after all, the President of the United States. But among his audiences, in the May days of 1912, there were many who had listened to the attacks made on him by Theodore Roosevelt. Many of the faces were closed against him.

"T.R." had branded him a failure and he could not rid himself of that brand.

As the voters turned toward Roosevelt, some associates and supporters of Taft slipped quietly to the sidelines. Taft felt most keenly the coolness of Senator Elihu Root, the lawyer and statesman, the man who had served in Roosevelt's cabinet as secretary of state when he had been a cabinet member, the conservative adviser upon whom he himself had relied so heavily.

In these days of disappointment Taft saw his friends and fellow officials in a new light. Root had refused to enter Ohio to help him. The secretary of the interior, Walter Fisher, and Henry Stimson, his secretary of war, hung back —not wishing to draw "T.R.'s" wrath. Taft wrote to his brother Horace: "Seats in the bandwagon are popular and I shall expect many more will turn to him when it becomes apparent, as it may and probably will become after Ohio and California, that I cannot win."

Root had plenty of excellent excuses for not intervening then in the wrestling match between Judge Taft and Colonel Roosevelt. In a note to Taft, Root said he could not jump on a former President who had loaded him with honors. The Colonel had been laudatory of Root, even in the current conflict, and Root had no zest for injecting himself into the fray.

Beyond all that, Senator Root felt that his fighting days were over. He did want Taft, his "old friend," to realize how deeply he sympathized with the beleaguered man in the White House. He hoped that Taft would pull through.

Taft understood Root's reluctance to get into the free-for-all, but the senator's sympathy did not do him much good. He needed outstanding men to make speeches for him, and he discovered that very few would do so. He had to take the stump himself, night and day. He hated the feelings of futility and exhaustion that speech-making gave him.

He made more than fifty speeches in Ohio, denying all the charges hurled by Roosevelt, reminding the people over and over that he had done many things for them. He had fostered the civil service, prosecuted the "trusts" more vigorously than "T.R.," signed bills to increase veterans' pensions, established a federal Children's Bureau to promote the health and welfare of children, and had created a Commission on Efficiency and Economy to make the government operate more effectively. He had inherited a deficit from Roosevelt, and he had developed a system of spending control which entitled him to be called the "Father of the Federal Budget." He had turned the Roosevelt deficit into a surplus.

Unfortunately, Taft recited his achievements in a plodding, pedestrian style. His speeches were often too long. He did not have the gift of exciting his audiences. They listened to him respectfully, but he lacked the glamor and showmanship of "T.R."

In the districts where workingmen and their families were numerous, Taft was seldom applauded. In union circles Taft was regarded as an enemy of labor or a "stuffed shirt" who knew nothing about the troubles and anxieties of the workingman's life—and cared less. He did not know what it was like to raise a family on ten dollars a week at a time when the cost of living was shooting upward.

Taft was, indeed, a man from a comfortable, well-to-do family. He had little first-hand experience of what the hand-to-mouth existence of the average laborer was really like. He felt that some labor agitators were dangerous and violent men.

Yet he could claim credit for many steps taken to improve the conditions of labor. In Fostoria, Ohio, he truthfully told an audience: "We passed a mining bureau bill to discover the nature of those dreadful explosions and loss of life in mines. We passed safety appliance bills to reduce the loss of life and limbs to railroad employees. We passed an employers' liability act to make easier recovery of damages by injured employees. We have just passed through the Senate a workman's compensation act . . . requiring the railroads to insure their employees against the accidents of a dangerous employment. We passed the children's bureau bill calculated to prevent children from being employed too early in factories. We passed the white phosphorus match bill to stamp out the making of white phosphorus matches which results in dreadful diseases to those engaged in their manufacture."

But these measures had not mollified the anti-Taft feelings of labor leaders, who remembered him as a federal judge who had used court injunctions against strikers. Taft had consistently recognized the right of men to strike—and then had consistently insisted that courts had the right to use injunctions against violence and "illegal forms" of boycotts. But the union organizers believed that strikes could not be effective without the power to resort to violence against strikebreakers.

Violence in any form was abhorrent to Taft. He saw clearly that men could not be forbidden to withhold their labor from their employers. And yet he was outraged when strikers beat up strikebreakers. He could not give the sanction of the law to such brutality: he did not realize that their violence was motivated by a desperate struggle for bread.

Taft's doubts about saving Ohio from Roosevelt were thoroughly justified by the results of the primary. On May 22 the New York *Times* carried a headline saying: ROOSEVELT TRIUMPHANT IN OHIO—CLAIMS 15 DISTRICTS OUT OF THE 24. The people of his home state had not been as loyal to Taft as the people of New Jersey had been to Wilson.

Soon afterward, California's Republicans also gave a majority of their votes to Roosevelt. Taft suffered an equally humiliating defeat in New Jersey on May 28, and said to a friend: "There appears to be nothing saved."

With mournful humor, referring to his own physical bulk of more than 300 pounds, Taft wrote to another supporter: "I do not think you need to be overcome with mortification. You had a pretty heavy candidate to carry . . . we are fighting on." "How can they be so dumb?" was the question running through his letters during the month of May, when Roosevelt was riding roughshod over him everywhere. Taft didn't use these words, but the cry of protest was hovering above the stream of letters that poured from the White House.

Taft was angrily amused by the fact that Roosevelt called him the candidate of Wall Street and big business. In fact, Roosevelt was getting much more campaign money from corporation executives than Taft could raise. The Roosevelt committee in New York had filed a statement showing that $59,200 had been spent in Manhattan alone to produce 15,000 votes for Roosevelt—an expenditure of nearly $4 per head. Three men—George Perkins, Frank Munsey, and Alexander S. Cochran, a millionaire carpet manufacturer, who shared the Perkins-Munsey view that Roosevelt would help "good" corporations—had given $15,000 apiece to the Roosevelt cause. The three gifts accounted for nearly four-fifths of the amount collected.

Reports circulated that the Roosevelt forces in Ohio had large sums to get their voters to the polls. At hearings held by a Senate committee later on, the Ohio political boss, Walter Brown, admitted that about $50,000 had been spent there in the primary fight against Taft.

"The businessmen are fools, like some of the voters," the President said in a letter to Charles P. Taft, after the catastrophes of the May primaries. ". . . They don't see beyond their noses. They only think of their particular interest and don't take a broader view. They are in favor of special privilege in the sense of having themselves favored and everybody else prosecuted. . . ."

Fools or not, the businessmen and the voters made it very clear to every observer except William Howard Taft that the Republican choice for the Presidency—among the rank and file, as well as in Wall Street—was not Mr. Taft.

THE COMPLEXITIES OF COLONEL ROOSEVELT

Whatever else might be said of Theodore Roosevelt, nobody stamped him as a fool. His complexities baffled his closest friends as well as enemies. His motives were many and mixed —and often hidden even from himself.

What could explain his behavior in the spring of 1912, the ferocity of his attacks on Taft, his snarls at Wilson, his contemptuous gibes at Clark? What could explain his readiness to accept the financial aid of men like Perkins, Munsey, and Cochran—and his equal readiness to denounce the "malefactors of great wealth"? He knew the pain he was inflicting on Taft, the unfairness of his barbs at Wilson, the absurdity of the treatment he gave to Clark. He must have realized the anomaly of his position with relation to his friends from the great corporations.

When Taft released the documents showing that Roosevelt had not pressed the government's case against the International Harvester Company after a meeting with Perkins, Taft threw suspicion on the relationship between Roosevelt and Perkins.

Discussing the Harvester Company case in Ohio, Taft said: "I don't charge that there is any corruption there, but I ask you to look at and consider the courageous audacity of a man who comes and impeaches me with belonging to the interests when there is that evidence on the record. . . . I ask you, with your knowledge of the method by which Theodore Roosevelt has brought charges against me, what he would say if the case were reversed and George Perkins were supporting me, and I had not sued the Steel Trust and the Harvester Trust."

Roosevelt now declared that Taft, as a cabinet member during "T.R.'s" administration, had gone along with the decision to defer any action against the International Harvester Company. In actual fact, Taft, then secretary of war, had departed from Washington on August 18, 1907, six days before the arrival of Perkins at the White House for the conference on the International Harvester case. Taft was in San Francisco sailing for the Philippines at the time the federal Commissioner of Corporations recommended to Roosevelt that nothing be done. It was impossible for Taft to have taken any part in the deliberations on the Harvester case.

When Charles D. Hilles, the assistant secretary of the treasury under Taft, challenged Roosevelt by presenting these facts to the public, the Colonel was not a bit abashed. He simply asserted that Taft had expressed approval of the decision in January, 1908, after Taft had returned to American shores. Hilles told the press that he was skeptical about Roosevelt's memory of what had really happened. Taft was outraged anew. Roosevelt hurried on, scattering charges over the countryside.

Oddly enough, Roosevelt was just as pessimistic about his own future as Taft was, even when he was sweeping state after state in the preferential primaries. He wrote to a friend, saying: "Do not get the idea into your head that I am going to win in this fight. It was a fight that had to be made and there was no alternative to my making it."

He did not feel that he was driven by excessive personal ambition. He felt that his duty to the nation, as a former President, made it necessary to sacrifice himself in order that the people's rights might be preserved. He felt that those who supported him with their money and energy were aware of the true nature of the goals he sought.

He had thoroughly approved of the statement issued by

Senator Dixon of Montana, who was serving as the head of the executive committee of the National Committee for Roosevelt. The statement had been issued after he had gone over every word of it.

Dixon had pointed out that the lack of positive leadership during the Taft administration had severely damaged the G.O.P. A Republican majority of sixty in the House of Representatives had been overturned, and the Democrats now had a majority of seventy. Before 1910, two-thirds of the senators had been Republicans. In the spring of 1912 the party held only a bare majority in the Senate.

Many small businesses had gone into bankruptcy. Many farmers had sold their holdings and were looking for jobs in the cities. The number of unemployed men had increased at an alarming rate. Taft seemed to have no bold proposals to meet these conditions.

In his speeches in the thirteen states where Republican primaries were held—in California, Georgia, Illinois, Maryland, Massachusetts, Nebraska, New Jersey, North Dakota, Ohio, Oregon, Pennsylvania, South Dakota, and Wisconsin—Roosevelt had declared that he would use the power of the government to stimulate "constructive activity" in every field. Over and over again he had voiced his belief in "pure democracy."

"We Progressives believe that the people have the right, the power, and the duty to protect themselves and their own welfare," he said in many cities and towns. "We believe that human rights are supreme over all other rights; that wealth should be the servant, not the master, of the people. . . . We are engaged in one of the great battles of the age-long contest waged against privilege on behalf of the common welfare. We hold it a prime duty of the people to free our government from the control of money in politics."

He did not say how these things were to be accomplished, and the people did not question him. They turned out to see the hunter, the President who had walked with kings, the Defender of the Common Man who placed the people's opinion on constitutional questions above the rulings of judges on the bench. He drew enormous and enthusiastic crowds.

Except for North Dakota and Wisconsin, where La Follette was the popular choice, Roosevelt won in every state primary he entered. He defeated Taft in Illinois by 139,436 votes, in Pennsylvania by 105,899, in California by 69,218, in Ohio by 47,447. He got 16,769 more votes in Nebraska than La Follette and Taft put together.

Out of the 388 Republican delegates chosen in the primaries, Roosevelt won 281. Taft had 71, and La Follette had 36. In these primaries the signs all pointed in one direction: Theodore Roosevelt was the man the people loved and admired.

Yet the ward heelers and precinct captains of the Republican Party, like the anti-Clark groups in the Democratic camp, were positive that the people did not know what they were doing. The primaries were confusing, the politicians said. The primaries really meant nothing. And the politicians controlled the 690 delegates who were not chosen through primaries.

Men of cabinet rank were hesitant about throwing their full weight to Taft. But in the states where delegates were selected by conventions composed of lower-level politicians, Taft's men were in charge and Taft got the votes. The President professed to believe that these conventions represented the will of the people more accurately than the primary votes.

By the end of May no one knew whether Taft or Roosevelt had a majority of the delegates. The New York *Tribune,* favoring Taft, asserted that he had 410 delegates and gave only 251 to Roosevelt. The New York *Mail,* supporting Roosevelt, said the Colonel had 292 delegates, as against 232 for the President. Each tabulation indicated that the preferences of hundreds of delegates were unknown or undecided.

With friends in the White House, Taft talked privately of his willingness to withdraw for a compromise candidate, such as Charles Evans Hughes. He made it plain that he had no personal desire to run, but he would never permit his delegates to be thrown to Roosevelt.

Before Senator Root boarded a train for Chicago, he went to the White House and asked Taft what the President would advise the delegates to do if the convention became deadlocked. Root was scheduled to serve as the convention chairman. Taft said he would accept Root or Hughes or "somebody who does not represent what Theodore Roosevelt represents."

To Taft, Colonel Roosevelt had come to represent lying and unscrupulous methods, deception of the public, and the setting of class against class for radical purposes. To Roosevelt, Taft now represented corruption and the evils of the arrogant elite-group who exploited the people—and in his own eyes Roosevelt was the embodiment of righteousness.

The Colonel revised his plans from day to day, from hour to hour. Those close to him predicted that he would lead his men personally at Chicago. But when these reports got in the papers, he growled: "Fake, pure fake." And then he added, through his clenched teeth: "If circumstances demand, of course I'll go!"

He assured the nation that the identity of the Republican candidate had been definitely settled. Talk of compromise was utterly foolish. He snapped to the press: "I'll name the compromise candidate. He'll be me. I'll name the compromise platform. It will be our platform."

SUFFRAGISTS MARCH: COST OF LIVING RISES: SOCIALISTS MEET

While most of the nation's attention centered on the see-saw struggles between Roosevelt and Taft, Clark and Wilson, the currents of change surged through America and other lands.

The first Sunday in May witnessed a parade of 10,000 women and men sympathizers with banners urging votes for females. The paraders stepped briskly along Fifth Avenue, headed by ladies on horseback. The streets around the avenue were choked with spectators, some booing, many cheering.

Men were deeply divided on whether women should have the ballot. "T.R." was opposed to the idea, although most progressives favored it. Wilson was uncertain about whether it was desirable. Taft wanted to leave the decision to the states, although his personal hostility to the notion was well known.

But the feminists and suffragettes were active, stubborn, and determined. It was evident to most observers that votes for women could not be long delayed. The barriers against them were crumbling.

In the middle of May the House of Representatives approved a Senate resolution authorizing a constitutional amendment for the direct election of senators—and a week later the Massachusetts legislature became the first assembly to give consent to the amendment. Popular sentiment in the other states was overwhelmingly for it. All the Presidential candidates accepted the inevitability of the amendment's adoption.

On May 17 the national convention of the Socialist Party nominated Eugene V. Debs of Indiana for President. At the meeting in Indianapolis, the Socialists advocated public ownership of all mines, quarries, oil wells, forests, water power, land, banking, grain elevators, stockyards, and warehouses. They demanded federal income and inheritance taxes to be used for the socialization of industry. They were for women's suffrage, national balloting on major questions of public policy, recall of public officials through special elections when necessary, and the establishment of minimum wage laws, unemployment insurance, and old-age pensions.

Under the leadership of Debs, the Socialists asked for abolition of the Senate and of the President's power to veto legislation. They urged the direct election of the President and Vice-President, the relief of unemployment by public works, reduction of the hours of labor in factories, and the elimination of child labor and prison contract labor.

Unemployment and increases in the cost of living were two issues that came up repeatedly in the summer of 1912. A New York *Times* headline proclaimed: BEEF NEVER SO HIGH IN 30 YEARS—COSTS 13½¢ A POUND WHOLESALE. That meant a price of 15½¢ a pound to the public. To American workingmen, often bringing home little more than two dollars a day, any rise in meat prices meant a lower standard of life. In millions of households meat was considered as essential as bread.

Hardships caused by rising prices had driven miners to go on strike. Late in May riots flared at the coal pits in Mt. Carmel and Shenandoah, Pennsylvania. Collieries were overrun by angry men. Strikebreakers were clubbed and stoned. The hunger for food led to the spilling of blood.

None of the Presidential candidates knew how to deal with these storms of violence or the increasing inflation. Each told audiences that remedies would be found if the voters picked the right man for the White House and elected a Congress willing to take bold measures.

Both the Democrats and the Progressives suspected that the "trusts" were the prime movers in pushing prices higher. Since the "trusts" controlled the supplies of many products and supposedly could set prices at any level, this explanation appealed to the public. The candidates were against the evils of the "trusts" but could not solve the problem of how to curb them effectively without damaging or destroying "freedom of enterprise."

When Roosevelt talked about boards of experts who would overcome these problems, his audiences were responsive yet skeptical about how his idea would work. Wilson's pledges to "regulate competition" also seemed vague and unsatisfactory to many. And Taft evidently had no answer to the cost-of-living squeeze, except to urge people to budget their money.

On May 24 an uprising of Negroes in Cuba against the government there brought demands for American action to maintain order. The next day Taft sent a squadron of American warships to the waters near Cuba and announced that he was prepared to take additional steps to prevent anarchy. Slow-moving at home, Taft often astonished the world by the speed with which he acted to protect U.S. lives and property abroad.

Late in May, when a Senate committee published its report on its investigation of the sinking of the *Titanic,* public attention shifted for a few days to the tragic fate of the great ship which had met disaster in a collision with an iceberg.

TITANIC VERDICT IS NEGLIGENCE, the *Times* said in its headline on the report. And the people shuddered, reading the committee's statements about the derelictions of the White Star Line and the slipshod style in which some of the ship's officers had handled their duties.

For a while there was anger and disturbance over the *Titanic* and concern about Cuba. And then people began to talk again about the prices of beef and bread, the behavior of Mr. Taft, the chances of Colonel Roosevelt, and what would happen at the Republican convention in Chicago. . . .

VI. June: The Old Guard
Stands by Taft

In the smoky railroad stations of Chicago, hour by hour in the first days of June, the solid men who supported the big man in the White House arrived to do their duty and nominate the President. They were the strong foot soldiers, the phalanx of the Grand Old Party, surging in to meet the last charge of Roosevelt and his lieutenants.

Many of the professional politicians were almost as broad in the beam and stately in stride as their commander, William Howard Taft. They were well-dressed, well-brushed, well-trained men, substantial in girth and worth, genial in their manners yet capable of cool combat. They strode through the windy streets of Chicago with purpose in their rubicund faces, ready for the fray.

One of the handsomest men among them was a tall editor-politician from Ohio, a man with a quick laugh and a joyful appreciation of poker games, parties, and girls. Warren G. Harding had a special mission at this convention. He had been invited by Mr. Taft to place the President's name in nomination when the time came.

"I know you can do it well," Taft had said in his letter to Harding, "and I should be delighted to . . . have it done by a man who represents the state so worthily as you do."

Another leader who came to Chicago to do the President's bidding was D. T. Flynn. He was prepared for fisticuffs and blows with cudgels. Taft had given him instructions: "I am counting on your presence in Chicago to call the bluff and bluster of the Roosevelt people. There is a suggestion of physical force in their attitude that it will gratify me to have met in a proper spirit."

If physical combat had developed between the Taft and Roosevelt contingents at Chicago, the Taft men would have been at a disadvantage. Admirers of Roosevelt had obtained Rough Rider uniforms and were galloping through the city on horseback, eager to demonstrate their devotion to the Colonel. If any such encounter had occurred, the Roosevelt cavalry might have routed the Taft infantry.

But the struggle in this case was carried on in the hotel rooms of the Republican National Committee, where the Taft men were in full control. Under the party rules, the 53 members of the committee had been picked at the closing session of the 1908 convention—which had nominated Taft—and they would remain as members until the close of the 1912 meeting.

Although these rules had been in effect for a good many years and Roosevelt had accepted them as President, his followers now tried to get them changed as quickly as possible. They knew that the Taft group had a large majority on the committee. The committee would decide, in the case of the contesting claims of delegates, which delegates would be recognized as legal participants in the 1912 convention.

Through his representatives in Chicago, Roosevelt asserted that the membership of the National Committee should reflect the votes taken in the states just before the convention gathered. His followers pointed out that Victor Rosewater, acting chairman of the committee, had been defeated by R. B. Howell in a Nebraska election. For this reason Howell should represent Nebraska on the committee and take Rosewater's seat.

There were other members of the committee who had also been defeated in local elections. They did not wish to be dislodged by newcomers when the rules entitled them to hold their places and their power until the end of the 1912 meeting.

Colonel Harry S. New, a member of the committee, blasted the Roosevelt proposal. Beating on a table, he asserted that a national committeeman held his chair for four years, like the President. Taft couldn't have claimed the Presidency right after the election of November, 1908, because the law stated that the outgoing officeholder was President until the term expired in March, 1909. Committee members elected in 1908 were entitled to stay on the committee until their terms expired, regardless of elections.

Roosevelt's lieutenants were gloomy after the committee accepted the position advocated by New. With Taft's men in command, it did not seem possible to oust the 238 Taft delegates whose standing had been challenged. And if Taft got nearly all of those delegates, the fight for the Republican nomination was really over.

Before the formal sessions of the National Committee began, Taft asked it to open its meetings to reporters from the press associations. Roosevelt immediately expressed hearty approval of the idea; he said that the public would be strongly behind him if the press showed what was going on.

Then, speaking as a former federal judge, Taft urged the members of the committee to consider the contested delegates with the strict and stern impartiality existing in a carefully conducted trial. Taft wanted to win, and he felt that he could win fairly. He was reasonably sure that he had a majority of the delegates already pinned down. He was also sure that many of Roosevelt's contests were based on the flimsiest kind of evidence. So he sought to expose the flamboyant Colonel.

While the National Committee was wrangling over the preparations for the hearings on the delegates, the Republican state convention was rumbling into action in Ohio. Although Taft had been thoroughly whipped in the popular primary, he was still angling for the six Ohio delegates-at-large to be chosen by the state gathering. He had a burning determination to make significant gains in his home area.

Roosevelt had been depressed and Taft had been encouraged by the results of county conventions in Ohio. In the first seven counties reporting, Taft got 46 delegates and Roosevelt only 15. Taft's managers boasted that they would dominate the state meeting—and they did.

When the Ohio convention opened on June 3, the Taft men won all the early skirmishes, gaining majorities on all the committees. And when the showdown came on June 4, the vote in the convention was close—390 to 362 in favor of sending six Taft delegates to Chicago. The Roosevelt men kept the Columbus convention in an uproar, bellowing "fraud" and "trickery," but lost all along the line.

The quiet men in the derby hats, the heavy-faced imperturbable men with long experience in politics, outnumbered and outmaneuvered the few professionals and the many amateurs on Roosevelt's side. The outcome in Columbus foreshadowed the outcome in Chicago.

With cool precision, the quiet men took Roosevelt's claims apart—and never put them back together again. In the hearings concerning rival delegations held by the National Committee, the Roosevelt group was knocked down again and again.

Actually in nearly every case the decisions were almost

unanimous. Even Roosevelt's friends—and they included such committee members as William E. Borah of Idaho, T. Coleman du Pont of Delaware, Frank B. Kellogg of Minnesota, Cecil Lyon of Texas, and William Ward of New York—discovered nothing to justify his accusations against 23 of the 24 Taft delegates from Alabama, the first group challenged.

After seven hours of questions and answers, arguments, and feverish discussions, the committee on June 7 awarded 24 disputed delegates from Alabama and Arkansas to Taft. The next day the committee announced the seating of 48 more delegates pledged to the President, and Senator Borah said that "the 9th Alabama district and the 5th in Arkansas were the only contests heard thus far which in my opinion had any merit." And on Monday, June 10, twelve contests over Indiana men were decided unanimously in favor of Taft.

Roosevelt foamed. The New York *Times* reported that he had assailed the morals of the committee men, and asserted that election officials had gone to jail for deeds no worse than those committed in Chicago. He indicated to reporters that if he continued to receive such treatment he would bolt the Republican Party and run on an independent ticket.

Borah and the other committee members who admired Roosevelt did not take kindly to his insinuations and his cries of rage. Borah said coldly: "There have been many frauds at the primaries. I don't say there were not. But there was no evidence of that fact presented. . . . Under the circumstances, I could not vote to sustain the Roosevelt delegates."

On June 11, however, Borah and Governor Herbert S. Hadley of Missouri saw grounds for opposing the seating of some Taft delegates from Kentucky. They fought the Taft forces—and still the committee approved 17 delegates for Taft and one for Roosevelt.

It became evident, as the committee went from vote to

vote, that Taft could count on 37 of the 53 members to approve his delegates under virtually any circumstances. The *Times* on June 12 tabulated the numbers of delegates seated in the first four days of the committee's deliberations, and stated that 101 were for Taft and 1 for Roosevelt.

The Colonel's ire soared. "Thieves!" he cried. He accused members of the committee of engaging in behavior "dangerously near being treason to the whole spirit of our institutions; to the whole spirit of free democratic government."

Blithely oblivious of his name-calling and his charges of "brigandage" and "treason," the committee went on chopping down Roosevelt's strength, giving Taft 40 more delegates at the next meeting. On June 13, the committee divided the Missouri delegation on Taft's advice, awarding 8 delegates to Roosevelt and 6 to the President. Roosevelt was not appeased by this magnanimous gesture.

"There is no form of rascality which the Taft men have not resorted to," shouted the Colonel to the press. He announced in New York that he would leave on Friday, June 14, or on Saturday, June 15, to take personal charge of his troops "on the battlefield" at Chicago. His friends had urged him to advance to the firing line.

With the cheers of a large crowd ringing in his ears, Roosevelt left on Saturday aboard the Lake Shore Limited, in a belligerent mood and surrounded by excited friends. The train struck some rocks on the track not far from New York, and narrowly escaped being wrecked.

ROOSEVELT AT THE FRONT, "FEELING LIKE A BULL MOOSE"

Waving a black felt hat with a broad brim—his Rough Rider hat, the one he had worn in so many campaigns—Roosevelt rolled into Chicago with fire in his eyes. He was greeted by a mass of people that stretched for many blocks beyond the railroad station. Fathers lifted their children to see him.

Bands were playing, women were screaming, men were booming, "Teddy! Teddy! Come on, Teddy!"

He was in his element. He was with the people, and the people loved him. The people knew a leader when they saw one. He doffed his hat, he grinned and his big teeth gleamed; he waved his arms to embrace them all.

When his car reached the Congress Hotel, crowds were still trailing him. A fast band played "There'll Be a Hot Time in the Old Town Tonight." Teddy appeared on a balcony, ground his teeth together, and roared: "It is a fight against theft—and the thieves will not win!"

A banner rose from the crowds, a banner proclaiming that California's 26 votes must go for Roosevelt. He nodded his head briskly.

"They are mine and shall be counted for me!" he promised. "The people have spoken and the politicians will be made to understand that they are the servants and not the masters of the plain citizens of the Republican Party."

The crowd responded as crowds have always responded to men who have sounded deep notes of righteous rage.

"Soak 'em, Teddy," came the roar as he went back into his rooms.

Newspapermen were there, as they always were when he was on a rampage. Was he set for a tough fight? Was he in shape for it? Did he welcome it, or did he hate to get into it?

"I feel fine," he said. His face was glowing. "I'm feeling like a bull moose!"

The phrase delighted them. It delighted him, too. He decided to use it again—and so he did and so did his followers in the months between the Chicago convention and the election. It became the symbol of freedom for him and his faithful ones, a symbol of nobility and natural dignity and unfettered vitality.

But on Sunday, June 16, Roosevelt had a sad awakening. The newspapers listed 566 delegates definitely in Taft's camp, only 466 in his. Out of the total of 1,078, Senator La Follette had 36 and a few others were scattered here and there.

The arithmetic was grim. The number necessary for the nomination was 540, and Taft was apparently 26 beyond that figure. All the contests had been decided, and Taft had triumphed in nearly every one. Roosevelt could not accept the arithmetic. He refused to accept it.

He sent his lieutenants out to all the hotels where the delegates were gathering. He knew how bewildered, how confused, how uncertain many of them were. He had been to other conventions, and he knew the score. He was out of office, but he was the most famous American alive and he had the aura of the Presidency still clinging to him. He was Teddy Roosevelt, and that was more than anybody else was.

Through the night hours he paced his rooms, he met with his aides, he planned statements, he talked on the telephone, he wrote notes, he sent messages, using senators as errand boys. He asked the doubtful delegates to come to his hotel, to give him a chance to explain to them what the real issues were, to tell them why he thought their future and the country's future were at stake.

In a night and a day he shifted 22 votes—or he thought he had. He persuaded ten southern delegates, two from New York, and ten from Iowa to join his legions. Taft men claimed that the delegates had shifted as a result of gifts and extravagant promises made by "T.R.'s" lieutenants. "T.R." scoffed at such claims. He regained his buoyancy. He felt he had brought Taft within reach, and he had just begun to fight.

Taft's margin was getting thin, Roosevelt exulted. If he held the 22, he had cut Taft from 566 to 544, granting that Taft actually had 566 to start with. And he doubted that Taft had even had that many votes; he doubted it very much.

In the corridors of the hotels, in the bars and dining rooms of the city, his messengers passed Taft men who were very, very busy. The heavy men, the solid men for Taft, were not missing any bets. They were trying to lure over some of the Roosevelt delegates—and human nature being what it was, they were sure to succeed in a few instances.

Ugly stories appeared in the papers. Taft headquarters hinted that they had uncovered a Roosevelt plan to seize the convention gavel by force. Roosevelt's men renewed their insinuations that Taft's "boodle boys" were slipping money into the pockets of wavering delegates. Taft's managers renewed their charges of attempted bribery by Roosevelt adherents.

It was a strange and unsavory battle—a battle fought in the poisonous fog that shrouds every political convention, a struggle in which wicked whispers were as sharp as swords, a contest of lies and plots behind closed doors. And the two men whose fates were being settled behaved, for a while at least, like beasts in a jungle.

The tabulations of delegate totals in the press were sheer guesswork. Nobody could keep track of what was going on in the minds of the delegates under the pressures to which all of them were subjected. Delegations were divided into factions, and the factions were split into cliques, and the cliques had leaders and rival leaders.

The muddiest current in the whirlpool came to the surface on the eve of the convention's first session. Negro delegates emerged with affidavits stating that Roosevelt's followers had offered them bribes to join the bolters deserting Taft. Some of the Roosevelt people countered with stories of the corruption of Negro Republicans in the South.

Perhaps the shabbiest aspect of the whole convention was the manner in which both sides went after these particular delegates. The Negroes were substantially represented in Republican gatherings because Abraham Lincoln, a Republican President, had freed the black slaves of the South. The Republican Party in the South was composed mainly of Negroes, and the colored delegates were too often regarded as political pawns to be shifted back and forth by white leaders.

Both Roosevelt and Taft seem to have considered Negroes as childish and unstable people, who might some day reach the level of the white race but would certainly require many years of tutelage by their superiors. While Roosevelt said he was a radical and Taft labeled himself a conservative-progressive, neither man gave sustained support to measures designed to improve the sorry lot of the dark-skinned people.

The Negroes had not forgotten how Roosevelt as President had treated three companies of soldiers who belonged to the 25th United States Infantry, Colored. In 1906 some soldiers in these companies had been accused by excitable citizens of Brownsville, Texas, of firing their guns and rioting in the Brownsville streets at night. After an investigation which turned up some conflicting and confusing testimony, Roosevelt ordered the men of all three companies dishonorably discharged. About 160 Negro soldiers were thrown out of the army, although only a few had been accused of rioting. Among those dismissed were men who had served for fifteen years, six soldiers who had won Congressional Medals of Honor, and thirteen who had certificates of merit for bravery.

Taft, Roosevelt's secretary of war, had backed up the Colonel in the Brownsville affair, although Senator James Foraker of Ohio had produced evidence that the shooting had actually been done by residents of Brownsville. The Texans had put the blame on the Negro troops in order to have them removed from the area. Foraker's statements were brushed aside.

Consequently, neither Taft nor Roosevelt now aroused much enthusiasm among the colored voters. So the Negro delegates at the 1912 convention found it relatively easy to swing from one to the other, knowing the attitudes of both and not caring much about either candidate.

Still there was plenty of moral fervor at the convention, plenty of excitement about "the rights of the people" generated by Roosevelt and his dedicated followers. The lobby of Roosevelt's hotel was packed day and night by his faithful supporters, and he was cheered and serenaded by bands whenever he left his suite.

On the night of June 17, the night before the convention was to begin, the Roosevelt people assembled at the auditorium to sing "Onward, Christian Soldiers" and hear the gospel from "T.R." himself, the Apostle of the Square Deal. About 5,000 persons crammed into the hall, and another 15,000 stood outside, stamping and shouting, tossing hats into the air and seething with excitement.

Colonel Roosevelt made a magnificent speech. Many felt that the talk was one of the finest in his career. It was blistering on Taft, it was harsh and defiant, it chastised the evildoers, it plucked the strings of self-sacrifice, and ended as a song of martial glory.

The Colonel said he had studied the evidence in the contests over the delegates, and he could see "no element of doubt" that his own men, not Taft's, were "honorably and lawfully chosen by the people." No matter what happened, he intended to see that justice was done.

"Our cause is the cause of justice for all in the interest of all," Roosevelt insisted. "The present contest is but a phase of the larger struggle. Assuredly the fight will go on whether we win or lose; but it will be a sore disaster to lose." He paused, and the crowd roared its devotion to him.

"What happens to me is not of the slightest consequence," he said, and the hall was hushed. "I am to be used, as in a doubtful battle any man is used, to his hurt or not, so long as he is useful, and is then cast aside or left to die. I wish you to feel this. I mean it; and I shall need no sympathy when you are through with me, for this fight is far too great to permit us to concern ourselves about any one man's welfare."

He stood straight before them, every inch a warrior, a man who believed in the dangerous life, who was willing to be consumed in the flames of a righteous war.

"If we are true to ourselves by putting far above our own interests the triumph of the high cause for which we battle, we shall not lose," Roosevelt said. "It would be far better to fail honorably for the cause we champion than it would be to win by foul methods the foul victory for which our opponents hope."

His words moved on the wires of the news agencies; his words went quickly to the White House and inflamed the huge man who huddled there. Yet Taft was not shaken; Taft had declared that he would rather die than bend his knees to Roosevelt.

"But the victory shall be ours," Roosevelt screamed in his falsetto voice. "And it shall be won as we have already won so many victories, by clean and honest fighting for the loftiest of causes. We fight in honorable fashion for the good of mankind; fearless of the future; unheeding of our individual fates; with unflinching hearts and undimmed eyes; we stand at Armageddon, and we battle for the Lord."

The bands played. Thousands cheered, and thousands wept. Roosevelt moved in majesty from the auditorium.

Yet all his art and all his oratory could not halt the Taft machine. When the delegates gathered in the Coliseum the next day, the torches of the Roosevelt crusaders were flickering faintly. In the first crucial hours the strength of the quiet men in the derby hats was shown to be overwhelming.

Taft's friend Job E. Hedges proposed Elihu Root as the temporary chairman of the convention, and said that Roosevelt had described Root as "the ablest man that has appeared in the public life of any country in any position in my time."

However, Roosevelt's men pushed forward Governor Francis E. McGovern of Wisconsin to challenge Senator Root. They hoped that Robert La Follette, despite his fury over Roosevelt's betrayal of his own Presidential ambitions, might let the Wisconsin delegates support McGovern.

La Follette sneered at Roosevelt, and would not budge. Some of his men stood with him. The Wisconsin delegation divided its votes between Root and McGovern, and Roosevelt's chance to control the convention went down the drain. Root won the chairmanship, getting 558 votes against McGovern's total of 502.

The bell had tolled for Roosevelt, and the few political veterans around him knew it. Still he would not concede a thing. There were other rounds to come, and he was still in the ring. He demanded that the Credentials Committee of the Convention seat 72 of the Roosevelt delegates rejected by the National Committee.

On the afternoon of the second day of the convention, the Credentials Committee held a session to consider Roosevelt's claims. While the committee went through the motions and solemnly decided to shut the doors on the Roosevelt men, the sweating delegates in the Coliseum miserably shuffled from place to place. Fists were clenched, eyes glared, threats were thrown from one aisle to another.

Hundreds of the political leaders of the United States were in that enormous room, and the air crackled with hostility. Extra policemen were on hand, patrolling the aisles, swinging their clubs, telling some delegates to be quiet and others to sit down. The faces of the policemen were pale with tension. In the presence of dozens of reporters, they might have to quell a mob by cracking the heads of delegates including congressmen, senators, governors and judges.

While the Roosevelt forces were being ground down, his adherents in the galleries chanted: "Teddy! Teddy! We want Teddy!" And suddenly a girl among them leaned over a railing and unrolled a wide campaign picture of the Colonel. "A cheer for Teddy!" she screamed.

Men leaped to their seats. Fist fights popped in all parts of the hall. Policemen plunged frantically through the mob. The Roosevelt delegates ran to the gallery, pulled the girl into their ranks, and marched around the Coliseum, cheering and challenging the Taft men to meet them head on. While they paraded around the platform, Chairman Root stood staring calmly into space, ignoring the tumult.

After an hour of this uproar, Root banged his gavel and ordered a vote on the motion made by the Roosevelt men to remove the Taft delegates. The motion was defeated.

The meeting of the Credentials Committee broke up at ten-thirty that night when the Roosevelt men burst from the session, saying that they were being smashed by the Taft steamroller. Many of the Roosevelt men left the Coliseum and streamed to the Congress Hotel for a series of frenzied meetings. Nothing could stop Taft: that was clear now.

Would Roosevelt quit the Republican Party? Would he form his own party and continue the struggle? These questions were hurled at the delegates by reporters who rushed from room to room.

Some of "T.R.'s" lieutenants had definite ideas about what he should do. Others urged caution. At two o'clock in the morning of June 20, his fieriest followers packed the Florentine Room of the hotel and he went down to speak to them. Their enthusiasm aroused his fervor.

"So far as I am concerned, I am through," Roosevelt said. "If you are voted down I hope you, the real and lawful majority of the convention, will organize as such. . . . I hope you will refuse any longer to recognize a majority thus composed as having any title in law or morals to be called a Republican Convention."

Yells greeted that stern statement. Governor Hiram Johnson of California, a passionate Progressive, jumped to a table.

The right time had come for a new political party, Johnson declared. Plans were made for a rump convention to be held later in Orchestra Hall.

When Roosevelt got back into the comparatively calm atmosphere of his hotel suite, he wasn't so sure that he should lead a new party. Then he called in his financial advisers, George Perkins and Frank Munsey, and they promised that they would raise whatever money he needed.

Still he hesitated. Senators Borah and Beveridge were not in favor of a bolt from the Republican fold. Borah was running for re-election in 1912, and needed the help of the regular Republicans in his state. Beveridge didn't believe in third-party movements.

But Roosevelt's more fanatical friends told him that he had to run for the sake of the country. Perkins and Munsey renewed their promises to get the funds. And finally, on June 21, Munsey was authorized to make the momentous announcement.

"Mr. Roosevelt will be nominated for President by a new party," Munsey said, standing in a circle of newspapermen. "He refuses to have anything more to do with the Republican Convention now in session in this city. He would not now take a nomination from that body if it were given to him."

And so the Rough Rider mounted a different horse and started on a long, hard ride. The hunter who had been so sure of good hunting in Chicago admitted defeat. The man who had said that he would be the candidate and he would dictate the Republican platform had been forced to swallow his boastful words.

The day after Roosevelt's decision to form a new party the delegates remaining in the Republican convention formally endorsed Taft as their Presidential candidate.

Warren G. Harding droned through a speech listing Taft's virtues and extolling the achievements of this administration. Most of the delegates applauded politely. Some of those in the hall, however, did not join. Some of the Roosevelt men had refused to leave.

On the first ballot William Howard Taft got 561 votes—more than enough to win. Roosevelt received 107; La Follette, 41; Cummins, 17; Hughes, 2. To Root's shock, 344 delegates asked to be registered as present and not voting.

The cynical and witty senator from New York, Chauncey M. Depew, pronounced the verdict in a statement to a reporter: "The only question now is which corpse gets the most flowers."

Mr. Taft had his bitter triumph. He had blocked Roosevelt's road to the White House. He was positive of that. "It is really a great victory to remove the danger of Roosevelt's accession to the Presidency," he told friends. "He will now do his best to beat me, but the country can much better stand such a result than Roosevelt's success and the consequences. November is a full four months away, and much may happen in that time."

"MAY THE LORD HAVE MERCY ON ME!" WILSON PLEADS

The ferocity of the combat in Chicago was depressing to Woodrow Wilson, as it was to many other Americans of both parties who read about it in the newspapers. Wilson had moved his family from the steamy atmosphere of Trenton to the cool and peaceful Governor's Cottage at Sea Girt, New Jersey, but the rumbling of the far-off battle was oppressive to Wilson's spirit.

The day of the Wilsons' arrival at the cottage had been gray and drizzly, and the sea had made a melancholy sound upon the shore. Wilson and his daughters had started a cheerful blaze in the huge fireplace to drive off the dampness. Yet the telephone kept ringing, political advisers were coming and going, and tents had been erected on the lawns for reporters and telegraphers. The Wilsons had little chance to rest or relax.

On June 17 Wilson wrote to his old friend Mary Hulbert. After describing the rain and the dismal mourning of the sea, he told her: "Now that the possibility is immediately at hand (it is no more than a possibility, as things stand) I find myself dreading it and wishing most devoutly that I may escape. Not that I dread what would be really big and essential and worth while in the whole thing, but all that would go with it—all that is *non*-essential, *not* of the *business,* merely distracting and exhausting and hateful without counting—the excessive personal tax of a campaign. May the Lord have mercy on me! My heart is not faint, but my taste and my preference for what is genuine and at the opposite pole from mere personal notoriety revolts at the thought of what I may be in for! . . . I am well (I do not count a teasing sick headache!) and underneath, deep down, my soul is quiet."

He wanted to escape, he pleaded with the Lord for mercy, he hated the notoriety, his head was aching, and his mind raced from plan to plan—and under it all his soul was still, relying upon Providence, certain of his destiny.

What a mystery Wilson was—to himself, to his family, to those who adored him and those who hated him. Like Roosevelt, his moods changed swiftly and ranged from exuberance to profound despair. Like Roosevelt, he had endless endurance and an underlying quality of metal that could not be smashed.

Everyone knew that the gouging and throatcutting tactics of the Republicans at Chicago would affect the Democratic contenders. Bryan, who was observing the G.O.P. convention as a newspaper correspondent, felt that the Republican meeting demonstrated beyond a doubt that the Democrats must nominate a "real progressive."

In his dispatch to the afternoon papers of June 21, Bryan declared: "If the Democrats are guilty of the criminal folly of nominating a reactionary, they will supply Mr. Roosevelt with the one thing needful in case he becomes an independent candidate, namely, an issue, and with two reactionaries running for President he might run and thus entrench himself in power."

Unfortunately, Bryan did not indicate whether Clark or Wilson was the "real progressive" to carry the Democratic banner. Some professional politicians suspected that the Great Commoner, seeing the Republicans torn into warring factions, hoped once again to become the Democratic candidate. To be sure, he had been defeated three times—in 1896, in 1900, and in 1908—but he had never had the opportunity of running when the Republicans were badly divided.

On the other hand, the mildly progressive and conservative groups supporting Champ Clark interpreted the results of the Republican fracas to mean that any Democratic nominee could gain the White House. In their view Clark was a tested man; Wilson was an intellectual, and not really a politician by profession. Why should the Democratic Party reach out for Wilson, when the regular Democrats in many primaries had called for Clark?

With the primaries and state conventions finished, the figures in the newspapers pointed definitely to Champ Clark. The speaker had 436 delegates pledged him, Wilson had 248, Oscar Underwood of Alabama had 84, the "favorite sons" of other states had a total of 102, and 224 of the delegates were rated "uncertain." The delegates pledged to "favorite sons" or "uncertain" were dominated by the organizations in their states—Tammany Hall in New York, the Martin-Ryan organization in Virginia, and others—and were more likely to go over to Clark than to Wilson.

The odds seemed to be as much against Wilson as they

had been against Theodore Roosevelt in a convention containing a majority of political veterans and members of big-city machines. And Wilson did not have the frenzied followers Roosevelt had drawn to his cause.

McCombs and some of the other practical Wilson campaigners wanted to make a deal as quickly as possible with Charles Murphy, the boss of Tammany, to gain New York's 90 votes. McAdoo and some of the more cautious Wilson men felt it was politically dangerous to attempt any agreement with Murphy and Thomas F. Ryan, the financier behind Murphy.

The hostility of Bryan toward the Tammany group, toward Ryan and August Belmont and other wealthy Democrats who had opposed him over the years, was known to be implacable. Wilson himself, after his skirmish with Colonel Harvey, was wary of any alliance with men who were identified with the Wall Street wing of the party.

While Wilson was at Sea Girt and the Democratic clans were descending upon Baltimore, an issue arose giving Bryan the chance to put all the avowed candidates in a difficult position. When covering the Republican shindig in Chicago, Bryan learned that the Democratic National Committee planned to choose Alton B. Parker, the conservative who had been nominated for President in 1904, as the temporary chairman of the Democratic convention.

Bryan fired off a telegram to Norman Mack, chairman of the National Committee, opposing the choice of Parker. "When four fifths of the whole country is radically progressive, I cannot believe such criminal folly is possible," Bryan declared.

The committee went ahead and picked Parker. Bryan then declared that he would oppose Parker at the convention. He sent telegrams to Clark, Wilson, and the other Presidential contestants, asking them to take a stand for or against Parker. He demanded replies by return telegraph.

Before Wilson received Bryan's message, the Baltimore *Sun* had already sought his opinion of the choice of Parker. Wilson answered: "My friends in Baltimore, who are on the ground, will know how to act in the interest of the people's cause in everything that affects the organization of the convention. They are certain not to forget their standards as they have already shown. It is not necessary that I should remind them of those standards from Sea Girt; and I have neither the right nor the desire to direct the organization of a convention of which I am not even a member."

McCombs was pleased by that statement. He felt that it placed the decision in his hands, since he was in charge of Wilson's Baltimore headquarters. He himself wanted to evade the whole issue, to keep from angering Murphy, an admirer of Parker.

Then Bryan's telegram was delivered to Wilson at Sea Girt. He consulted McCombs by phone, and McCombs begged him to repeat his *Sun* statement. Wilson paced up and down, and talked the question over with his wife and with Joseph Tumulty, his secretary. Both felt that Bryan was entitled to know where he stood.

It was one of the decisive moments in Woodrow Wilson's career. He decided to give Bryan a clear and positive answer. And his answer was more important than any speech he had made in the exhausting weeks of campaigning, more important than the maneuvering of all his lieutenants in Baltimore.

"You are quite right," he telegraphed Bryan. "The Baltimore convention is to be a convention of progressives—of men who are progressive on principle and by conviction. It must, if it is not to be put in a wrong light before the country, express its convictions in its organization and in its choice of the men who are to speak for it. You are to be a member of the convention and are entirely within your rights

in doing everything within your power to bring that result
about. . . ."

Wilson's words delighted Bryan. Clark's reply was equivo-
cal; he had many followers who favored Parker, so he made
a call for harmony which did not satisfy anybody. Oscar
Underwood and Governor Judson Harmon of Ohio, the two
most conservative candidates, backed Parker.

In his newspaper column Bryan told the nation of the
answers he had received. To the country it seemed clear
that Wilson and Bryan were standing together on the progressive side—and the other candidates were straddling, or
on the other side of the fence.

As the Democratic delegations poured into Baltimore,
Wilson's star was beginning to rise once more.

U.S. MARINES LAND IN CUBA: FRENCH KILL 600 MOORS

While Republican politicians quarreled in Chicago and the
Democrats prepared to frolic and fight in Baltimore, other
things were happening in that golden month of June.

American Marines went ashore in Cuba to restore peace
and quiet there. General Estenoz, a rebel leader, was slain
in a skirmish and his death ended the Negro rebellion.

Pacifying the dark people in another land, French troops
killed 600 Moors near Fez, Morocco. In the eyes of the
French, civilization prevailed over an uprising of barbaric
tribes.

VII. June: The Battle of Baltimore

SEE THE BANNERS, HEAR THE DRUMS

With a band playing and flags flying, the stalwarts of Tammany Hall marched to their hotel over the hot pavements of Baltimore in the afternoon of June 24, Boss Murphy striding cockily at the head of his cohorts. Judge Alton Parker and August Belmont, the diamond-studded Democrat, marched with the mighty Murphy. Thomas Fortune Ryan, the archenemy of Bryan, did not accompany them but he was in town: he had arrived in his private railroad car.

Stimulated by the crashing music of three brass bands, the New Jersey delegation also paced through the streets under the blazing sun. Drums were pounding, and Wilson banners were rippling in the summer light. Woodrow Wilson was no longer deserted—no longer regarded as a man who had stumbled and fallen. The delegates lifted pictures of their governor high in the air and waved the portraits happily before the crowds.

The New Jersey delegation, shouting and cheering for Wilson, took over the fifth floor of the Stafford Hotel. At the Hotel Emerson a gigantic picture of Wilson dominated the lobby. Some of the delegates were Princeton graduates. Wearing orange hatbands, showing the Princeton colors, they paraded vigorously and strained their voices in college songs.

The Clark headquarters, too, was full of noise and strenuous men who stamped in and out. The Clark men and the Wilson men were spoiling for a fight, and made no bones about it. The Democrats seemed determined to make the Republican ruckus in Chicago look tame, and the Baltimore police were as nervous as their colleagues in the Windy City had been.

It was a wild way to choose a Presidential candidate, but it was the only way the politicians knew. And they loved all the smoke and racket and all the foolish sounds and sudden gusts of fury. This was their big show.

In the afternoon of the next day, June 25, the delegates and the gallery visitors hurried into the flag-wrapped armory. Pushing and sweating, shoving back the mobs that struggled to get in, the police finally got the doors closed.

On the platform at the far end of the echoing hall stood a white-haired man in scarlet robes. He raised one hand, and the chattering of the crowd died down. He was James Cardinal Gibbons, the Catholic Archbishop of Baltimore, an ascetic man with a commanding presence.

He invoked the guidance of God and sought to bring some serenity into the boiling hall: "Let the light of Thy divine wisdom direct the deliberations of this convention. . . ." Directly behind him, stern and grizzled, sat the Commoner from Nebraska, the stormy old man from the prairies, William Jennings Bryan. Light gleamed on his huge bald head.

When the Cardinal had finished, Chairman Mack of the Democratic National Committee declared that he had been instructed to offer the name of Alton Parker for temporary chairman. The Commoner rose at once. A roar went through the hall, a wave of cheering for the old campaigner, a salute to the man who had been nominated three times for the Presidency.

A reporter for the New York *World* noted Bryan's appearance: "His heavy black brows were contracted over his piercing eyes. His hawk nose had an extra downward twist. His lipless mouth was like a thin dagger-slit across his broad face. He held his head erect. . . . The grizzled fringe of his dark hair was ruffled and moist with perspiration. He made a fine figure, standing up there, in an old dark sack suit, with a low collar and white string tie."

He could not halt the cheers. He made motions for silence, but the crowd was letting off steam and would not heed him. The band played some of his old campaign tunes. He took his seat and began to fan himself with a large palm leaf. His face was set and grim.

At last the delegates grew tired and quiet. Bryan rose again and went to the edge of the platform. He nominated Senator John W. Kern of Indiana for the chairmanship. Kern had been the Democratic candidate for Vice-President when Bryan tried for the White House in 1908.

Bryan glared at the New York delegation, which occupied solid rows in the center of the convention floor. Parker, a heavy man in a well-tailored suit, was sitting with the Tammany chieftains.

After denouncing Judge Parker as the candidate of the reactionaries and as the tool of the rich men who sought to own the Democratic Party, Bryan finished the major part of his speech with a fervent plea for righteousness.

"I appeal to you," he said. "Let the commencement of this convention be such a commencement that the Democrats of this country may raise their heads among their fellows and say: 'The Democratic Party is true to the people. You cannot frighten it with your Ryans nor buy it with your Belmonts.'"

Men leaped to their feet, waved their banners, and bellowed. The crowd was with him then. But the Commoner did not know when to stop. He had delivered too many speeches, he had been carried away too often on the torrent of his own eloquence. He was carried away again. He kept on lashing Parker, repeating accusations of "predatory wealth" and "sinister forces" until the temper of the crowd flared against him.

Some delegates began to shout interruptions. Others wondered aloud why he didn't sit down. Still others called: "Parker! Parker! We'll take Parker!" When Bryan concluded his long oration, he had blurred the picture he had drawn so effectively at first.

Senator Kern followed Bryan and astonished the audience by offering to abandon the chairmanship contest if Judge Parker would also withdraw and agree to support a compromise candidate. Parker did not respond. The New York delegation sat in stubborn silence.

Kern then stunned everyone in the hall by declaring that he would not seek the chairmanship himself. He presented his candidate: William Jennings Bryan. Once more the crowd was in turmoil, many of the delegates cheering for Bryan, others booing.

Now the Wilson men and the Clark managers suspected that the Commoner might be trying to maneuver the convention into another stampede for himself. The Clark leaders rallied their forces against the old Nebraska orator. But the Wilson group, since the issue had been raised in terms of the progressives vs. the conservatives, supported Bryan for chairman.

Cone Johnson of Texas, a burly delegate with a voice like "a human fog-horn," shoved his way to the edge of the speakers' platform, got the mob quiet, and immediately bellowed: "This one thing I know—the fight is on and Bryan is on one side and Wall Street is on the other."

Champ Clark refused to accept those terms. He insisted that he was not on one side or the other. Bryan observed, in an article written later for the press, that "Mr. Clark himself was not taking sides, but his managers worked manfully for Parker." That was enough to convince Bryan that Clark was the front man for the reactionaries.

Nevertheless, Judge Parker won the temporary chairmanship, getting 579 votes to Bryan's 508. The victory of Parker, however, was a dreary one. Galleryites rose and stamped noisily from the armory when Parker started to read his keynote speech. William Allen White, the Kansas editor, depicted the scene: "The galleries rose . . . a brutal, noisy crowd . . . and left a rather dazed old gentleman reading a long manuscript, nervously looking over his glasses occasionally at the vanishing crowd."

In Bryan's newspaper dispatches he warned that the convention was about to be taken over by the bankers and the corporation lawyers who had backed Parker in 1908. Within twenty-four hours the delegates were struck by a barrage of telegrams urging him to back Bryan against the "money trust." More than 100,000 wired messages were delivered to the convention members in the next three days.

Aided by the telegrams, the Bryan-Wilson delegates defeated a movement to keep Parker as the permanent chairman. In his place they established a huge congressman from Kentucky, Representative Ollie James, who had a booming voice as powerful as Cone Johnson's and an equal devotion to Mr. Bryan.

Heartened and hopeful, the liberals in the convention then united in an effort to destroy the "unit rule"—a party regulation providing that all members of state delegations must vote as a unit. The regulation had 76 years of tradition behind it, but the liberals appealed to the rules committee and then took the fight to the convention floor.

Leader of the revolt was a young delegate from Ohio, an

intellectual lawyer named Newton D. Baker, an admirer of Woodrow Wilson. Baker made a fiery address. He took the position Wilson had described earlier in clear terms: "The unit rule can have no legitimate place where delegates are elected by direct primary. It violates every principle of popular rule in such circumstances as to prevent their voting as their constituents instructed them to vote."

Senator John Sharp Williams of Mississippi, a fervent follower of Wilson, also ripped into the unit rule. He declared that if the convention supported "the most damnable thing" the delegates should "quit your talk about 'popular government.'"

Mention of Wilson's name in a speech by another delegate set off a thundering demonstration for the man from Princeton. Senator Williams sprang to his feet, twirled his hat above his head, and called for more cheers for Woodrow Wilson. Hundreds of delegates poured into the aisles and began to swing around the hall, waving Wilson pictures.

The band suddenly launched into "The Star Spangled Banner." An orange and black banner more than thirty feet long was hauled through the galleries by Wilson's friends from Staunton, Virginia, his birthplace. As they swung the banner, they chanted: "We want Wilson! We want Wilson!"

Another banner, bearing the words "Give us Wilson and we'll give you Pennsylvania," appeared in the Pennsylvania delegation. Texans tossed up a large white streamer carrying the inscription: "40 FOR WILSON." The hundreds of marchers on the floor hailed the appearance of each new banner.

The Wilson demonstration subsided at the end of thirty minutes of uproar. The floor leader for Wilson—Congressman Robert L. Henry—then announced that Virginia, "the mother of the doctrine of state sovereignty," had signed the report made by delegates opposing the unit rule. Other states joined the Wilson group. The unit rule was overthrown.

Wilson's chances had now improved greatly. Yet the Clark-

Tammany combination was still immensely strong. Bryan searched for a way to break it apart.

In the world of William Jennings Bryan there was an incessant warfare between the plain people and the plutocrats. He did not believe the Democratic Party could serve them both. He did not believe the plutocrats were entitled to participate in a Democratic convention.

And so he was roused to instant rage when his brother, Charles W. Bryan, reported to him at three o'clock in the morning of Thursday, June 27, that Champ Clark's men had evidently made a deal with the Murphy-Ryan tribe to deliver New York's 90 votes to Clark at some time during the balloting.

If Clark got the nomination under such an arrangement, Charles Bryan felt, the speaker would be in the hands of Wall Street and could never be a progressive President. The Commoner agreed, and his wrath increased. He was receptive when Charles suggested that a resolution be introduced in the convention calling for the expulsion of Thomas Ryan and Ryan's friend, August Belmont. That would force Tammany's crowd into the open, and separate the sheep from the goats.

Charles thought that a Wilson leader should place such a resolution before the delegates, and the Commoner approved. Charles volunteered to get a group of the Wilson men together in his rooms. William Jennings Bryan retired, and Charles offered his idea to the Wilson leaders— Thomas P. Gore, Luke Lea, Cone Johnson, and others. All of them were Bryan men as well as devoted to Wilson. But they were horrified by the resolution, and would not present it.

When Charles again visited his brother at his hotel Thursday evening, he was depressed. William Bryan said he might offer the resolution himself, and wrote a draft of it. He thrust it into his coat, promising to think it over. On the way to the night session of the convention, he made up his mind to take the plunge.

Soon after the session opened, he rose in his place and asked consent to present a resolution. Congressman James, unaware of what the Commoner proposed to do, gave him the floor. Pale and stately, with the dignity of a man who had endured much and was prepared to endure more, William Jennings Bryan read what he had written:

"Resolved, that in this crisis in our party's career and in our country's history, this convention sends greeting to the people of the United States, and assures them that the party of Jefferson and of Jackson is still the champion of popular government and equality before the law. As proof of our fidelity to the people, we hereby declare ourselves opposed to the nomination of any candidate for President who is the representative of or under obligation to J. Pierpont Morgan, Thomas F. Ryan, August Belmont, or any other member of the privilege-hunting and favor-seeking class.

"Be it further resolved, that we demand the withdrawal from this convention of any delegate or delegates constituting the above-named interests."

Quiet fell upon the convention for a moment. The delegates could not believe that they understood what Bryan was saying.

"My God, Josephus, what's the matter with Bryan?" gasped Congressman James, the chairman who had let the Commoner throw a hornets' nest into the auditorium. He was speaking to Josephus Daniels, the North Carolina editor, who stood beside him on the speakers' platform. "Does he want to destroy the Democratic Party?" James cried.

Delegates began to scream at one another. Thomas Ryan, who had secured a seat with the Virginia delegation, tried to walk from the hall but was restrained by fellow delegates.

Another man rushed over to Bryan, excoriated the Commoner until he frothed at the mouth, and toppled into the arms of friends.

Bryan waited until the howling at last halted. "This is an extraordinary resolution," he admitted. "But extraordinary conditions need extraordinary remedies. . . ."

His face growing red, the Commoner went on: "There is not a delegate in this convention who does not know that an effort is being made right now to sell the Democratic Party into bondage to the predatory interests of this nation."

He looked at Ryan. He looked at Belmont. He continued: "It is the most brazen, the most insolent, the most impudent attempt that has been made in the history of American politics to dominate a convention, stifle the honest sentiment of a people, and make the nominee the bond-slave of the men who exploit the people of this country."

To his enemies, Bryan's performance was pure demagoguery. To his admirers, it was one of his great moments—one of the times when the Commoner, who had not been able to reach the Presidency, demonstrated how eloquently he could whiplash the rich and the insolent men who regarded the people as cattle to be bought and sold.

To the Wilson men, Bryan's resolution brought joy and uneasiness—joy because Bryan was finally committed to stop Clark, and uneasiness because Bryan himself might want to run one more time. With the Republicans split, the candidate of the Baltimore convention was almost certain to enter the White House. After three defeats, Bryan undoubtedly yearned for a great vindicating victory. Perhaps he aimed to create a Wilson-Clark deadlock—and a final turn to himself.

Yet the Wilson leaders had no choice. The fate of their candidate was now bound up with Bryan. Bryan had stated the issue in terms which made it practically impossible to oppose him. Who wanted to favor the nomination of a candidate obligated to "the privilege-hunting and favor-seeking class"? Bryan was asking every delegate to reject such a dubious nominee.

Delegates did rise and assert that they could not accept the second part of the resolution—the part that called for the expulsion of delegates constituting "or representing" the Morgan-Ryan-Belmont interests—because a convention had no legal power to expel delegates sent there by "the sovereign states." Bryan reluctantly dropped that part of his resolution, but he insisted on a recorded vote on the first section, opposing the nomination of any man under obligations to the Morgan-Ryan-Belmont class.

When the vote was taken, the Tammany men from New York and Ryan's friends from Virginia were suddenly on Bryan's side. Boss Murphy had accepted the advice of Senator-elect James K. Vardaman of Mississippi. Vardaman, an old friend of Bryan's, had been infuriated by the resolution and had rushed over to Murphy, saying: "Vote for it. If you do, Murphy, we will make Bryan look like a fool."

After he had announced that New York would support the resolution, Murphy grinned at August Belmont and grunted: "Augie, listen and hear yourself vote yourself out of the convention." Virginia accepted the Bryan proposal in the same ironic style.

Murphy, Vardaman, Ryan, and their henchmen overlooked one very important fact. People across the country were reading the dispatches of Bryan and other newspaper correspondents dramatizing in simple sentences the vote on the resolution. In these articles the approval of the resolution (883 to 201½) appeared as a triumph for righteousness, personified in Bryan, over the evil forces of Wall Street.

The impact of Bryan's articles on the people was evident in another torrential flow of messages. These messages were phrased differently by different citizens, but their import was clear to the delegates: "Back Bryan." The efforts of Murphy and Vardaman to ridicule the Commoner were washed out of the minds of the plodding, sweating delegates by a stream of telegrams.

Although it was nearly midnight before the Bryan resolution was disposed of, the names of Presidential candidates were called for by the chairman that same night. Alabama started the parade, with Senator John H. Bankhead asking his son William to sing the virtues of Oscar W. Underwood. The strains of "Dixie" sounded. Demonstrators from Georgia, Florida, and Mississippi joined the sturdy Alabamans in stomping around the hall for Underwood. The demonstration faded at the end of half an hour.

Then came Senator James A. Reed of Missouri, exalting Champ Clark and attacking Woodrow Wilson. "Give me no political dilettante who comes into camp when honors are most ripe to pluck," cried Reed, referring to Wilson. He hailed Clark, saying that the man most fit to lead the United States was one "whose breast is covered with the scars of honor; who leads today and should lead tomorrow—the Lion of Democracy, Champ Clark of Missouri."

Delegates by the hundreds were ready to roar for the lion. They surged through the aisles, seized the speakers' platform, yelled and waved their banners. One Clark man mounted a table and moved that Champ Clark "be nominated by acclamation." Consulting himself, the delegate declared that the motion had been adopted.

Then an ancient southern gentleman climbed to the platform, carrying a hunting horn. He played the old tune "Off Hounds," and the Clark men swept into a new outburst. The cheering, clapping and singing went on for an hour and five minutes.

A few minutes after two o'clock in the morning of June 28, Judge John W. Wescott stepped forward to nominate Wilson. He took one stride toward the lectern, but it was an hour and fifteen minutes later before he had a chance to swing into his speech. The Wilson men went wild.

Horns blew, whistles rose piercingly through the steamy air of the packed hall, shouts and screeches came from the galleries. Banners waved again, as the delegates supporting Wilson scrambled through the aisles. One floating streamer proclaimed that Wilson was the "Yankee Doodle Dixie Candidate." The Wilson demonstration exceeded the Clark parade in size and duration.

Judge Wescott had opposed Wilson in the New Jersey state convention in 1910, but had been converted into a strong supporter by Wilson's achievements as governor. The judge was an old-fashioned, flag-waving orator, but his enthusiasm for Wilson was obviously genuine—and he had a voice that reached into every corner of the armory.

"The Democratic Party is commissioned to carry on a great constructive program, having for its end a complete restoration of the doctrine of equal rights and equal opportunity," Wescott said. "Providence has given us, in the exalted character of New Jersey's Executive, the mental and moral equipment to accomplish this reincarnation of Democracy."

Wescott declared that Wilson had smashed a bipartisan political machine in his state and had built upon the wreckage "an ideal commonwealth." Wilson had been in politics less than two years, but his accomplishments had been magnificent.

"Every crisis evolves its master," Judge Wescott said. "Time and circumstance have evolved the immortal governor of New Jersey. . . . New Jersey appreciates the honor . . . of placing before this convention as a candidate for the Presidency of the United States the seer and philosopher of Princeton, the Princeton schoolmaster, Woodrow Wilson."

Another demonstration followed. Speeches seconding Wilson's candidacy were made by Senator Thomas P. Gore of Oklahoma, Governor John Burks of North Dakota, John Walsh of Wisconsin, Senator Ellison D. ("Cotton Ed") Smith of South Carolina, Alfred Jacques of Minnesota,

A. Mitchell Palmer of Pennsylvania, and P. H. O'Brien of Michigan. Judging by the variety of states represented, Wilson was truly the "Yankee Doodle Dixie Candidate."

Wilson had the backing of influential men in the North and the South. He had the unshakable support and enthusiasm of many delegates. But he lacked the necessary votes; he was still far short of the total amassed by Clark.

Enthusiasm could not compensate for the lack of numbers. William McCombs, Wilson's chief commander at Baltimore, still felt frustrated when he contemplated New York's big block of 90 delegates. Yet it was too late to attempt any arrangement with Boss Murphy; Wilson was already committed to Bryan.

The first ballot on Presidential candidates was tabulated at seven o'clock in the morning, after Governors Baldwin of Connecticut, Marshall of Indiana, and Harmon of Ohio had been placed before the assembly by their friends.

The totals were:

Clark: 440½	Marshall: 31
Wilson: 324	Baldwin: 22
Harmon: 148	Sulzer: 2
Underwood: 117½	Bryan: 1

(Sulzer was Representative William Sulzer, a congressman who later became governor of New York.)

As the tired delegates walked slowly from the hall, they all knew that a fierce, knockdown, tooth-and-claw struggle between the Clark and Wilson forces lay ahead. On that warm June morning, no man knew what the outcome would be.

WILSON ON THE EDGE OF SURRENDER

At Sea Girt, Wilson played golf, walked along the beach, gazed out at the gleaming sea, talked with his wife and his daughters, laughed and joked with his friends. He had lines of anxiety between his brows, but those marks of worry did not seem to get any deeper. He apparently regarded the future with the deep serenity of the true philosopher.

His hopes were rapidly ebbing. When he talked on the phone with McCombs and William Gibbs McAdoo, he realized that his nomination was unlikely. His managers were not defeatist, but they could not hide the truth from him.

In the evening of June 28, while the balloting was progressing inconclusively—on the first few ballots, Clark gained 14 votes and Wilson added 28, but no trend was evident—the governor sat near the fireplace with his wife. His face was full of melancholy at times; she reassured him and he felt comforted. He read for a while, looking at a biography of Gladstone. Gladstone had been his earliest hero, and he knew that Gladstone had endured many situations as trying to the soul as the one in which he now found himself.

Friends came in. One of them was J. Franklin Fort, a former governor of New Jersey. While Fort and others were present, Wilson was asked his reaction to the battle in Baltimore. He declared that it reminded him of the man in the buggy, who was told over and over that the distance to the next town was twenty miles, although the buggy seemed to be in motion. The man in the buggy said to his companion: "Well, John, I'm glad we're holding our own."

Wilson was not really holding his own in Baltimore. Boss Murphy was just waiting for the strategic moment to throw the New York delegation into Champ Clark's camp. Murphy and the Clark leaders were sure that the New York announcement would make hundreds of delegates clamber aboard the Clark bandwagon.

Not long after midnight, as the early hours of June 29 were expiring, Murphy made his move. On the tenth ballot the Tammany chieftain rose slowly from his chair. "New York casts 90 votes for Champ Clark of Missouri," Murphy said. He had shifted the delegation from Harmon to Clark.

The Clark delegates went wild again, leaping and dancing around the convention floor. The 90 votes from New York gave the speaker a total of 556—more than a majority of the convention. No Democratic convention since 1844 had failed to nominate a man who gained a majority.

While the Clark delegates paraded, Wilson's floor managers—McCombs, McAdoo, Palmer, and Representative Albert Hurleson of Texas—begged the Underwood delegates to stand firm. Underwood had more than 100 votes. Without those votes, Clark could not get the two-thirds of the convention required for the Democratic nomination.

In Sea Girt, Wilson wrestled with his conscience. He had repeatedly denounced the "two-thirds rule." He felt that a plain majority should be enough to entitle a man to the nomination. Clark now had the majority. In Washington the speaker was preparing a telegram of acceptance for the nomination, feeling certain that Wilson would drop from the race. Wilson paced up and down, talking with his wife. He was on the edge of surrender, and yet he could not bring himself to take the terrible step. He postponed action.

McCombs then telephoned from Baltimore. The faithful McCombs was depressed. He told Wilson that a message should be drafted, releasing his delegates if the Clark trend continued. McCombs asked whether Wilson wanted to name a candidate to receive the delegates, and suggested Underwood. Wilson said he had no right to give his delegates to another man; he wouldn't try to tell them what to do.

When he left the phone, Wilson turned to his wife. She faced him with tears in her eyes. Evidently he thought that he had lost, and she saw the depth of his pain.

She told the reporter later: "We tried to pretend to think we were glad that it was over."

Wilson finally telegraphed McCombs, authorizing him to free the delegates when McCombs decided the time was right. He felt the fight was over.

From his youth Wilson had carried inside him a belief that

Providence would summon him to a high destiny. His father had encouraged him to think of himself as a future President of the United States. Could his father's encouragement have been only the foolish pride of a doting parent? Could his own faith in Providence have been wrong? Had he suffered all these years from a delusion, a kind of madness?

He talked with his wife about a possible trip to the lake country in Great Britain, the beautiful and gracious country he loved so much. They made plans for a visit there as soon as his term as governor was finished. He wondered again whether he should telegraph congratulations to Clark. He could not compose a message. He accepted, and yet could not accept, the reality of his defeat.

So Wilson still hesitated, and while he tried to reach a decision, conditions in the convention underwent another sudden and drastic change. William Jennings Bryan, who had been absent when Murphy cast the Tammany vote for Clark, had returned to the hall. As soon as he discovered what had happened, he rose and protested: "A progressive candidate must not be besmirched by New York's vote." One of his daughters, in the gallery, led a cheer for Woodrow Wilson. The applause for Wilson spread.

Would the next state in line go with New York to Clark, or hold fast? In the roll call of states North Dakota came after New York. The armory was completely quiet when Chairman James asked the leader of the North Dakota delegation to tell the state's vote. North Dakota had been for Wilson. If its delegates abandoned him at this moment, the New Jersey governor might be done for.

"Ten votes for Wilson!" shouted the North Dakota leader, and the Wilson men yelled with glee. The fight wasn't over. It was getting rougher, that was all.

Oklahoma came next. One delegate stood up. He had been for Wilson, he said, but apparently Clark was the convention's choice. He asked for a poll of the delegation.

Once again, a strange ally came to Wilson's rescue. Wil-

liam H. ("Alfalfa Bill") Murray, a skinny man with snap-
ping suspenders and a red bandana kerchief around his neck,
vowed that he didn't mind a poll of his delegation. Then
"Alfalfa Bill" bellowed like a bull: "But we do insist that we
shall not join Tammany in making the nomination!"

Abashed by the thought of joining the dangerous men
from Tammany Hall, the Oklahomans stayed in Wilson's
column. The Wilson men raised the roof with a series of
happy howls, and staged a demonstration lasting for nearly
an hour. By the time the demonstration concluded, the peril
of a stampede for Clark had vanished.

The Clark men and the Wilson men closed in on the Underwood delegates on the eleventh ballot because they held the
balance of power. But Underwood wouldn't yield to any
offers. His men were stubbornly loyal. Perhaps Underwood
felt that a long stalemate between Clark and Wilson would
eventually win him a compromise nomination. Perhaps the
promises made by Wilson leaders, that their delegates would
go to Underwood and not to Clark if Wilson couldn't win,
helped to keep the Underwood men firmly in line.

After the eleventh ballot, the convention adjourned. It was
three minutes past four o'clock in the morning of June 29. The
exhausted delegates plodded wearily from the hall. No one
then could see how the struggle could be ended.

CLARK HURRIES TO BALTIMORE

As Colonel Roosevelt had done in the Republican combat,
Champ Clark did now in the Democratic conflict—he hurried to the scene of battle. His lieutenants in the field were
demoralized and disrupted by what happened on the thirteenth and fourteenth ballots, taken after the delegates re-
convened in the afternoon of June 29.

On the thirteenth ballot Speaker Clark gained only 7½
votes, despite the intensive efforts of his men on the convention floor. Wilson gained two votes—a very small sign of

progress—but the atmosphere was definitely becoming more favorable to the professor's cause.

And on the fourteenth ballot, after the Nebraska delegation had been polled by special request of one of the delegates, Bryan cast his vote for Wilson. The poll of the Nebraska group showed that thirteen of them wanted Wilson, while Clark held six. Clark, however, had been the choice of the voters in the Nebraska primary, so Bryan felt that he could not switch to Wilson without making a public explanation.

The Commoner demanded recognition. The presiding officer, perhaps afraid of another long speech, inquired: "For what purpose does the gentleman from Nebraska rise?" Bryan answered: "To explain my vote."

Some delegates derisively shouted at him, and asked the chairman to maintain the regular order. Bryan could not be stopped. He told the crowd: "As long as Mr. Ryan's agent— as long as New York's 90 votes are recorded for Mr. Clark— I withhold my vote from him and cast it. . . ."

He was interrupted by a wave of cheers and jeers. He went right on, reminding the delegates that Nebraska was a land of progressives and the Nebraskans had voted for Clark "with the distinct understanding that Mr. Clark stood for progressive democracy." By welcoming Tammany's 90 votes, Clark had violated that understanding.

The indomitable Commoner, who had not left the convention floor for more than a few minutes at a time since Tammany had gone to Clark on the tenth ballot, was a rumpled and weary old man. But his voice had a ring of power when he said: "With the understanding that I shall stand ready to withdraw my vote from the one for whom I am going to cast it whenever New York casts her vote for him, I cast my vote for Nebraska's second choice, Governor Wilson. . . ."

Clark delegates groaned and booed, while the Wilson men roared their approval. Actually McCombs and other Wilson leaders were not ecstatic about Bryan's statement. Bryan was clearly trying to hold a veto power over Wilson as well as Clark. Convinced of his own righteousness, Bryan was striving to run the whole convention.

Delegates resented Bryan's arrogance. One man cried: "Are you a Democrat?" Another, an Underwood man from Alabama, shouted: "There are a thousand delegates here, and we have something else to do besides listening to Mr. Bryan make his four or fifth speech."

Yet Bryan felt that he spoke for the people—and the people were mightier than a thousand delegates or ten thousand delegates or any number of delegates who did not voice their will.

But few delegates followed him immediately into the Wilson camp. The Clark lines did not break under the weight of the Commoner's prestige. Boos and catcalls were hurled at Bryan from the Tammany ranks. John Stanchfield, a New York delegate, branded him as "a money-grabbing, selfish, office-seeking, favor-hunting, publicity-seeking marplot."

Hearing of Bryan's action, Speaker Clark held a meeting in Washington with his advisers and with Wilson's foe, William Randolph Hearst. He issued a statement, saying that Bryan's charge that he was influenced by Wall Street was "an outrageous aspersion" on his character. He asked Bryan to prove such charges or retract them.

Then Clark hastened to Baltimore. He arrived just as the convention was adjourning. Thus he missed the chance to go on the floor and make a personal appeal to the delegates. With a majority already listed for him, he might have captured the few extra votes he needed—if he had reached the armory a few minutes earlier.

At every crucial moment, chance or destiny or Providence seemed to work for Wilson. Bryan's endorsement had been reluctant and hesitant, but hatred of Tammany and rich Democrats had strengthened his will to fight for Wilson.

Every step Clark took now—revealing his frantic reach for the prize—carried the nomination farther away from the Missourian and closer to the New Jersey governor.

On Saturday, June 29, the balloting went on during the whole day, with gradual gains for Wilson and a gradual decline for Clark. The speaker's majority melted slowly but surely.

Kansas made a significant switch on the twentieth ballot. This delegation had been told to stay with Clark until his nomination appeared to be out of the question. On the twentieth tally Kansas jumped from Clark to Wilson.

A little later the 43 Massachusetts delegates transferred from Clark to the governor of their own state, Eugene N. Foss. After twenty-six roll calls, the totals were:

| Clark | 463½ | Underwood | 112½ | Marshall | 30 |
| Wilson | 407½ | Harmon | 29 | Foss | 43 |

(One delegate stood fast for William Jennings Bryan.)

On Sunday, June 30, the convention did not meet. But in hotel rooms and in lobbies, in restaurants and in private homes, the bargaining among political managers was fast and furious.

That Sunday, Woodrow Wilson got in a motor car with his family and traveled to Spring Lake, New Jersey, to attend church services there. After the prayers, the minister voiced astonishment that the governor had traveled so far over dusty roads to participate in the services.

"Where should a man in my straits be on such a day, except in the House of God?" Wilson asked. "I could not remain at the camp."

Wilson felt that prayers were urgently required to carry him to his goal. At Sea Girt, after studying the results of Saturday's balloting, he had told a reporter: "We have been figuring that at the present rate of gain I will be nominated in 175 more ballots."

Clark had given notice that he would not release his delegates to Wilson under any circumstances. If he could not win himself, he was going to be sure that Wilson did not win—if the convention had to stay in session all through the summer.

Clark's floor leader, Senator Stone of Missouri, had asked Wilson to follow the Democratic tradition which called for support of the man who obtained a majority. Stone had telegraphed Wilson: "A majority of the national convention has voted for the candidacy of Champ Clark. No one questions his fitness and loyalty to Democracy and for seventy years the practice has been established of giving the nomination to the candidate who received a majority. We ask you in the interests of the party and in vindication of the democratic principle of majority rule to assist in making his nomination unanimous by the withdrawal of your candidacy."

Wilson had not heeded that plea. He could not go contrary to the voice within him, the voice that had assured him of the Presidency when his hour came.

Whether Wilson had divine guidance, good fortune, or a very keen political mind, during the convention he invariably avoided disastrous mistakes and took full advantage of every opportunity that came his way. He had wavered only momentarily, infected by the defeatist mood of William Mc-Combs, after Clark had leaped to a majority on the tenth ballot.

He did not waver now when McCombs telephoned him on Sunday afternoon and urged him to state publicly that he would not, if nominated and elected, appoint Bryan secretary of state. McCombs protested that many delegates would not swing to Wilson until he offered that guarantee against Bryan, who had incurred the hostility of a great number.

"I will not bargain for this office," Wilson said. "It would be foolish for me at this time to decide upon a cabinet officer, and it would be outrageous to eliminate anybody from consideration now, particularly Mr. Bryan, who has rendered such fine service to the party in all seasons."

The Wilson who spoke those words was a different man from the conservative college professor of 1896, who had refused to vote for the Commoner when Bryan had been the nominee of the Democratic Party in that year. Wilson had considered Bryan's advocacy of free silver a misleading and inflationary doctrine, and had regarded Mr. Bryan as much too radical to be President.

Whether Wilson had moved with the times or whether he believed that he needed the support of Bryan in 1912—whatever the reasons might be—he had certainly changed his position rather drastically. He was willing to take the risk of a sudden Bryan drive for the nomination; he had been warned repeatedly of that possibility. Yet he could not abandon Bryan, because Bryan had been loyal to him.

Bryan's dispatches to the newspapers, the articles appearing in the Baltimore *Sun* and other publications reaching the delegates, had increasing effects upon those leaning toward Wilson. The delegates at last became convinced that the ordinary people now wanted Wilson as their standard-bearer. The delegates began to believe that Wilson was the man who could win in November.

On Monday, July 1, when the convention resumed balloting, many of the men in the hall carried copies of the New York *World* with an editorial demanding the choice of Wilson. The editorial was harsh and stern: "Ryanism and Murphyism have created an issue that makes the nomination of Woodrow Wilson a matter of Democratic life or death. To compromise now is to send a Democratic ticket into the campaign shackled to bossism and plutocracy. To compromise now is to give Theodore Roosevelt the supreme issue that he needs.

"Compromise is no longer possible. There can be no Democratic harmony, there can be no Democratic unity, there can be no Democratic integrity, until the convention overwhelms this shameful alliance between corrupt finance and corrupt politics. . . . As Stephen A. Douglas once said, 'There can be no neutrals in this war—only patriots or traitors.' "

What irony for Champ Clark! He had been the victor in the state primaries; he had piled up many more votes than Wilson; he had been endorsed by a majority of the delegates at the convention; he had spent his life in the Democratic Party—and now his cause was described as a "shameful alliance between corrupt finance and corrupt politics" and those who stood with him were tarred as "traitors" to true democracy. His mournful rage burned still more fiercely.

Wilson took the lead on the thirtieth ballot, with 460 votes to the speaker's 455. Yet it was a narrow lead, and Clark would not quit. Wilson's lead continued to grow on ballot after ballot. Still the speaker struggled, rallying his men, refusing to bow.

The Illinois delegation held a meeting at midnight on July 1. By one o'clock in the morning of July 2, Clark knew the worst. The Illinois delegates had voted, 41 to 13, in favor of swinging to Woodrow Wilson. Clark's leaders went to him, told him the time had come to concede that he had been beaten. He had to face it.

Clark pleaded for more time. He tried desperately to make a deal with Oscar Underwood. He was prepared to accept anybody except Wilson. Wherever he turned, he struck stone walls. The Wilson flood was swelling and sweeping everything before it.

On the forty-third ballot, William McCombs came to a personal breaking point. The nomination of Wilson seemed absolutely certain, but the Illinois leader, Roger Sullivan, had not committed the block of votes needed to end the tension.

"Roger, we've got to have Illinois, or I'll withdraw," Mc-

Combs said; he was a sick man, trembling with fatigue, aching from lack of sleep, thirsting for the triumph so long delayed. He had known the terrible tensions of politics for many years, but this convention was too much for him.

Sullivan's hard face did not relax. "Sit steady, boy," said the Illinois boss. Sullivan seemed to be prepared to stay in the inferno of that steaming hall forever.

But five minutes later, Sullivan announced that the votes of Illinois were going to Governor Wilson. Virginia and West Virginia jumped on the bandwagon, and by the end of that ballot Wilson had 602 votes and Clark had dropped to 329. Underwood grimly held 98½.

Senator Bankhead was shocked by Sullivan's shift. Bankhead thought he had established an understanding with Sullivan to deliver the Illinois votes to Underwood at some point during the July 2 balloting. With Tom Heflin and Henry Clayton, Bankhead went over and asked Sullivan what he intended to do on future ballots. Sullivan said he was going to swing Illinois back to Clark again on the forty-sixth roll call.

One delegate in the hall, T. P. Gore, later reported that Clark had made a quick visit to the armory after Sullivan had announced the shift to Wilson. Sullivan had gone to Clark's cab, outside the hall, and had agreed to vote for him again if the balloting went on long enough. Clark apparently promised to recognize Sullivan as the distributor of federal jobs in Illinois if Clark got the Presidency.

Irked by Sullivan, Bankhead went to the platform on the forty-sixth ballot. Alabama, of course, was the first state called. The senator declared that he was withdrawing Underwood's name. The convention was thrown into another uproar: the delegates and the people in the galleries recognized that the moment of decision was upon them.

"Wilson! Wilson!" came the chant from the galleries.

Weary and sorrowful, Senator Stone of Missouri rose and

released the delegates from every state supporting Clark, except his own. Out of love and respect for the speaker, Missouri would stay irrevocably enrolled under the banner of "Old Champ Clark."

Massachusetts withdrew the name of Governor Foss and the delegation went to Wilson. The cheers grew louder, pictures of Wilson were lifted and waved. A political miracle was about to happen in Baltimore.

At three-thirty in the afternoon of July 2, 1912, the miracle happened—as Woodrow Wilson had known it would. He became the Democratic nominee for President of the United States.

When the news reached Sea Girt, the forty men in a band waiting there picked up their instruments and blared forth a burst of joyful music. The band marched toward the rambling house by the sea, toward a large white cottage where Wilson and his family were suddenly conscious of the weight of the responsibilities that had come to him at last.

VIII. July: Roosevelt Sounds a Trumpet

THE COLONEL'S GAMBLE

When did Theodore Roosevelt, the friend of millionaires and radicals, the man who hobnobbed with kings and loved the common people, really decide to take the greatest gamble of his life—the attempt to gain the Presidency on a third-party ticket?

President Taft was sure that Roosevelt had been set to bolt the Republican Party from that day in February, 1912, when the Colonel said that he would not refuse another nomination for the White House.

Amos Pinchot, a liberal friend of the Colonel, felt that the decision had come in Roosevelt's Chicago hotel suite when it became evident that Taft could not be blocked. When Pinchot entered the suite, he found Roosevelt pacing up and down. Some of "T.R.'s" advisers sat in silence around him; others leaned against walls. Frank Munsey and George Perkins halted Roosevelt's pacing by extending their hands and touching his shoulders. One of them said: "Colonel, we will see you through."

William Draper Lewis, another friend of Roosevelt—Dean

of the Law School of the University of Pennsylvania—who later served as chairman of the resolutions committee at the Progressive convention, saw things in a different light.

Lewis went to a meeting called by supporters of Roosevelt after Taft's nomination had been announced. Governor Hiram Johnson of California presided at this gathering of excited Roosevelt admirers. Everyone present felt that the Colonel had to stay in the fight for progressive principles.

Roosevelt came in. Speeches and resolutions were forgotten in the group's desire to hear from the leader. He said that the time had come when all men who believed in the maxims of public and private morality underlying free government should join in the insurgent cause. He asked the men there to go back to their states, to sound out the sentiment of the people, and to come together again in the near future to nominate a Progressive candidate on a Progressive platform.

Those at the meeting assured the Colonel that he was the man they wanted. Roosevelt replied: "If you wish me to make the fight I will make it, even if only one state should support me. The only condition I impose is that you shall feel entirely free, when you come together, to substitute any other man in my place, if you deem it better for the movement. In that case, I will give him my heartiest support."

Yet in the early days of July rumors began to circulate that Roosevelt would not run after all. The impassioned delegates who had supported him in Chicago were scattered throughout the country. No organization had been formed to make arrangements for a Progressive assembly. Doubts and misgivings assailed some of those who had been in the vanguard of the Roosevelt movement.

The adoption of a progressive platform by the Democrats and the nomination of Wilson had dismayed many who had talked of unfurling a new party banner. Some said publicly that it might be better to unite with the Wilson forces.

On July 3 a chill breeze blew through the Roosevelt followers. Governor Chase S. Osborn of Michigan, one of the seven Republican governors who had pleaded with Roosevelt to seek the nomination, said he didn't think there was any reason to establish a third party.

Mark Fagan, who had been mayor of Jersey City on a reform ticket, resisted the invitation of Roosevelt men who asked his endorsement of the Colonel. Fagan declared that he would support Wilson.

Senator Robert La Follette, still smarting from the Colonel's treatment of him, startled the country by insisting that he would not leave the Republican Party in spite of the scathing criticisms he had made of Taft. La Follette asserted that the third-party idea was inspired solely by Roosevelt's desire for a third term as President.

Did Roosevelt actually believe that a new party could carry him into the White House? He indicated to some of his friends that he was doubtful of the outcome. He was capable of convincing himself of many things, but he had been in politics for many years—and he knew the obstacles in the path of any candidate running on an independent ticket.

His shrewdest political advisers informed him that his wisest course would be to accept the verdict of the Republican convention, to say that he would vote for the candidate of his party, and then to retire to his home on Sagamore Hill until Taft went down to a crashing defeat. After that, he would certainly become once more the unquestioned leader of the Republican Party with the next Presidential nomination in his pocket.

That was the advice given him by the professional politicians and by some of his friends who were concerned about his personal future. He heard what they said—and he did not heed them. He was a crusader, with his armor already buckled on, and he could not retreat to his castle.

Wilson might be an intelligent man. Wilson might be sincere. Yet Roosevelt did not think that Wilson could accomplish anything as the head of a party that was "rotten" and "boss-controlled." To Roosevelt, Wilson was just as much at the mercy of the bosses as William Howard Taft.

So he decided to run. He told Lewis and others closely associated with him: "If we form a third party and go out and fight for better social conditions in this country, we will accomplish more in three months than could be accomplished under ordinary conditions in a dozen years."

On July 3 he informed the press that he was in the fight to the finish, even though he failed to get a single electoral vote. He was going to educate the voters as they had never been educated before. He was ready to lead his new army.

CALL OF THE BULL MOOSE

When Roosevelt spoke, the trumpeting cry of the Bull Moose sounded through the land. On July 7, over the signatures of sixty-three Roosevelt men from forty states, the summons went out to the faithful followers of the Colonel in towns and cities, in villages and farms across the nation.

The Colonel had been unjustly deprived of a Presidential nomination at the Republican convention. The people deserved a chance to vote for him in the November election. The two old parties were hollow shells, no longer representing the healthy strength of America. A new party had to be brought into being to take control from the tired and cynical men who dominated the old ones.

Those were the ideas contained in the message sent out by the Roosevelt committee. The call produced a response which shocked and surprised the regulars in both the Democratic and Republican headquarters.

Dozens of leading citizens in many states declared that they would go to the National Progressive Convention, opening on August 5 in the same building where the Colonel had been defeated in June. The taint of Taftism was to be wiped clean. Delegates would pay their own expenses. The convention was to be a sober, thoughtful gathering of devoted citizens.

The trend toward Wilson among disaffected Republicans was swiftly halted. Michigan's Governor Osborn returned to the Roosevelt tent. The Kansas City *Star*, the Philadelphia *North American*, and other publications which had supported Wilson against Clark, regretfully abandoned him because they did not believe he could make the Democratic Party into a truly progressive organization. They began again to beat the drums for Roosevelt.

Perhaps Woodrow Wilson was a true progressive. They were willing to believe in Wilson's sincerity and ability. But they could not see how a party which appeared to be reactionary and corrupt in the South and other areas could suddenly be made progressive by a new leader of Wilson's type.

There were millions of citizens who saw the American scene in this perspective. What had the Democratic leaders in Congress really done to meet the problems that faced the nation in 1912? Did they have a coherent, intelligent, long-range program? What fruitful efforts had they made to give farmers a fair share of the national income? What had they done to improve the country's educational system? Had the Democratic bosses in Virginia and Illinois—or their counterparts in the Republican organization—tried strenuously to eliminate corruption? Were they fighting the spiritual darkness which seemed to be creeping across America? To millions the answers to all these questions could be given in a few words—the Democrats were boss-ridden "boodle-grabbers."

Those who heeded Roosevelt's trumpet had many motives. Some were genuinely altruistic, and sought nothing for themselves. Others were far-sighted lawyers, teachers, businessmen, and clergymen who thought the country was headed for disaster under the professional politicians. Others were politicians who thought Roosevelt might be riding the wave of the future—and they wanted to be on the crest of the wave.

With his outstretched arms, with his elastic and restive mind, Roosevelt was eager to receive supporters of all kinds, from Wall Street bankers to radical Socialists to liberal-minded ministers who had been ejected from their pulpits by wealthy parishioners alarmed by their dangerous notions of equality among men.

Exulting in the knowledge that an aroused multitude would be with him at the Progressive convention, Roosevelt began to make practical arrangements for the coming campaign. He conferred with advisers on possible planks in the new party's platform, met with Munsey and Perkins to raise funds, and discussed a proposal to support various Democratic and Republican candidates who might in turn help support him in their local districts.

Roosevelt knew that it was impossible to organize a new party on a national scale in the few months remaining before the November voting. He must appeal to dissidents in both major parties who might throw their followers into his column.

One of the conflicts that plagued him was the question of whether Negroes from the southern states would be accepted as full-fledged delegates at the Progressive assembly. While insisting that he was a firm friend of the Negroes, Roosevelt thought the only hope of gaining higher status for colored voters lay in persuading prominent whites to take the lead in admitting Negroes as political associates.

He wanted to place entirely in the hands of white southern Progressives the decision on whether Negro delegates should be admitted. If the white southerners wanted to include Negroes in their delegations, that was fine with him.

If they wanted to exclude them—until the Progressive Party could build enough strength among white voters to challenge the Democrats—that policy was also satisfactory to Roosevelt.

There were some Progressive leaders who felt that Christian justice required more consideration for the Negroes. These leaders believed that the acceptance of Negro delegates should not depend on the attitudes of the southern whites. They thought the Progressive Party should demonstrate its superiority over the other parties by encouraging Negro delegates to attend the Progressive meeting in proportion to their numbers in the South.

It was decided that the question should be settled by the Credentials Committee at the convention under Roosevelt's direction.

Through the month of July the Colonel worked furiously, attacking Taft and Wilson with blunt statements that landed on their heads like bludgeons, writing letters and articles defining his ideas, telephoning his friends, reassuring the doubtful ones, renewing the enthusiasm of the fire-eaters, keeping his lieutenants in line, and adding recruits to the Progressive cause day by day. He exhausted his assistants and never seemed to get tired himself.

WILSON BINDS UP WOUNDS, PREPARES FOR OTHER WARS

The factional wars of the early spring and summer were over for Woodrow Wilson. He spent the last weeks at Sea Girt shaking the hands of Democratic potentates who came from all corners of the United States to give advice, seek his blessing, and remind him of their availability for big federal jobs if he won the Presidency. He was affable to all.

Not fearing Taft but knowing that Roosevelt was a fierce battler, Wilson now tried to heal the injuries caused by the Baltimore convention. He wanted a united party for the stormy months ahead. He told funny stories, he laughed and joked, he showed that he appreciated the good qualities of anyone sincerely dedicated to the Democratic Party.

On the Fourth of July, he received thirty-five members of the Democratic National Committee, who stayed for three hours at the rambling cottage and left in a glow of happiness. He wasn't the cold, reserved, distant scholar they had anticipated. He had warm blood in his veins, a twinkle in his eye, and a gift of gab that matched theirs.

Senator James O'Gorman of New York, who had fought Boss Murphy in the pre-convention period and had once been suggested by Bryan as a compromise candidate for the White House, arrived the next day with Dudley Field Malone. The anti-Tammany men and the Tammany chiefs were floating on a sea of harmony, O'Gorman and Malone reported. New York would do its bit for his candidacy.

From Alabama, Wilson learned that Oscar Underwood's legions would be at his side through thick and thin. That meant he would have a solid core of southern support. And Underwood's backers would contribute much needed campaign money as well.

The labor vote was not as important in 1912 as it became later. Yet Wilson and his friends were anxious to get a sizable fraction of it. He went to Trenton on July 9 for a meeting with Samuel Gompers and other leaders of the American Federation of Labor.

Gompers later wrote: "In that meeting I felt my prejudices disappearing before the sincerity and obvious humanitarianism of the man. . . . I left Trenton feeling very much relieved."

There remained the problem of mollifying Speaker Clark. Clark was a dyed-in-the-wool party man, and would not bolt to Roosevelt under any circumstances. But Wilson knew that thousands of voters had supported Clark in the primaries, so at least a semblance of friendliness with the speaker was essential.

The ill fortune which had dogged Clark at the convention continued to pursue him at Sea Girt. Reaching the town an hour ahead of his expected arrival, Clark found no one to greet him. When he reached the governor's cottage, Wilson was in a conference with two Progressive Republicans— Charles Crane of Chicago and President Charles Van Hise of the University of Wisconsin.

When Wilson and Clark finally got together, they had little to talk about except the necessity of a Democratic victory in the fall. Clark snapped at the reporters questioning him after his visit: "I do not care to talk about national politics unless they relate directly to the Ninth Congressional District of Missouri." Then he hurried away.

The atmosphere was somewhat warmer when he made a second trip to Sea Girt on July 20, bringing with him Democratic members of the House of Representatives. Wilson was gracefully respectful to the speaker in the presence of the House members, and Clark responded to Wilson's overtures.

Two days later Wilson invited the two senators from Missouri, both staunch admirers of Clark, to aid him in drawing plans for the campaign. Senator James A. Reed, who had heaped sarcasm on Wilson at Baltimore, and Senator William J. Stone, who had demanded his withdrawal, now expressed their willingness to assist him at every stage.

Meanwhile, Wilson was reading and trying to answer the thousands of letters and telegrams which had flooded the cottage after his nomination. He was also trying to compose a speech for August 7, when he would formally accept his nomination.

His affability and calm began to crack under the terrible strain of the first two weeks of July. He wrote to Mary Hulbert on July 14: "The life I am leading now can't keep up. . . . Not a moment am I left free to do what I would. I thought last night I should go crazy with the strain and confusion of it."

His wife and daughters soothed him, as always, and his friends invited him to slip from the crowded cottage to quieter places. He took refuge once with Melvin Rice, at Rice's secluded estate near Atlantic Highlands, and then had six days aboard the *Corona,* a yacht belonging to Cleveland H. Dodge, a heavy contributor to his campaign funds. He took along a bound copy of the Democratic platform and some newspaper clippings about it. Among them was an editorial from the *World* entitled: "Planks To Be Broken."

Then he proceeded to jot down in shorthand his address of acceptance.

It was a thoughtful, yet rather vague, rather wordy and ponderous speech, without the brilliant phrases which later appeared in his oratory. The address ran to more than twenty typewritten pages, and covered every plank in the platform except two—the section urging a single term for the President and the proposed exemption of American ships from Panama Canal tolls. He was opposed to these two ideas.

1912 was one of the exceptional years in American politics —a year when people paid close attention to the party platforms, a year when men argued in their homes, in clubs and saloons, on the streets and at meetings in halls and in the parks, about the party planks. There was a positive demand for reform in the air, a demand for doing something about "the trusts" and "the tariff" and "the high costs of living," a demand for more individual freedom and at the same time more effective action by the government.

The Democratic platform said the tariff should be lowered; the tariff, in fact, should be used for revenue only and not to protect particular industries with lobbies in Washington. Wilson strongly favored that policy, and said so in his acceptance speech.

The platform promised the voters that prosecution of "the trusts" would be swifter and sterner under a Democratic President than under Taft or Roosevelt. Wilson endorsed that promise, saying that he would seek more stringent laws than the Sherman Anti-Trust Act.

Perhaps the most revolutionary section of the Democratic platform was the call for an income tax. Such a tax had been one of the drastic proposals of the Populist Party in the 1890's and had led conservatives to refer to the Populists as "lunatics." Now it was part of the Democratic program, and Wilson accepted it.

The 1912 Democratic platform also favored direct election of United States senators, instead of by graft-haunted state legislatures. Wilson approved that idea as well, although he was well aware that it, too, was a Populist proposal. The wild notions of the '90s no longer seemed so wild to him.

Strict federal regulations for railway, express, telephone and telegraph companies were pledged in the Democratic document. That pledge, too, stemmed from Populist outcries. So did the proposals to safeguard the rights of organized labor, to foster the health of workingmen, to stimulate industrial, agricultural, and vocational education, and to establish a better program for the conservation of natural resources.

In general terms Wilson embraced all of these planks, as well as the promises of banking reforms and expansion of the credit system to aid small businesses. A President must be strong to carry out these pledges; Wilson was sure he was strong enough.

At the same time he said: "We represent the desire to set up an unentangled government, a government that cannot be used for private purposes, either in the field of business or in the field of politics; a government that will not tolerate the use of the organization of a great party to serve the personal aims and ambitions of any individual, and that will not permit legislation to be employed to further any private interests. . . ."

Seeking the unity of his own party and hoping to draw as many Republicans and Progressives as possible to his ticket, Wilson ended his speech by saying that he should seek the counsel of the wisest men he could find, regardless of their personal backgrounds.

The address was permeated by the moral fervor and the religious intensity so characteristic of Wilson, who thought of himself as a participant in the making of history.

Perhaps his prayers to the God he counted upon for guidance, his own passionate determination, the steady backing of editors and reporters, and the last-minute surrender of tough politicians had combined to place him where he was and had influenced him when he wrote that speech. But his words were shaped to a large degree—perhaps more than he realized—by the barricade-storming of William Jennings Bryan and the Populists in the past.

Then with the speech completed and the steering committee for the new campaign chosen, Wilson's tensions diminished. He relaxed again at Sea Girt, laughing and singing with his family, enjoying pleasant evenings by his fireside, receiving visitors again with relish.

To be sure, he had some difficulties with McCombs, his choice for chairman of the Democratic National Committee. McCombs had not fully recovered from the exhaustion he had suffered in the pre-convention struggles and the hard conflict in Baltimore. He tried to handle too many details now, and got into troubles which had to be smoothed over by Wilson. Yet Wilson appreciated McCombs' loyalty and devotion, and did not allow anything to break their friendship.

Wilson had other difficulties, too. His advisers were horrified when he told them that he did not want to engage in long trips around the country. He tried to convince them that "extended stumping tours are not the most impressive method of conducting a campaign." He had been worn down by his spring trips; and he knew that he could not equal Roosevelt or Taft in sheer physical stamina and lungpower.

Confident of his election because of the Republican schism, he hoped to conduct a dignified course of lectures explaining the issues in reasonable sequence. As always, he was sure that the voters would heed his appeals to their reason.

His plans were much too academic, his advisers insisted. They said he was overlooking the irrational element in politics. People might be interested in his ideas, but they were also curious about him as a person. Taft and Roosevelt had been in the limelight for many years; Wilson, in spite of his renown in university circles and his nation-wide appearances during his drive for the Democratic nomination, was still comparatively unknown.

His campaign committee convinced him at last that he must satisfy this type of inquisitive yearning, so he yielded to their wishes. He did stipulate, however, that he would not start the campaign train until the second week of August. He wanted a little more time by the sea, drawing refreshment from his family.

A LONELY PRESIDENT, MR. TAFT SEEKS HELP

The weary occupant of the White House, William Howard Taft, tried to put some fight into the moribund Republican National Committee, played golf whenever possible, and searched for men to help him stem the tides of "general radicalism" that threatened to wash Wilson or Roosevelt into the Executive Mansion.

After his triumph at Chicago, the President had been swamped with hundreds of letters and telegrams from people who hated Roosevelt or admired Taft. Yet when he tried to get some of these gentlemen and ladies to work in the campaign, he had to do quite a bit of pulling and hauling.

His friends, on the other hand, criticized him for failing

to use the office of the President to get more headlines than his opponents. Some advisers even wanted him to issue belligerent statements every day.

"I seem to have heard that before," Taft snorted. "It always makes me impatient, as if I were running a P. T. Barnum show, with two or three shows across the street, and as if I ought to have as much advertising as the rest. . . . I decline to take any responsibility."

Roosevelt had staged the Barnum show for him in 1908, when he ran as the Colonel's heir apparent. Making statements just for publicity, kissing babies and going to exhibitions, pumping hands and slapping backs, were activities that Taft despised. His dislike for such performances was all too obvious.

But the Age of Publicity was well under way in 1912. Press agents, speech-writers, advance men distributing bits of news before the arrival of candidates, were becoming standard campaign equipment. Taft's inability to play this game was a severe handicap.

He planned to make only one speech—his address formally accepting the Republican nomination, scheduled for August 1. In that speech he would tear to shreds Roosevelt's accusations, summarize again the achievements of his own administration, point out that the Democrats "do not know how to run a government," and then rest his case with the voters.

His advisers, like Wilson's, insisted that this was not practical. So Taft finally stirred himself from his lethargy. He begged Elihu Root to go to the large cities and make speeches for him. Root was widely known, highly respected, and an able speaker. Yet he answered that health would not permit him to take a leading role in the campaign.

Root was not the only man who showed reluctance. Senator Borah, who had refused to bolt the Republican Party with Roosevelt, was now on the fence. Governor Herbert

Hadley of Missouri also seemed undecided about which way to jump.

Taft and Charles Hilles, who had been assistant secretary of the treasury and then had become secretary to the President, dined together in the White House on July 13. Hilles told the President bluntly that it was very hard to find men and money to carry on the campaign. They also talked about how Mrs. Taft felt when she learned that the President was likely to be badly defeated. She was pleased that her husband had beaten Roosevelt in Chicago, and Taft assured Hilles that would console her for many disappointments.

Taft was still unable to understand why he had suddenly become so unpopular. He had been accustomed to being loved and admired throughout his life. As a federal judge, as the head of the United States commission in the Philippines, as secretary of war, and as President in the first years of his administration, he had been hailed and saluted. Now the cold shadow of dislike seemed to be darkening over him.

"Sometimes I think I might as well give up, so far as being a candidate is concerned," he wrote to his wife on July 22. "There are so many people in the country who don't like me. Without knowing much about me, they don't like me—apparently on the Dr. Fell principle. . . . 'I don't like you, Dr. Fell, The reason why I can not tell, But this I know and know full well, I don't like you, Dr. Fell!' "

Yet a week later he was more optimistic. Senator Borah had dinner with him at the White House and seemed friendly. He told the lonely Taft that La Follette had weaned away from Roosevelt all but two or three insurgent senators. They had found Roosevelt to be intensely selfish and completely self-absorbed. They were not going to join the Colonel in the third-party movement. Borah predicted that the whole Bull Moose business would collapse in October. Taft couldn't be convinced that Roosevelt would permit such a collapse.

While he was receiving senators at the White House and striving to get Root and others to stump for him, Taft was hunting for an aggressive man to be chairman of the G.O.P.'s National Committee. This was a thorny and thankless task. Those who grabbed for the job—such as the odoriferous Republican boss in New York, Bill Barnes, and the lobbyist Harry Daugherty, an Ohio politician with numerous blots on his record—would have lent credence to Roosevelt's charge that Taft was ruled by the corrupt bosses. Those who refused to consider it were the respectable bankers and merchants on whose support Taft had counted.

Hilles at last succumbed to the President's pleading and took the job himself. Then he had to find a treasurer for the committee. But in Wall Street and elsewhere the financial giants who had been the pillars of solid Republicanism did not care to be involved in a hopeless cause. Charles G. Dawes, E. T. Stotesbury, John Wanamaker, and other tycoons expressed their "regrets" that such a deplorable situation had developed.

Taft learned that the New York "money men" were turning now to Wilson as a candidate to defeat Roosevelt. The financiers did not believe that Professor Wilson's "radicalism" was more than skin-deep; they knew that he came from a conservative southern family, and they were sure that his background and his scholarly caution would keep him safe and sane.

During the July weeks while Hilles scurried frantically from office to office, imploring wealthy men to aid the Grand Old Party, Taft drudged at his desk, composed his acceptance speech, golfed with a few old cronies, and sometimes hoped that the people would get disgusted with the antics of Roosevelt and Wilson.

Taft told Archbishop John Ireland that "the real character of Wilson may be so disclosed to the people . . . as to render his election improbable." He wrote to another friend:

"I have very little confidence in the judgment of Wilson. He has changed his views so often that he seems an utter opportunist." Judging by Wilson's statements, Taft was justified in feeling that the Democratic candidate was windy and vague.

In his happier moments Taft felt that the people would become quickly disillusioned with Wilson's speeches. "The people will doubtless flock to hear him," he acknowledged in a note to a friend. "But he is academic rather than soul-stirring. . . . They are conscious of a pleasurable sensation, but they don't carry away much."

When he drafted his own acceptance speech, Taft was not as much of a stand-patter as he seemed to be in his letters to his wife and friends. The Republican platform had paid its usual obeisance to Lincoln, and Taft tried to show that he was in the Lincolnian tradition by describing what he had done for the common people.

The platform declared that the Republican Party was "opposed to special privilege and monopoly." And Taft felt that he had shown his opposition to the cohorts of greed by his enforcement of the Sherman Anti-Trust Act. He accepted the platform proposal for additional legislation to "define as criminal offenses those specific acts that uniformly mark attempts to restrain and monopolize trade, to the end that those who honestly intend to obey the law may have a guide for their action and that those who aim to violate the law may the more surely be punished."

Taft affirmed the platform planks calling for a sound but more elastic monetary system, extension of the civil service, full publicity for campaign contributions, and conservation of natural resources. These were threadbare policies, familiar to all those who had attended Republican rallies through the years.

On the question of federal action to give women the right to vote, the platform was silent. This was in accordance with

Taft's views. He thought the settlement of such questions was a matter for the states. Personally, he did not relish the idea of having women as active participants in politics.

During the Republican convention many delegates had been deluged with demands for planks favoring suffrage for women. Hilles had informed the President of this development. Taft had held stubbornly to his previous statements.

In his acceptance speech Taft asserted that the paramount issue in the campaign was the maintenance of constitutional government against those who might destroy it. Denouncing Roosevelt, he declared that the Colonel's "recently avowed political views would have committed the party to radical proposals involving dangerous changes in our present constitutional form of representative government and our independent judiciary."

With regard to the judiciary, the Republican platform had attempted to appeal to every school of thought—defending the independence of judges and then saying that "we favor such action as may be necessary to simplify the process by which any judge who is found to be derelict in his duty may be removed from office."

Taft was forthright on this point. He could see no compromise between giving the judges the permanent positions they needed to be impartial and subjecting them to the whims of popular passions. He did not, however, believe that judges should be kept in office if it became evident that they were not able to perform their duties.

The day was over, Taft felt, when judges and members of the executive branch of government had to act on the principle that the least government was the best. He thought that "positive law" had established the duty of government to help the weaker groups in society.

"It has been suggested that under our Constitution, such a tendency to so-called paternalism was impossible," Taft said. "Nothing is further from the fact." And he went on to say: "The Republican Party stands for the Constitution as it is, *with such amendments adopted according to its provisions as new conditions thoroughly understood may require.*"

This opened the door for drastic change. Of course, it meant change at a very slow rate. Adoption of constitutional amendments usually took years of debate—first the debate in both branches of Congress before an amendment could be submitted to the states, and then the debate in the state legislatures, with the approval of three-fourths of the states necessary for ratification.

To Taft, who had grown to manhood in a well-established family in the relatively calm and stable state of Ohio, such a procedure was adequate enough for the needs of the United States.

It was not enough for those who were forming battle lines under the leadership of Theodore Roosevelt. It was not enough for Senator Albert J. Beveridge of Indiana, the idealist who felt that a new Roosevelt had been born—a Roosevelt who was not simply trumpeting a war cry to old followers, but a Roosevelt who would create a firm basis for a truly liberal party dedicated to the interests of the ordinary voters without wealth or lobbyists to serve them in Washington.

Beveridge had agreed to be chairman of the Progressive Convention and to deliver the keynote address; he did not waver in his devotion to the Progressive cause. Beveridge and Hiram Johnson, the rampaging independent leader from California, were hoping to reform the country in a very short time.

The ponderous man in the White House, the dignified man with the thick white mustache and the round benign face, recoiled at the sound of the Bull Moose call. Mr. Taft watched with horror the signs of the times.

CORRUPTION COSTS A SENATOR HIS SEAT: MURDER SHAKES NEW YORK

July was a month in which the results of corruption burst into the light in Washington, in New York, and in Detroit.

In Washington the Senate voted 55 to 28 to declare the seat occupied by Senator William Lorimer of Illinois a vacant chair—because of the corrupt methods used by Lorimer to attain election. "It was my fight and my victory," cried Colonel Roosevelt, who had refused to associate with Lorimer and had supported a Senate investigation of Lorimer's election.

New York was shaken by the slaying of Herman Rosenthal, a gambler who had placed evidence of bribe-taking by New York policemen in the hands of reporters. A police lieutenant was accused of Rosenthal's murder.

In Detroit eight Aldermen—members of the city's governing council—were arrested for taking bribes. Newspapers disclosed that thievery and venality were widespread in political circles.

With these revelations before them, millions of Americans looked to the Progressive Party headed by Roosevelt. They knew that Mr. Taft was personally decent, personally above corruption, but they felt that America had grown slack and slothful in the Taft era. They wanted Teddy Roosevelt at the head of the nation again; he would chastise the evildoers.

IX. August: No Rest for the Fighters

A RAGE FOR RIGHTEOUSNESS

The gathering of the Progressives in Chicago on August 5, 1912, had the outward trappings of a political convention—the bands, the banners, the placards bearing the names of the states, the delegates wearing badges, the onlookers in the galleries swinging huge pictures of their favorite candidate.

And yet this meeting was totally different from the assemblies of the Republicans and the Democrats. To be sure, the other conventions had explosive emotions, moments of tragedy and scenes of comedy. But their sessions were business meetings, moving on schedules, dominated by shrewd men who argued and bargained in the manner of practical politicians. The Progressive gathering had a very different quality: the exalted excitement of a religious revival.

More than 10,000 people—including 1,200 delegates and alternates—were in the hall when Hiram Johnson led in his California crowd singing a brand-new song: "I want to be a Bull Moose, and with the Bull Moose stand!" The singing rose to a roar, and then suddenly Oscar S. Straus, the Jewish philanthropist, joined the New York delegation in "Onward, Christian Soldiers."

After the opening ceremonies the keynote speaker, Senator Beveridge, came forward to define the Roosevelt crusade.

"We stand for a nobler America," he said. He felt that the two old parties had been corrupted by evil bosses and the evil combinations of wealth—"the money trust," "the meat trust," "the steel trust."

Owing to the greed of some men and the indifference of others, laboring people were not getting enough to live on, Beveridge declared. Children were poorly nourished; old people, without pensions, were underfed or starved.

"Hunger should never walk in these thinly peopled gardens of plenty," Beveridge said, and the people in the auditorium voiced their agreement.

Beveridge assured decent businessmen that they had nothing to fear from Roosevelt. The Progressive Party would "try to make little business big, and all business honest, instead of striving to make Big Business little, and yet letting it remain dishonest."

In closing, Beveridge called for social security for the aged. He thought a measure of such security could be created under the Constitution, if the Constitution were properly considered as "a living thing, growing with the people's growth . . . aiding the people in their struggles for life, liberty, and the pursuit of happiness."

He was given an ovation which lasted for some minutes. As the applause grew fainter, someone started to sing "The Battle Hymn of the Republic" and thousands of voices joined in the majestic Civil War song that begins:

> He is trampling out the vintage where the grapes
>   of wrath are stored.
> He has loosed the fateful lightning of His terrible,
>   swift sword.
> His truth is marching on.

While the thousands there were singing, one man in the crowd looked around at the sea of upturned faces. To Amos Pinchot, the thoughtful reformer who tried always to keep cool and objective, the sight was not pleasing. The temper of the thousands shook and disturbed him.

It was true that there were a large number of superior, intelligent, and deeply earnest people, who had seen the inside of the political cup and were disgusted with the uselessness of the Republican Party as an instrument for attacking social problems, Pinchot felt. But outnumbering them was a distinct majority composed of people bent chiefly on riding to power or prestige on Roosevelt's broad back. Pinchot saw sharp-faced southern Republican politicians looking for patronage; eastern disgruntled hangers-on of the old party, some too good and some too bad for it; far westerners and middle westerners shouting for industrial justice, but mainly attracted by the idea of getting in on the ground floor of a growing concern. And there were many restless sentimentalists who always cluttered new movements that might satisfy their craving for good in the abstract—weak men who would fade away when they were asked to work for concrete proposals.

The power-hungry, the cynical, the disgruntled, the opportunists, and the sentimentalists might have been in a majority, as Pinchot felt they were. Yet they did not set the tone for the convention, and Pinchot had to admit that the tone was clearly religious.

"This nondescript army, with aims as far apart as the poles from the equator, was miraculously kept united by the magnetism of one electric personality," Pinchot wrote later. "And through them all a sort of rage for righteousness presently began to surge. . . . The Progressive Party, under Roosevelt, was going to free the United States not only from political and economic but from spiritual night. It was to rout Taft's Republican hosts, but this was merely a prelude to routing all the hosts of darkness."

Colonel Roosevelt appeared before the delegates and the visitors in the galleries on August 6, the second day of the assemblage. This time the total audience was more than 15,000 persons, and they made it plain that they were ready to follow Roosevelt wherever he went. When he led the charge up the hill of danger, they would be with him to the last man—or so they believed in their hours of ecstasy.

Roosevelt read from a manuscript many pages in length. It was, he said, his "Confession of Faith" in the American people and the future of America. As he read it, he was interrupted by handclapping and cheers 145 times—and with each interruption the cheers seemed to grow louder.

The Republican and Democratic parties, as Roosevelt saw them on that day of acclamation, were "husks, with no real soul within either, divided on artificial lines, boss-ridden and privilege controlled, each a jumble of incongruous elements, and neither daring to speak out wisely and fearlessly what should be said on the vital issues of the day." It was the year of decision, he declared. 1912 was the year in which the people had their chance to destroy these rotting "husks."

Roosevelt promised that the Progressives would "put forth a platform which shall . . . be a contract with the people." And he shouted: "We shall hold ourselves under honorable obligations to fulfill every promise it contains as loyally as if it were actually enforceable under penalties of the law."

Yet when the actual preparation of the platform reached the final stages, the Progressive delegates discovered that they were really united on only one thing: the leadership of Theodore Roosevelt. Throughout the night of Tuesday, August 6, and the morning of Wednesday, August 7, the wrangling proceeded.

By their very nature the Progressives were men of strong convictions. None of them liked to compromise. It took all the persuasive skills and force of the Colonel to get them to agree on the most controversial planks.

Many deplored Roosevelt's policy on the admission of colored delegates to the convention. Friction over this issue was carried over into the platform discussions. Roosevelt, as we have seen, had compelled the Committee on Credentials to decide that the acceptance of Negro delegates from a southern state should depend on the consent of white Progressives from that state. To some of the northern Progressive leaders, this obviously placed the Negroes in a dependent and inferior position. Yet Roosevelt was sure that his way of dealing with the question was correct.

Upon completion, the Progessive platform had planks to cover almost everything, ranging from suffrage for women to reorganization of the federal departments for efficiency and economy. The platform advocated flood control; good roads; lowering the cost of living; conserving natural resources; developing the territory of Alaska; a better patent law; protection against fraudulent investments; teaching more people to read and write; the registration of lobbyists; publication of campaign contributions, and dozens of other proposals to make life better and easier for every American.

Many of the ideas in the Progressive document, like the ideas in the Democratic platform and a few of those in the Republican platform, came from radical slogans which had been condemned by William McKinley and solid Republicans in the dark past. Among them were promises of farm relief, social welfare assistance for women and children, restrictions on court injunctions, and the recall of judicial decisions.

Even if Roosevelt had been seeking a twenty-year term in the White House, the Colonel would have found it impossible to carry out, as he had promised the convention, all these proposals. Such practical difficulties did not bother "T.R." when he stood before his assembled followers. He showed them the vision of an America in which the government took a benign paternal interest in every American from birth to death. And the spectators and delegates loved him, and admired his vision.

There was some confusion about his attitude toward the trusts. He had bared his teeth at "the bad millionaires" often enough for the delegates to be sure that he would be rough on those who violated the Sherman Act. Yet he was in consultation, all through the convention, with Perkins and Munsey, who did not approve of that act and certainly did not want to see it tightened.

When the platform was read to the convention on August 7, Roosevelt was not in the hall much of the time. He was not present when Dean Lewis droned through the section that stated: "We favor strengthening the Sherman law by prohibiting agreements to divide territory or limit output; refusing to sell to customers who buy from business rivals; to sell below cost in certain areas while maintaining high prices in other places; using the power of transportation to aid or injure special business concerns; and other unfair trade practices."

George Perkins, who was sitting next to Amos Pinchot, turned to Pinchot and whispered: "Lewis has made a mistake. That doesn't belong in the platform. We cut it out last night." Bounding to his feet, Perkins vanished in search of the Colonel.

A conference was held shortly afterward, attended by Roosevelt and O. K. Davis, secretary of the National Committee. Davis sent a note to the press associations and the newspaper correspondents, saying that the plank was not officially included in the platform and should not be printed. The section favoring a stronger Sherman Act did not appear in the published version of the Progressive platform, which was distributed in large quantities later in the campaign.

The disappearance of the plank presented to the convention by Dean Lewis created little discussion at the time. Only a few delegates were deeply interested in it. And they accepted, as the others did, the Colonel's decision. He was their leader. His wisdom and courage would take them in the right direction.

Few delegates realized that preliminary drafts of the platform had been sent to the Colonel's hotel suite for revision or rejection—and that Perkins and Munsey had the determining voices in a number of planks. As a matter of fact, very few of the delegates considered themselves qualified to produce a platform—that was up to Theodore Roosevelt and the men around him.

And in spite of the removal of the stern Sherman Act section, the Progressive Party still appealed to many liberals of the nation. Jane Addams, the social worker and founder of Chicago's Hull House, expressed the feelings of many high-minded delegates when she said: "I second the nomination of Theodore Roosevelt because he is one of the few men in our public life who has been responsive to modern movement. Because of that, because the program will need a leader of invincible courage, of open mind, of democratic sympathies—one endowed with power to interpret the common man and to identify himself with the common lot—I heartily second the nomination."

Roosevelt certainly had courage, an open mind, and democratic sympathies. But he had never wanted to identify himself fully with "the common man" or "the common lot." He was a general, a commander, leading troops to the front.

The Colonel's real conception of himself was quite evident in his speech to the crowd after he had been nominated by acclamation and after Governor Johnson of California had been selected for the Vice-Presidency. Roosevelt and Johnson walked to the platform and took their places beneath a placard bearing a verse from Rudyard Kipling:

> For there is neither East nor West,
> Border nor breed nor birth,
> When two strong men stand face to face,
> Though they come from the ends of the earth.

As Roosevelt and Johnson eulogized one another and shouted their plans to fight for righteousness, it was clear that here were "two strong men" standing face to face. When they had finished, the entire audience rose and sang the hymn beginning, "Praise God from whom all blessings flow."

As the delegates and the people from the galleries poured from the hall their faces glowed with dedication to the nation's welfare. Woodrow Wilson might believe that Providence had chosen him to be America's prophet, but the Progressive thousands who streamed into the humid streets of Chicago on August 7 were positive that the anointment of the Almighty had been given to Theodore Roosevelt.

Amos Pinchot found it both a stirring spectacle and a pitiful sight. In his opinion the delegates and the gallery worshippers were deceived or self-deluded. Pinchot hoped that the Progressive Party, in addition to defeating Taft, would substitute something better for the sordid game of practical politics. And yet he wondered how it could possibly do so.

To Pinchot, the tragic irony of the Progressive rally was the absence of the senator from Wisconsin, the zealous and angry tribune of the people, Robert La Follette. Pinchot was one of those who had moved from the La Follette camp to the Roosevelt banner. Yet he was capable of contrasting and comparing the two men—and recognizing that La Follette had been the logical leader.

"La Follette really hated the great figures of Wall Street undermining American civilization," Pinchot wrote. "Roosevelt, like Lincoln Steffens, looked at big-business men, even the most reactionary and apparently reckless among them, as good men gone wrong. . . . La Follette was sure no one could ever use men of this kind for useful purposes. Roosevelt was under the impression that he, at all events, could so use them. . . .

"La Follette did not care a damn for the pomps and glories of life. There was no Lorenzo the Magnificent or Louis XIV or William Hohenzollern in his makeup. Roosevelt was a patron of the arts and letters, and friend and protector of scientists, writers, and philosophers. He loved to be cronies with the great, the near-great, and the about-to-be great. . . .

"La Follette was unromantic to a degree, except in his conception of a Hegelian world, in which the romance was one of the undying struggle between right and wrong, in which he saw himself as a leader in an uphill conflict against sinister forces. . . . Both men were egotists. But La Follette was modestly egotistical, while Roosevelt flaunted his egotism with youthful and attractive bravado."

With bravado and a full conviction that he was sacrificing himself for his country, Roosevelt went gallantly forward. The Progressive Party, the party of "the common man," was under the dashing command of a man who tried to combine the qualities of Lorenzo the Magnificent, Louis XIV, Kaiser William, and a Colonel of the Rough Riders.

MR. TAFT FINDS ODD ALLIES

In quiet ceremonies held in Washington on August 1, William Howard Taft was formally notified of the Republican Presidential nomination.

Senator Root, rather gray and wan, delivered a speech informing the President of the action taken by the G.O.P. convention. Mr. Taft, in a labored address marked only by occasional flashes of indignation at Colonel Roosevelt, accepted the honor.

Taft again enumerated the achievements of his administration, and it was a substantial list. He then asserted that most of the progress in the United States for the past half-century had been due to the sober management of Republican administrators. The Republican Party knew how to govern, Taft said, and he felt capable of continuing its excellent record.

After making this speech, he withdrew for a while into the White House. Those of his associates who took any interest in his electoral fate tried to break through his obstinacy and get him to take his case to the people.

On August 12 he did talk with a group of newspaper correspondents. He did not endear himself to them when he said that he considered it beneath his dignity to attract attention to himself through the press.

"I have been told that I ought to do this, ought to do that, . . . that I do not keep myself in the headlines," Taft said. "I know it, but I can't do it. I couldn't if I would, and I wouldn't if I could."

Then to his astonishment, he suddenly received unusual assistance from two senators who were ordinarily in violent opposition to one another—Boies Penrose, the reactionary and notorious boss of Pennsylvania, and Robert La Follette, who seemed willing to do almost anything to revenge himself on Roosevelt.

Congress had resumed its meetings, and La Follette and Penrose teamed together to get the Senate to establish a special committee to investigate campaign contributions of previous elections. Senator Moses E. Clapp, an independent Republican friend of La Follette, was appointed chairman. Clapp and his associates began to dig immediately into the gifts made to Roosevelt's 1904 campaign fund by corporations.

President Taft was quite willing to encourage Penrose and La Follette in this investigation. He was eager to damage or destroy Roosevelt's claim to be the representative of the "plain people."

The revelations of the immense sums gathered by the Roosevelt managers in 1904 came as a shock to the country. And for the first time the role of wealthy contributors in paying for Roosevelt's campaign trips was fully exposed. Under the rules then prevailing, corporations and corporation heads were free to give as much money to a candidate's campaign committee as they wished. Ledgers and other records of these contributions were usually burned, but some contributors testified frankly before the Clapp committee—and their testimony was pieced together in a revealing pattern. Senator Clapp's committee officially stated that 72½ per cent of the $2,195,000 collected for Roosevelt in 1904 had been donated by corporations. J. P. Morgan admitted that he had turned over $150,000 in cash, and Edward T. Stotesbury, a Philadelphia banker closely linked to Morgan, said he had collected more than $165,000. E. H. Harriman, the railroad king, said he had given $50,000 and had rounded up another $200,000.

The part played by the Standard Oil Company in Roosevelt's 1904 election became a vital issue now in 1912. John D. Archbold, a top executive of the oil company, testified that a total of $125,000 had been passed to the 1904 Republican National Committee "in currency." Under oath before the Clapp committee he said the money had been sought from Standard Oil by Cornelius N. Bliss, then treasurer of the Republican Committee. Bliss had died some years after the 1904 campaign and had left no record of any conversation with Archbold. However, Archbold testified that Bliss had given him the understanding that Roosevelt knew about the solicitation of money from Standard Oil.

Reacting swiftly to the 1912 testimony, Roosevelt now denied that he had known about the gift. He quoted from a 1911 newspaper, in which Bliss had declared that Roosevelt's orders against the soliciting of gifts from corporations had been "ignored."

Actually, in 1904 rumors of large gifts made by Standard Oil to the Roosevelt campaign had led Judge Alton Parker, the Democratic Presidential candidate, to charge that George B. Cortelyou, Roosevelt's secretary of the Department of Commerce and Labor, had obtained big donations through "blackmail." Cortelyou had jurisdiction over the Bureau of Corporations and could threaten the corporations with government suits, Parker declared.

In 1904 Roosevelt had denied that money had been extorted, but tacitly acknowledged that corporations had made gifts to his campaign.

"That contributions have been made . . . is not the question at issue," Roosevelt had declared in his 1904 statement. "Mr. Parker's accusations against Mr. Cortelyou and me are monstrous. If true they would brand both of us forever with infamy; and inasmuch as they are false, heavy must be the condemnation of the man making them. . . . The assertion that there has been any blackmail, direct or indirect, by Mr. Cortelyou or by me is a falsehood."

The Roosevelt statement disposed of the question in 1904, but it rose to plague him again in 1912.

A parade of witnesses appeared before the Senate committee. The names of many wealthy donors to Roosevelt's 1904 campaign went into the record and made headlines in the papers opposed to the Colonel's Bull Moose Party. Among the contributors, in addition to Morgan, Stotesbury, and Standard Oil, were such millionaires as James Speyer, who gave $25,000; James Stillman, who put in $10,000; James Hazen Hyde, $25,000; H. C. Frick, $50,000; George J. Gould, $100,000; C. S. Mellen of the New York, New Haven and Hartford Railway, $50,000.

Both the papers supporting Taft and those supporting Wilson joined now in asking how Colonel Roosevelt could be so close to so many rich men and still pose as the defender of the poor against the predatory wolves of Wall Street.

Roosevelt usually ignored their attacks, or cited his public repudiation of a $100,000 gift from Standard Oil. He quoted from the letter he had written to Treasurer Bliss is 1904, ordering Bliss to send back the oil company's contribution.

But in a letter to his wife, written on August 22, 1912, Taft relayed to her a conversation he had enjoyed with Philander Knox, his secretary of state: "Knox said he came into the office of Roosevelt one day in October, 1904, and heard him dictating a letter directing the return of $100,000 to the Standard Oil Company. He said to him, 'Why, Mr. President, the money has been spent. They (meaning the National Committee) cannot pay it back—they haven't got it.' 'Well,' said the President, 'the letter will look well on the record, anyhow,' and so he let it go. He is referring to this letter now as an evidence that he never approved the receipt of the money."

The furor over the 1904 contributions did not keep wealthy men from contributing generously to Roosevelt's drive in 1912. With his supreme self-confidence, Roosevelt evidently felt that he could accept such contributions without committing himself to granting the donors any favors if he became President once again. After all, he had not hesitated to chastise the railroads and the Standard Oil Company after they had helped him to get elected in 1904.

As a matter of fact, Roosevelt had started twenty-five legal proceedings leading to indictments of corporations and individuals under the Sherman Act. He had pushed through Congress legislation which gave the Interstate Commerce Commission more power to regulate the railroads. He had denounced the Standard Oil Company for its "secret rates" and "enormous profits." He had advocated a national licensing law to place "all corporations engaged in inter-state commerce" directly "under the supervision of the national Government."

His opponents promptly replied that he had talked vigorously but had moved slowly and timidly against the abuses perpetrated by giant corporations, always expressing fears of action that might be "too drastic." Taft, on the other hand, had begun forty-five proceedings against the corporate combinations, and had pushed them much farther.

During the month of August, 1912, Taft drew what comfort he could from the disclosures of the Clapp committee. He did not have the disposition to carry the battle to Roosevelt or Wilson; besides, the Republican National Committee could not raise the money to pay for special trains, bands, bunting, and the necessary paraphernalia of a standard campaign tour.

The loyal and valiant Charles Hilles tried everything he could think of—but the men with large incomes, the men who had benefited most from the efforts of the Republican Party to maintain the status quo, kept their wallets in their pockets and their checkbooks closed. They admired Taft, but saw him as a loser. Andrew Carnegie, devoted to Taft because of the President's attempts to secure the passage of international arbitration treaties, was an outstanding exception. Carnegie gave a total of $35,000, and Taft was effusively grateful.

Then, horrified by the realization that he might lose his home state, Taft sent his own check for $2,500 to the regular Republicans who were fighting for him there. The President also gave $7,500 to Hilles for the National Committee, which was barely able to keep functioning.

In 1912, as in all Presidential contests of the twentieth century, it took millions of dollars to stage an effective campaign. Ironically, William Howard Taft, the only avowed conservative in the struggle couldn't raise enough money to compete with his rivals. His oddly matched allies—Robert La Follette and Boies Penrose—did what they could to aid him, but it was far from adequate. It was just enough to sting Roosevelt into higher frenzies, and to keep Wilson on his toes.

WILSON DECLARES: "THERE IS NO INDISPENSABLE MAN"

On the sunlit afternoon of August 7, after an enthusiastic and good-humored audience had assembled on the lawn before the Governor's Cottage in Sea Girt, Woodrow Wilson came out on the porch and read his carefully composed speech accepting the Democratic nomination.

The crowd admired the polished phrases, the scholarly style, the moral tone of the address, and then grew restless as Wilson went on and on, dissecting and discussing every major section in the Democratic platform. The women in their light summer dresses, the men fanning themselves with their straw hats, were in a mood to sing and cheer—not to meditate upon the fate of the nation.

Yet they were respectful. They were deeply impressed by Wilson's mind and Wilson's manner, and they found statements in the speech to roar happily about, such as his reference to Roosevelt: "There is no indispensable man." They liked his humor and humility when he said: "The government will not collapse and go to pieces if any one of the gentlemen who are seeking to be entrusted with its guidance should be left at home."

They sensed his serenity, his belief that his election was almost a foregone conclusion, and they liked that: they wanted to share such a buoyant exuberance. He was forward-looking, but moderate. He was prepared to lead, but not to push beyond the limits imposed by reality.

Wilson said: "The nation has been unnecessarily, unreasonably, at war within itself. Interest has clashed with interest when there were common principles of right and of fair dealing which might and should have bound them all together, not as rivals, but as partners." He felt certain that he could bring these clashing forces into partnership.

"We stand in the presence of an awakened nation," the idealistic governor of New Jersey told his audience. In his view there was "a turning back from what is abnormal to what is normal"; the country had "lost certain cherished liberties" but these were now going to be restored.

To Wilson, this meant that "every form of special privilege and private control" had to be abolished. All unjust practices had to be corrected "in order to vindicate once more the essential rights of human life."

"Plainly, it is a new age," Wilson declared. "The tonic of such a time is very exhilarating. It requires self-restraint not to attempt too much, and yet it would be cowardly to attempt too little."

The Democrats at Sea Girt applauded such generalities, and the New York *World* lavished favorable adjectives on it: "Woodrow Wilson's speech of acceptance is the ablest, clearest, sanest statement of high public purpose this country has known in a generation." The cautious New York *Times* also went overboard: "It is a proclamation that will satisfy all save those who are determined not to be satisfied."

Yet some articulate people were not satisfied. Lillian Wald, of the Henry Street Settlement House in New York, did not see in it much hope of improving the miserable lot of the poor. She wrote to Jane Addams: "I read it with a cold chilly feeling of disappointment. It is an essay of lofty sentiments, in my judgment, but might be construed as a political hedge and an evasion of the sturdy things Bryan practiced in Baltimore."

The mayor of Toledo, Brand Whitlock, was critical of the speech in a letter to a friend: "Wilson seems to be piping a very low note; or trying to conciliate the reactionaries in his party, when he ought to know that you can conciliate privilege only by surrendering abjectly to it." Bryan and Oswald

Garrison Villard of the New York *Evening Post* also wanted Wilson to be more specific, to strike at definite enemies instead of talking about right and wrong.

Wilson, however, kept going along his own road. He listened to the counsel of many advisers; at their request he traveled from town to town; he began to tell more jokes and talk in saltier, less academic tones; and yet he hammered away at general principles which he considered more important than specific issues. He wanted the country to face the basic problems of the age; he did not claim to offer easy or complete solutions.

"As a candidate for the Presidency I do not want to promise heaven unless I can bring it to you," Wilson said. "I can only see a little distance up the road."

During August he seemed to be still searching for the issues he really wanted to emphasize. His three speeches in New Jersey, after his acceptance address, were neither very thought-provoking nor particularly effective. He denounced high tariffs in a rambling talk on August 15 at Washington Park. A few days later he had a humiliating experience in Union Hill when he tried to address a beer-drinking crowd of German-Americans and was driven off the platform by the crash of four brass bands. Then on August 20 he made a platitudinous assault on "the representatives of privilege" in a Mercer County speech.

Nonetheless, the development of his campaign organization proceeded at a fairly rapid pace, despite bickering between McCombs and McAdoo. At a meeting in New York on August 3, Wilson made McAdoo the national vice-chairman in charge of the New York headquarters. McCombs continued to hold the title of chairman of the Democratic National Committee.

Wilson appointed Henry Morgenthau, the wealthy lawyer who had donated $4,000 a month to his pre-convention drive, chairman of the finance committee. He named Joseph E.

Davies, another wealthy lawyer, vice-chairman of the headquarters in Chicago, and a little later he announced that
Rolla Wells of St. Louis had agreed to serve as treasurer
of the National Committee and that Charles R. Crane, a rich
Chicago manufacturer, had accepted appointment as vice-
chairman of the finance committee.

Choosing men he trusted for the major campaign posts,
Wilson gave them much responsibility and much leeway. He
did not take on himself the burden of the day-to-day decisions concerning the distribution of pamphlets and posters,
the assignment of speakers, the preparation of releases for
the press, and the ten thousand other details. He spent most
of his time and thought in seeking the advice of experts in
various fields, writing and rewriting his speeches, and select-
ing places to deliver principal addresses.

Aware of the Progressive Party's strength in the Middle
West, Wilson established the Chicago headquarters on an
equal level with his New York campaign center. Senator
Gore of Oklahoma and Representative Albert Burleson of
Texas moved their speakers' bureau from New York to Chicago. Senator Reed of Missouri was given the chairmanship
of the senatorial campaign committee. Jerry South, a Champ
Clark supporter from Arkansas, headed a special group to
convert foreign-born voters to Wilson; John Borden, a Chicago millionaire, set up a college men's bureau to rally
former students for the ex-president of Princeton; and Judge
Martin Wade of Iowa went after the labor vote.

Emaciated and fatigued from months of overstrain, Chairman McCombs broke down on August 12 and left for a long
vacation in the Adirondacks. McAdoo took over as acting
chairman. Then McAdoo, Morgenthau, Wells, and Robert
Ewing of New Orleans, who had organized a press contributions bureau, launched an appeal for dollars from citizens—
the dollars to be sent to Democratic newspapers and then
forwarded to the Wilson headquarters. Many daily and

weekly papers proved willing to cooperate, and thousands of citizens dutifully mailed in their dollars.

The New York *World* was one of the most active. It printed a drawing of an open-faced citizen looking at a billboard. The inscription on the billboard read: "WANTED—100,000 Earnest Citizens to Contribute Each One Honest Dollar, to Elect a President Of and For the People—No Trust Money Accepted. Mail Your Contribution to Rolla Wells, Treasurer, Democratic National Committee, 200 Fifth Avenue, N. Y. City. Contributions Personally Acknowledged."

There were Dollar Dinners and Dollar Drives, and newspapers favorable to Wilson implored the people to aid his cause with their small gifts. However, the money did not come in fast enough to keep the campaign machinery running. So Crane, Morgenthau, Cleveland Dodge, Jacob Schiff, and other wealthy friends of Wilson had to fill the gaps in the treasury.

When he had asked Morgenthau to head the finance committee, Wilson had declared: "I shall insist that no contributions whatever be even indirectly accepted from any corporation. I want especial attention paid to the small contributors. And I want great care exercised over the way the money is spent."

Wilson had also informed Morgenthau: "There are three rich men in the Democratic Party whose political affiliations are so unworthy that I shall depend on you personally to see that none of their money is used in my campaign." Consequently, Morgenthau could not call upon J. P. Morgan, August Belmont, or Thomas Fortune Ryan.

Morgenthau did exercise great care over the spending; he put in a budget system for the first time in the history of American political campaigns, and accounted for every penny collected. Morgenthau's integrity persuaded many people to contribute.

In the organization and execution of the 1912 campaign,

the man who later became Wilson's closest adviser—Colonel Edward M. House—played only a minor role. The most significant influence upon Woodrow Wilson then was a brilliant, aggressive, energetic lawyer named Louis D. Brandeis. Brandeis and Wilson had their first meeting at the Governor's Cottage in Sea Girt on August 28. After that meeting, which lasted for more than three hours, Brandeis announced that he had joined the Wilson movement, abandoning his allegiance to Robert La Follette.

Brandeis had practiced law for many years in Boston, where his activities in the public interest had earned him the title of "the people's counsel." He had devised a sliding scale of rates and dividends for gas-utility regulation, opposed the New Haven Railroad merger and monopoly, developed the system of savings-bank life insurance at low premiums for people with small incomes, and had created a basic charter for labor-management relations in the New York garment industry. He was an authority on the control of monopolies and the regulation of railroads, and a passionate advocate of more freedom for small businessmen.

Asked by a reporter for the New York *Times* to explain why he preferred Wilson to La Follette or Roosevelt, Brandeis gave quick and direct answers. He said he thought the Progressive Party could not succeed because it sought the regulation of monopoly in an ineffectual manner.

"We must undertake to regulate competition instead of monopoly, for our industrial freedom and our civic freedom go hand in hand," Brandeis said. "I found Governor Wilson a man capable of broad, constructive statesmanship, and I found him to be entirely in accord with my own views of what we need to do to accomplish industrial freedom."

Wilson expressed his agreement. "Both of us have as an object the prevention of monopoly," Wilson said. "Monopoly is created by unregulated competition, by competition that overwhelms all other competitions, and the only way to enjoy industrial freedom is to destroy that condition."

Monopolies could be prevented, Brandeis believed, by the establishment of economic rules which would keep the large companies from devouring the small ones. Such rules, Brandeis felt, would liberate the energies of many thousands of young men who wanted to create new enterprises.

Until his encounter with Brandeis, Wilson had been groping for ways to meet the economic threats presented by trusts and monopolies. In the past he had suggested that corporation officers should be forced to take personal blame for "monopolistic practices." And he had asserted that protective tariffs fostered the trusts. Yet he had not been able to see any remedies for the conditions he denounced.

Before his session with Brandeis, he had worried about his ability to draw the issues clearly between Roosevelt and himself. In a letter written on August 25 to Mary Hulbert, he had confided: "I think Taft will run third—at any rate in the popular, if not in the electoral, vote. The country will have none of him. But just what will happen, as between Roosevelt and me, with party lines utterly confused and broken, is all guesswork."

The defeats he had suffered at the hands of Champ Clark in the primaries had made him dubious about his appeal to the masses. In the same letter, Wilson said: "He [Roosevelt] is a real, vivid person, whom they have seen and shouted themselves hoarse over and voted for, millions strong; I am a vague, conjectural personality, more made up of opinions and academic prepossessions than of human traits and red corpuscles. We shall see what will happen!"

In his efforts to become "a real, vivid person" for the ordinary voters, Wilson occasionally got himself into trouble. In a speech at the Monmouth County Fair in Redbank, New Jersey, he talked about men sitting around a stove in a country store, chewing tobacco and commenting on politics. Wilson said: "Whatever may be said against the chewing of tobacco, this at least can be said for it, that it gives a man time to think between sentences." He was chagrined by a newspaper headline which appeared the next day: WILSON ADVOCATES THE CHEWING OF TOBACCO. He insisted that he wasn't advocating the habit of tobacco-chewing; he was advocating "thinking between sentences."

He was trying to clarify the issues of the campaign and to make the people think. And he found it was very hard to do these things. Most of the voters were distracted by the demands of daily life, the necessities of making a living, and the pressing individual problems which loomed larger before them than the problems of the nation.

There were thousands of unemployed who went to hear Roosevelt and Wilson, and tried to figure out the differences between Wilson's New Freedom and Roosevelt's New Nationalism. There were thousands of businessmen, bankers, teachers, railroad workers, corporation lawyers, and other Americans who tried to develop rational explanations for preferring one candidate above the other—with Taft generally regarded as a man receding into the past.

Sometimes it seemed as though Wilson and Roosevelt were as close as twin brothers in their ideas for promoting prosperity, controlling big business, fattening the farmers, and providing better jobs for everybody. At other times the scholar from Princeton and the cavalryman from Sagamore Hill seemed as far apart as the opposite sides of the earth.

But when Wilson embraced more and more of the ideas of Louis Brandeis, he was viewed by the voters as a man with a definite plan—a man who had thought things through, and knew what the next President should do.

EXPLOSIONS IN HAITI, SHELLING IN MEXICO, REBELLION IN NICARAGUA

Outside the United States violence erupted throughout the month of August.

Haiti changed Presidents after an explosion. When a blast destroyed President Leconte's palace and killed Leconte and his aides, Tancrede Auguste was chosen as the nation's chief executive.

Triumphant in heavy fighting around Juarez, Mexican troops loyal to President Madero drove rebel forces from that city. The rebels fled to the hills and reformed their ranks.

The Sultan of Turkey dissolved his parliament and declared martial law in Constantinople. Mulai Hafid, Sultan of Morocco, abdicated his throne.

Late in August, Nicaraguan rebels massacred 450 government soldiers who had been taken as prisoners. The massacre stirred moral indignation in the United States, and Mr. Taft sent American cruisers and Marines there to show the Nicaraguans that America frowned upon such blood-baths.

In Washington the volleys of oratory which had been dropping on Capitol Hill died away with the adjournment of the first regular session of the 62nd Congress.

THE PROFESSOR REMOVES HIS GLOVES

When Colonel Roosevelt declared that Wilson should belong to his Ananias Club—a club named after a Biblical character who had been punished with death for uttering falsehoods—the New Jersey governor decided that the time had come to hit "T.R." with bare knuckles and to bite him in the clinches if necessary.

On the first Monday in September, at a Labor Day celebration attended by 10,000 workers, Wilson took off his gloves. He whacked the Colonel with blow after blow, and he got cheers from his listeners.

Roosevelt was "a self-appointed divinity," Wilson said. Roosevelt's proposal to make the trusts legal and then regulate them with a "Board of Experts" would actually turn over the economic power of the country to the trust officials, who would dominate the "Board of Experts" from behind the scenes. To Wilson, such a scheme meant that the working people of the United States would be "wage slaves" unable to break their bonds.

"As to the monopolies, which Mr. Roosevelt proposes to

legalize and to welcome, I know that they are so many cars of juggernaut," Wilson said. "And I do not look forward with pleasure to the time when the juggernauts are licensed and driven by commissioners of the United States. . . ."

(Wilson referred to the huge cars used to carry giant images of Juggernaut, a god worshiped in India. Each car was 45 feet high, 35 feet square, and supported on 16 wheels, with each wheel seven feet in diameter. Pilgrims at Juggernaut's festivals were sometimes crushed under the broad wheels of the enormous cars.)

"What has created these monopolies?" Wilson asked. "Unregulated competition. It has permitted these men [the heads of the large corporations with monopoly strength] to do anything they choose to do to squeeze their rivals out and crush their rivals to earth. We know the processes by which they have done those things. We can prevent these processes through remedial legislation, and so restrict the wrong use of competition that the right use of competition will destroy monopoly. Ours is a program of liberty; theirs is a program of regulation."

His way of regulating competition would not be "regulation" in the Rooseveltian sense, Wilson asserted. Perhaps afraid that his audience would not get the distinction between the two approaches, Wilson pleaded: "I want you workingmen to grasp that point, because I want to say to you right now that the program I propose does not look quite so much like acting as a Providence for you as the other program looks. I want frankly to say to you that I am not big enough to play Providence, and my objection to the other plan is that I do not believe there is any man who is big enough to play Providence. . . ."

Wilson went on: "When you have thought the whole thing out, therefore, you will find that the program of the new party legalizes monopolies and systematically subordinates workingmen to them and to plans made by the Government, both with regard to employment and with regard to wages." Then he demanded: "By what means, except open revolt, could we ever break the crust of our life again and become free men, breathing an air of our own, choosing and living lives that we wrought out for ourselves? Perhaps this new and all-conquering combination between money and government would be benevolent to us, perhaps it would carry out the noble program of social betterment, which so many credulously expect of it, but who can assure us of that? Who will give bond that it will be general and gracious and pitiful and righteous? What man or set of men can make us secure under it by their empty promise and assurance that it will take care of us and be good?"

Wilson revealed here his distrust of government as an instrument for "social betterment." Roosevelt felt that the only way to make the forces of capital and labor work in harness together was to have the government serve as the mediator—and, if necessary, as the final arbitrator. The officers of government, Colonel Roosevelt thought, would show as much self-restraint and as much respect for the people's liberty as the officers of corporations and trade unions.

The country had to have leadership, "T.R." asserted over and over, and the top leadership had to be supplied by a resourceful government headed by a powerful President. A similar philosophy, adopted twenty years later by his Democratic cousin, Franklin Roosevelt, resulted in government intervention in every area of American life under the New Deal.

To the Wilson of the early stages of the 1912 campaign, such a philosophy was paternalistic. Later, under the prodding of Brandeis, he came around to some of the ideas he scorned in his Labor Day address. On that day, he refused to accept the notion that the President should try to be a Great White Father for all citizens.

"My kind of leading will not be telling other people what they have got to do," Wilson told the cheering Buffalo crowd. "By leading I mean finding out what the interests of the community are agreed to be, and then trying my level best to find the methods of solution by common counsel. That is the only feasible program of social uplift that I can imagine."

This kind of leadership was not very inspiring—it was the concept of spineless leadership which contributed to the rise of public-opinion polls—but Wilson gave his views a fervent flavor which made them palatable to many voters. He had a plan, a flexible plan, and it did not come entirely out of his own head; he was open to suggestions from everybody. The voters liked that. He relied upon Providence and the people, and they liked that, too.

His speech at Buffalo, carried in newspapers across the country, drew to him many of the rank-and-file members of the American Federation of Labor. He had already captivated the head of the A.F. of L. His earlier meeting with Sam Gompers at Trenton had swept aside the prejudices of the old labor chieftain, and his performance at Buffalo caused Gompers to write: "My respect for him grew into a feeling of well-nigh reverential admiration. . . ."

In addition to winning over the labor votes, Wilson tackled several other tough tasks during September. The day after his Buffalo address, he spoke to a group of foreign-language newspaper editors in New York City, assuring them of his determination to aid immigrants who came to American shores with the purpose "of making a home and career for themselves." He did not succeed, however, in removing all their doubts about his supercilious attitude toward eastern Europeans.

He also fought to keep leading politicians in New York and New Jersey from ruining the Democratic campaign. Roosevelt was accusing him of being manipulated by "the corrupt bosses" and the "Wall Streeters." Wilson had already made it evident, through his instructions to Morgenthau about Morgan and Belmont and Ryan, that the "Wall Streeters" had no hold on him. But he had to prove again his independence of the bosses.

Charles Murphy, the Tammany ruler, had summoned the Tammany braves to renominate Murphy's friend, Governor John A. Dix, for another term in the Executive Mansion in Albany. Progressive Democrats, led by United States Senator James A. O'Gorman and State Senator Franklin D. Roosevelt, had formed an Empire State Democratic party and were prepared to run their own candidates against Dix and the Tammany ticket. Wilson was asked to aid them.

"There is no common ground for men who believe in the Woodrow Wilson kind of Democracy and for men who believe in the Charles F. Murphy kind of Democracy," warned the New York *World* in an editorial on September 11. "Murphy must go. So far as the *World* is concerned, he has already gone. If there is a Democratic machine in this state that is determined to retain him, it must take the consequences of its own folly and corruption."

Wilson needed New York's forty-five electoral votes for the Presidency. He realized that Murphy might cut the national ticket, as Boss David B. Hill had sliced down Cleveland in the 1892 election. Yet he knew he could not compromise with the Tammany potentate.

In a statement to New York leaders on September 12, Wilson took a crystal-clear position. Without attacking Murphy or Dix personally, he indicated that he could not accept them. He did not wish to intervene in state matters, and he had said so publicly a few days after his nomination. But everyone had to know where he stood on bossism.

"The example of New York State is marked as perhaps the example of no other state is marked," Wilson said in his

September 12 declaration. "And the people are waiting to see—I mean the people of the Nation are waiting to see—if we have our eyes open and see the lesson and the duty, or I should prefer to say, the privileges of the time."

He used McAdoo, the chairman of his New York headquarters, to pass the word along to the O'Gorman-Roosevelt forces and the Murphy-Dix organization that he would plunge openly into the New York situation.

And on September 29 Wilson gave a statement to the New York press which was firm and cold. New York's Democrats must have complete freedom in choosing their candidate for governor, he said. He was confident that they were "ready to choose a progressive man of a kind to be his own master and to adopt a platform to which men of progressive principles everywhere can heartily subscribe, if only . . . [the party] be left free from personal control of any sort." The reference to "personal control" was aimed at Charles Murphy, and everybody knew it. (A few days later, at the state convention in Syracuse, Murphy abandoned Dix and agreed to back a nominee acceptable to Wilson.)

While he was siding with the insurgent Democrats in New York, Wilson was also busy repelling another assault from his perennial opponent, former Senator James Smith of New Jersey. Smith had entered the contest for the Democratic senatorial nomination and most observers thought he had an excellent chance to get it. Three of Wilson's good friends —John Wescott, William Hughes, and William Gebhardt— were contending for the nomination and were expected to split the progressive vote between them.

Wilson had urged his three friends to get together and decide which one should make the race; he could not express a preference for one above the others. Gebhardt pulled out on September 11, and Wescott and Hughes at last offered to let a committee from the Democratic national headquarters decide which of them should run. Hughes got the nod, and Wescott withdrew, pledging his backing to Hughes in a gesture of good will.

That cleared the track for one Wilson man to go to the post against Smith. Because of Wilson's strength in New Jersey, Smith's political stock hit bottom again. Wilson did not show him any mercy.

"Mr. Smith's selection as the Democratic candidate for the Senate would be the most fatal step backwards that the Democrats of the State could possibly take. It would mean his restoration to political leadership in New Jersey the moment my service as Governor ended," Wilson declared to the New Jersey press.

The return of Smith, Wilson reminded the citizens of New Jersey, would mean "a return to the machine rule which so long kept every active Democrat in the State in subordination to him, and prevented every progressive program conceived in the interest of the people from being put into effect." Wilson ignored the influences of the corporations, the banks, and other conservative institutions which had maintained the status quo in New Jersey. He loaded the blame for the failures of the past entirely upon the shoulders of Smith.

To make certain of Smith's repulse, Wilson interrupted his Presidential campaign on September 21, rushed back to New Jersey, and made speeches in Hoboken and Jersey City, imploring a majority for Hughes. Wilson almost implied that it was just as important to defeat Smith as it was to elect the Democratic candidate to the White House.

Wilson's followers in New Jersey rallied to Hughes. Smith was overwhelmed and gave up politics altogether. Wilson proclaimed a victory for the cause of decent government.

Wilson's actions in New Jersey and New York, though somewhat self-righteous and scapegoat-hunting, convinced the people across the nation that he was a man who lived in accordance with his principles. He was against the bosses, and he battered the bosses with every weapon at his command. And the voters felt that he was justified.

THE PLEASURES OF CAMPAIGNING

As Wilson began to savor the pleasures of being a Presidential nominee who had Providence and the people quite evidently on his side, he enjoyed campaigning more and more. He had the admiration of the voters; now he sought their emotional allegiance. It was very difficult to win, much harder than anyone seemed to realize; but he kept trying.

He got off to a slow start. His special train, leaving New York on September 15, was not well handled by the railroads. It moved from side tracks to freight lines and did not keep to the schedule set for it. Consequently, Wilson had to pop out at odd moments, wave to a few people, and deliver brief off-the-cuff remarks on the evils of high tariffs and uncontrolled monopolies called "trusts." Before he could establish any sustained communication with the sparse audiences, the train was clacking on the rails again.

He warmed up a little on September 17 at Sioux City, Iowa, where a sizable crowd awaited him at the Interstate Live Stock Fair. Also in Sioux Falls, South Dakota, where he made two speeches that night, he lashed out successfully at Colonel Roosevelt.

Roosevelt was not really responsible for the idea of legalizing and regulating the trusts, Wilson said. Roosevelt was shouting about it from the housetops, but the idea had actually been developed by George Perkins, the former Morgan banker who was master-minding the Colonel's campaign, and Elbert H. Gary, the ruthless head of the U. S. Steel Corporation.

"They have thought this thing out," Wilson said. "It may be, for all I know, that they honestly think that is the way to safeguard the business of the country. But whatever they think, this they know, that it will save the United States Steel Corporation from the necessity of doing its business better than its competitors. For if you will look into the statistics of the United States Steel Corporation you will find that wherever it has competitors the amount of the product which it controls is decreasing; in other words, that it is less efficient than its competitors, and its control of product is increasing only in those branches of the business where, by purchase and otherwise, they have a practical monopoly."

From Sioux Falls he went to Minneapolis and Detroit; enthusiastic crowds responded warmly whenever he struck hard at Roosevelt or Taft. He was still a little uneasy about using popular phrases, but he was getting into the swing of campaign oratory.

Wilson received a tumultuous greeting in Columbus, Ohio, upon his arrival there on September 20. Hundreds of loyal Democrats, with a vanguard including Representative James M. Cox, the candidate for governor, were at the railroad station. Tubas and trumpets, drums and bugles, gave him a loud salute.

That night, in the company of Governor Harmon and Representative Cox, Wilson taunted Roosevelt and Taft with barbed phrases, asking why the two other Presidential candidates had tossed to him "the two great issues of the tariff and the trusts." The tariff and the trusts were bread-and-butter issues, he felt. High tariffs on imported products helped to keep all prices high, and the market-hogging practices of the trusts also contributed to the rising cost of living.

Only the Democrats, Wilson declared, were "bold enough and far-sighted enough to see that they must tackle frankly and directly this question: Upon what principle shall tariff duties be laid, and by what means shall monopoly be prevented?" Only the Democratic Party, he said, dared to challenge the economic powers of the giant corporations.

He then returned to New Jersey for a short rest at Sea Girt. After that, he went to Scranton, Pennsylvania, to take part in the Democratic drive in that big industrial state.

Heated by the cheers of the 10,000 persons packed into the Scranton auditorium, Wilson cried out: "I want to fight for the liberation of America. . . . I am fighting, not for the man who has made good, but for the man who is going to make good—the man who is knocking and fighting at the closed doors of opportunity."

He repeated his denunciations of paternalism, pitted the wealthy classes against the poor and the middle classes—and naturally took the side of the underdogs.

"There is no group of men big enough or wise enough to take care of a free people," Wilson shouted. "The small classes that are trying to govern us are finding that we are kicking over the traces. . . ."

His audience, made up largely of men from the coal mines around Scranton, gave him lusty bellows of approval. And the new Wilson, the Wilson who defied the ruling groups, roared to them: "And having once got the blood in my eye of the lust for the scalps of those who resist the liberties of the people, I don't care whether I am elected President or not. I'll find some way to keep fighting." He swung his hands in sharp gestures. He punched home his points with the delivery of a battler.

Of course, he did care about being President. And he wanted to show the crowd that he was a two-fisted fighter who deserved their votes. The miners admired him for it. He wasn't just a professor from Princeton, after all; he wasn't a stuffed shirt or a thin-necked bookworm; he was a man who really knew the score.

A week later, when traveling through New England, he was a different man in a different place. In Hartford, Connecticut, Wilson tried hard to assure the people of New England that his proposed reforms would preserve legitimate enterprises. He was a builder, not a destroyer. He told the crowd: "We ought to go very slowly and very carefully about the task of altering the institutions we have been a long time in building up. I believe that the ancient traditions of a people are its ballast."

But the next night, in Fall River, Massachusetts, he spoke as a friend of the trade unions. He reminded his factory-worker audience that Roosevelt's "third-term platform" had not recognized the necessity for legalizing labor's right to organize. "Any employer can dismiss all of his workmen for no other reason than that they belong to a union," Wilson snapped. "So the thing is absolutely one-sided. I believe we ought to hold a brief for the legal right of labor to organize."

In Boston two days later Wilson had a long meeting with Brandeis on what might be done specifically about the trusts. He had read Brandeis' article in the September 7 issue of *Collier's Weekly*, suggesting the creation of a Federal Trade Commission for the regulation of competition. And Wilson, who had scoffed at Roosevelt's advocacy of a federal commission to control the trusts, now suddenly made a public admission that such an agency might be needed.

Before a mixed audience of bluebloods from Back Bay and workingmen from South Boston, Wilson said: "We are not fighting the trusts, we are trying to put them upon an equality with everybody else." He took issue with Roosevelt's apparent acceptance of the inevitable domination of industry by the trusts, and denounced the Colonel for approving U. S. Steel's purchase of the Tennessee Coal, Iron & Railroad Company. "He thought that it was inevitable that the Chief Executive should consent to an illegal thing in order to build up an irresistible power," Wilson asserted.

His campaign trips in September gave Wilson a heady feeling that he could reach the people; he could sway some crowds with as much fire and fervor as Roosevelt could muster. He had absorbed the Brandeis program, had made it his own, and had given his followers an effective slogan— "the New Freedom."

It was a beginning that pulled many thousands of new voters into his camp, a beginning that thrust some burning needles under Roosevelt's skin and made Taft grumble and groan behind the walls of the White House.

Under the tutelage of Brandeis, under the influence of the fervent responses he had received from some audiences, Wilson had gone step by step toward a broader role for government as the protector of the individual American's welfare. He saw that labor's right to organize had to be established by federal law, to give workingmen the economic strength to counterbalance the financial weight of the corporations.

Wilson could not bring himself to go as far as Brandeis, who had sent him a memorandum containing some really radical declarations. Brandeis said: "You have asked me to state what the essential difference is between the Democratic Party's solution of the Trust Problem and that of the New Party [the Progressives]; and how to propose to regulate competition."

"The New Party declares that private monopoly in industry is not necessarily evil, but may do evil; and that legislation should be limited to such laws and regulations as should attempt merely to prevent the doing of evil," Brandeis said. "We believe that no methods of regulation ever have been or can be devised to remove the menace inherent in private monopoly and overweening commercial power."

Wilson shared Brandeis' revulsion at the "evil" which seemed to exist in corporations that crushed competition, fixed prices, and drew the last drop of useful sweat from human labor. Yet he sensed that "evil" might be equally present in a government monopoly—and the menace might be even greater than the danger inherent in "overweening commercial power."

In the memorandum Brandeis spoke of the possible need in the future of "a public monopoly—a monopoly owned by the people and not by the capitalists." In practice, such a monopoly would be administered by civil servants and the people would have only a remote control over the policy established by the government's administrators. Ownership and management could be two very different things. What the people "owned" in theory, they might not be able to manage in actual operation.

Wilson wanted to keep the people free—to give them a chance to run their own lives, to choose their own pursuits, to produce their own prosperity through their own efforts without too much interference from corporations, unions, mass pressures, or governmental guidance. He was still suspicious of any group or individual claiming to speak with complete authority.

He, of course, felt that he had some authority—the authority that came from his own conscience and the promptings of Providence. But any other American could have such authority—that had to be acknowledged, that had to be placed beyond dispute.

THE FRUSTRATIONS OF COLONEL ROOSEVELT

September, 1912, was a sickening month for Theodore Roosevelt. It sickened him to see so many of his fellow Americans succumbing to the blandishments of a pale scholar like Woodrow Wilson. It sickened him to see his own pupil, his own selected successor, skulking in the White House like a pouting schoolboy.

Why wouldn't Taft come out and fight him toe to toe, the way a man should fight? Why wouldn't Wilson stop dancing around the political ring, and really swap some body-blows?

Why wouldn't the country wake up and see what was going on?

To wake up as many people as he could, to try to make them see the perils he saw in Wilson and the perfidy he detected in Taft, Roosevelt crossed the country from one shore to another. In California he had difficulties with Governor Johnson, the Progressive Party's Vice-Presidential candidate. Johnson felt that Roosevelt was attempting to do too much, making too many speeches, and not giving him enough opportunities to share the load.

Roosevelt was impatient about such matters. Roosevelt knew that he was the heart and the head of the Progressive movement. Roosevelt was certain that the people in all the states expected him to appear in person, to deliver the Progressive gospel straight from the shoulder. He was positive that the voters would accept no substitutes.

The Bull Moose campaign became a chaos of confusion. Roosevelt stomped from platform to platform, pouring forth denunciations of Taft and Wilson until his throat grew sore and he could scarcely lift his voice above a whisper. He interpreted the Progressive platform to suit himself; he did not think the statements that appeared in pamphlets and party publications really mattered.

For the dedicated liberals around him—Amos and Gifford Pinchot, Chester Rowell, Albert Beveridge, Hiram Johnson, Raymond Robins, William Allen White, and others—the omission of a strong statement on the Sherman Anti-Trust Act was a grievous error. For the crusading conservatives— George Perkins, Frank Munsey, and the other men of money —the Sherman Act was a bad piece of legislation which did not deserve Roosevelt's endorsement.

With the knowledge he had gained as President, Roosevelt believed that he was better able to judge the value and the limitations of the Sherman Act than any of his advisers. He did not want monopolies and giant corporations to run wild, but he did not want to dismantle a business enterprise simply because it had grown huge.

The questions of what to do about "the trusts" and "the tariff," the questions of what to do about "the high cost of living" and "preventing War," the questions of child labor and social welfare and the income tax—all of these questions were secondary in Roosevelt's eyes. The central question of a Presidential campaign, in his view, was the character of the man to be chosen to fill the highest office in the United States.

Roosevelt had thought more and talked more about the Presidency than any other living American. He regarded the Presidency as an office with enormous powers—actual and potential powers. The Presidency was co-equal with Congress and the Supreme Court; and the President was responsible only to the American people.

He reminded his audiences that he had declared: "There inheres in the Presidency more power than in any other office in any great republic or constitutional monarchy of modern times." And he made his own approach to the job very clear to them: "I believe in a strong executive; I believe in power. . . ."

Taft, in his judgment, was not heroic enough to exercise that power as it had to be exercised. Wilson, in his judgment, was not even aware of the true demands of the Presidency.

"T.R." asked the people to believe in him, to trust him, and to follow him. He promised them that he would act, and act vigorously, to do what had to be done in their name. He pledged that he would never forget that a President "was a steward of the people bound actively and affirmatively to do all he could for the people."

The powers of the Presidency came from the people and had to be returned to the people or the people's representative when the time came for a President to leave office. He demonstrated his understanding of that, and the crowds applauded him.

Roosevelt could have been nominated and probably could have been elected in 1908, when he had voluntarily withdrawn his name from consideration. He had held the Presidential powers nearly eight years, and he had been tempted to continue then in the White House. But he had decided that possession of such powers for another four years might have given him a feeling of kingship, a sense of perpetual rulership, that might have corrupted him and would have damaged the American democracy.

In 1908 he had been only fifty years old. He had been in his prime physically and mentally. He had been fully capable of carrying the weight of the Presidency with all the zest and stamina he had shown during his period as the Chief Executive. His hands were steady on the political reins; his party was pretty firmly behind him; he had not aroused divisive antagonisms to prevent him from functioning effectively.

Yet he had supported Taft as his successor, and he had gone abroad to give Taft an opportunity to use a clean slate. He had governed and controlled his personal appetite for power, although he acknowledged frankly that his appetite was great. He had overcome the terrible temptation to stay in office for the sheer enjoyment of it.

Now in September, 1912, as he traveled across the country, he expected the public and the press to remember these facts. Some people did; some newspapers attempted to understand what he was trying to do. But too often he was surrounded by a cloud of suspicion—suspicion that he was suffering from a mania to make his views prevail over all others, suspicion that he was a sorehead who couldn't get along with Taft or anybody else, suspicion that he just had a weakness for the limelight and would stand on his head and talk nonsense for headlines.

He did not have the glow of power around him on that trip. Instead, he was a celebrity, a man people wanted to see, a man they sought out of curiosity, a man they watched and listened to eagerly, a man whose motives often seemed to baffle them.

Roosevelt discovered anew the horrible frustrations of an ex-President. He was not preceded by the signs and symbols of high office. He was not flanked by Secret Service men, he did not have the services of the government at his command, he did not have the possibilities of rewarding and punishing, he was merely a famous man with an honorary title. His statements did not shake the country and make foreign nations tremble.

How he must have wished that he could change places with Taft! If *he* had been in the White House, he would not have been a mournful prisoner there. If *he* had held the Presidency, he would have held press conferences at least once a day; he would have produced a stream of news that would have blanketed and smothered whatever Wilson and Taft might have had to say. If Wilson or Taft had challenged any of his statements, he would have produced a government report, issued with the Seal of the United States, to prove that he was right.

Perhaps his frustrations drove him into making attacks on Taft and Wilson that grew more and more personal, less and less dignified.

As Roosevelt pushed into the eastern states, he tried to pin the label of "tool of the trusts" on Woodrow Wilson. In spite of the disclosures of the Clapp Committee about the use of corporation funds and Standard Oil money in his own 1904 campaign, Roosevelt told the people in the towns and cities that Standard Oil and the "corrupt bosses" were putting on the drive for Wilson.

Roosevelt was able to convince himself of almost anything, as a number of his friends, as well as his enemies, had observed. Somewhere in his mind he must have realized the foolishness of his words, and yet he kept on saying them. He had convinced himself that the people had to be informed about the hidden forces behind Wilson—and he was the man to inform them.

He was not disturbed by the apparent inconsistency of his assaults because of his close associations with Perkins and Munsey. He did not mind Perkins using Progressive Party publications to say good things about the trusts, to blast the Sherman Act, and to glorify the virtues of George Perkins.

While Roosevelt was on the campaign trail during September, shouting himself hoarse for Progressive principles as he saw them, Perkins served as editor and publisher of a party organ named *The Progressive Bulletin.* In the opening issue of this *Bulletin,* released on September 1, there was an editorial reprinted from a paper friendly to Perkins and perhaps owned by his friends.

Entitled "George W. Perkins and the Roosevelt Progressive Party," the editorial contained eulogies of two very wealthy men, E. H. Harriman and J. Pierpont Morgan, and linked Perkins with them:

"The country needs the work of such men as E. H. Harriman, powerful enough and strong enough to build thousands upon thousands of miles of railroad in a life that ended too soon. The country needs the imagination and power of such men as J. Pierpont Morgan, wasting his energies now in the accumulation of money that does him no good, and spending the money in the accumulation of collections that will do him no good—although they may be useful to the country in the future. . . . One such man as George Perkins, giving to the business of the people the energy and capacity that he has given to private business undertakings, would be a good, new thing in politics and a useful man in government. . . . Mr. Perkins directs the financial and practical management of the Roosevelt Party—luckily for the party."

In the same issue of the *Bulletin* there was a long summary of the Progressive platform. There was no reference to the section on the Sherman Act which had been read to the convention by Dean Lewis. The policy on "trusts" was said to be one of popular regulation.

Two weeks later, when the second issue of the *Bulletin* went to Progressive Party organizers, there was another description of the platform—and again no mention of the Sherman Act section.

In the September 23 issue, the *Progressive Bulletin* carried an editorial denouncing the Sherman Act. Headed "The Only Honest Plank on Trusts," the editorial said: "The new party is the only one that has a single intelligent and honest word to say upon the trust problem. . . . The plank that Mr. Bryan wrote goes back of even the Sherman Law, and rests on the naive faith that the way out of the difficulty lies in 'busting' everything of size. . . . Both these platforms [the old parties' platforms] rely upon compelling competition; and no policy which relies upon that will bring us one step nearer to an actual grapple with the trust problem. . . . The Progressive Party begins with the sane belief—backed by the economic experience of the whole world for a full generation—that competition may be harmful and combination salutary. It is only from this point of view that any solution of the trust problem will ever be found."

During his terms as President, Colonel Roosevelt had repeatedly endorsed the Sherman Act in his messages to Congress. He had asked for its retention and enforcement. He had initiated federal suits under the act in dozens of cases.

So it was impossible for the Pinchots and others to understand how he could let Perkins use the new party's official publication to say that "competition may be harmful and combination salutary." For the liberals believed that the large corporations were taking money out of the pockets of working people by fixing prices at high levels and gaining enormous profits.

Colonel Roosevelt did not share Amos Pinchot's black and

white judgment of the swiftly changing economic picture. Roosevelt felt that the development of huge corporations, the growth of gigantic cities, the rise of organizations enrolling millions of farmers and laborers, might be inevitable under the industrial technology produced by science. And although he had supported the Sherman Act in the past, he now saw that it might really be a vain attempt to turn back the clock of history.

"This is an era of federation and combination," Roosevelt said. And later he declared: "A simple and poor society can exist as a democracy on a basis of sheer individualism. But a rich and complex industrial society cannot so exist; for some individuals, and especially those artificial individuals called corporations, become so very big that the ordinary individual . . . cannot deal with them on terms of equality. It therefore becomes necessary for these ordinary individuals to combine in their turn, first in order to act in their collective capacity through that biggest of all combinations called the government, and second, to act, also in their own self-defense, through private combinations, such as farmers' associations and trade-unions."

At times, Roosevelt saw the shape of the future much more clearly than Wilson or Taft did, and his vision was far more penetrating than the vision of many intellectuals who criticized or condemned him as a "wild buffalo" or a "mad Bull Moose." He felt that he was right about everything—(and in the light of events since 1912, he was certainly right about an astonishing number of things)—but his insistence on his own omniscience irritated and alienated a great many people.

Perhaps his realization that he was not stirring enough people to make his crusade successful, perhaps his increasing sense of frustration and depression, accounted for his refusal to pay much attention to the protests against George Perkins' articles in the *Bulletin*. If he himself could not convince the people that he knew what to do, and if they could not accept him as the proper man to govern the country, what did the *Bulletin* matter?

Probably his frustrations and his forebodings of defeat led him to say harsher and harsher things. He finally brought himself to tell his followers that "every big crooked financier is against us and in favor of either Mr. Wilson or Mr. Taft." The financiers who backed him might be big and powerful, but in Roosevelt's eyes they were a different breed of men from those who supported his opponents.

In Springfield, Missouri, exasperated by Mr. Taft's retreat into the White House and Taft's refusal to take notice of his savage assaults upon the current administration, Roosevelt bellowed to a crowd: "I have noticed several Taft badges in your town, and they are the appropriate color of yellow." Some members of the crowd gasped; even Roosevelt's admirers were shocked to hear a President of the United States described in such words.

Roosevelt could not be restrained. He had broken all the rules in politics, and in September he cast from him the prudence which had caused his opponents in previous campaigns to regard him as a vote-cadger and an opportunist.

Ironically enough, his passionate sincerity did not ring true to some of the men and women who had worked in the Progressive movement for many years before the formation of the Bull Moose Party. Jane Addams, who had seconded Roosevelt's nomination at Chicago with so much enthusiasm, found that her ardor was not shared by some of her friends. Ann Howard Shaw wrote to her: "I wish I could believe he intended to do a single honest thing, or that he would carry out a single plank in the platform if he were to be elected. . . . I cannot."

Brand Whitlock, who had been skeptical of Wilson and inclined toward Roosevelt in August, swung over to Wilson in September while the Colonel was crossing the country and making ferocious speeches. Whitlock did not like the Colonel's "partisan spirit."

"I was, of course, impressed by the enthusiasm with which the Progressive cause was launched, and I like the social program which it put forth," Whitlock said in a letter to Wilson's friend, Newton D. Baker. "To that extent the movement gave expression to a beautiful sentiment in this land, which you and I have been trying to make concrete in our cities for many years. But that sentiment did not get itself fully, or adequately, expressed in the movement, and now it seems to have fallen back into the old partisan spirit, which is the very antithesis of that sentiment. If Governor Wilson had not been nominated at Baltimore, we should have had a new liberal party in this country, and the alignment at last would have been clear.

"But in his personality Governor Wilson himself wholly satisfies and sums up that democratic spirit which means everything to you and me, and it is personality that counts, that tells, more than creeds or platforms."

In Roosevelt's eyes, Whitlock decided to support the wrong candidate—but arrived at the decision through the right reasons. "It is personality that counts, that tells, more than creeds or platforms," Whitlock had said. And that was exactly what Roosevelt was trying to tell the voters.

MR. TAFT GETS SOLACE FROM MAINE AND VERMONT

To William Howard Taft, the very idea that personality could count more than beliefs or principles was a dangerous step toward radicalism and anarchy. He believed in a government of laws, a government established in accordance with the fundamental order of the universe. Men might come and go, but the principles of law and justice went on forever.

Taft himself could not engage in a contest of personalities. He could not treat the selection of a President as a kind of beauty competition, in which the contestants bowed and pirouetted before the voters. He could only treat it as a solemn occasion, an event of great weight and dignity which occurred every four years under the Constitution.

In a letter to his brother Horace the President had described the Roosevelt party as "a religious cult with a fakir at the head of it." People who were swayed by the emotional bayings of Roosevelt were beyond Taft's ken. He looked upon them with mystified sorrow.

A man's personality, a man's character, certainly had to be considered by the voters when they picked a President. But to base *everything* upon personality was to go astray into chaos. The nation could not be governed entirely by the President's moods.

Taft's hopes that the people might return to sanity rose a little in September. Vermont and Maine held elections then —and in both states the regular Republicans did reasonably well. The regular Republican running for governor against a Progressive and a Democrat in Vermont won a close race. The Republicans in Maine had a substantial majority over the Democrats.

In a letter to his old friend Otto Bannard, Taft cited the outcome in Vermont as an indication that Roosevelt would not bag any electoral votes in the New England states. He thought Roosevelt was "on the toboggan and will run a poor third in the election."

Expressing similar ideas to another friend, Samuel Mather, later in the month, Taft said it was conceivable that the Republican ticket could win if "every lover of sane, constitutional government would take off his coat and work, refusing to be misled by the cajolings of Mr. Wilson or by Mr. Roosevelt's assertion that he is 'battling for the Lord.' " He knew it was a long shot; he knew that the number of lovers of "sane, constitutional government" outside of New England might be very limited.

In fact, he had sent to another of his brothers, Henry Taft, an acknowledgment that he was preparing himself for repudiation by a majority of the voters. In this letter Taft said he realized that he had "unprecedented difficulties and a most unscrupulous enemy." He added: "I believe I am already reconciled to defeat, although if it actually comes, I would doubtless find that uncertainty was pleasanter than certainty in that respect."

Taft had a dreadful suspicion that there might be disloyalty to his candidacy even among those who were publicly committed to him. Harry Daugherty of Ohio, who was active in his campaign organization, protested to Taft that Postmaster General Frank Hitchcock was sabotaging the President by installing severe disciplinary methods which angered the railway mail clerks.

Taft did not openly seek the votes of the postal workers. Actually, he had extended the Civil Service to cover many of the jobs in the Post Office Department. He was disturbed, however, by Daugherty's reports that some of the clerks were antagonistic and harmful to him.

"What under heaven is the matter with your people in Ohio?" he wrote to Hitchcock on September 13. "They are engaged in working against me at every hand. Now, can you give some attention to this, and see to it that the men who are there are at least neutral?"

While Taft took solace from the voting trends in Maine and Vermont, he was disturbed by many things in addition to the accusations of disloyalty among his associates. He was accused of playing into the hands of the Roman Catholic Church. His trip to the Vatican, to settle the problems raised by the Church's ownership of land in the Philippines, was cited as proof of his pro-Catholic sympathies. It was rumored that his late aide, Major Butt, had been sent to Rome on a secret assignment by the President.

Actually, Taft had made his position on Catholicism clear

in a White House memorandum issued before the Republican convention, and he had restated his views in letters to his friends. Among them was G. H. Grosvenor, to whom Taft wrote: "I deny utterly that I have ever cultivated the Catholic Church for political purposes. But it is useless to persuade a man with the anti-Catholic virus to look with patience at any treatment of the Catholic Church that does not involve . . . hostility."

Taft, who tried to treat everybody with justice, found that it was hard to get a fair hearing for his own views. In 1908 he had been attacked because he was a Unitarian. In 1912 he was falsely charged with leaning toward the Church of Rome.

He went on working at the job of being President, patiently, quietly, doggedly, serving the country in harmony with his own nature, his own concept of public service. He presented himself as the defender of "sane, constitutional government," he drew comfort from the stability of New England, and he awaited the verdict of the nation's voters.

SCIENTISTS SEE BRIGHT FUTURE—
MARINES COOL OFF NICARAGUA

Two international conventions of scientists met in Washington during September—the eighth Congress of Applied Chemistry and the fifteenth Congress of Hygiene and Demography (the branch of anthropology concerned with births, deaths, and diseases).

President Taft sent greetings to both groups, expressing hopes for the progress of humanity through science. Newspapers gave space to reports of astounding advances in chemistry and great gains made by hygiene against the illnesses of man. The scientists predicted that the new generation of children would have longer lives than any previous generation in history.

Meanwhile, American Marines methodically crushed the

rebellion in the small nation of Nicaragua. Railway and telegraphic communications were rebuilt, and the ragged rebel Nicaraguans were put to flight by well-armed and well-disciplined Americans. Hostility toward the United States grew in Latin America.

Martial law was established in Augusta, Georgia, to break a strike there conducted by employees of the street-railway system. Order was restored in Georgia as well as Nicaragua, and the streetcars ran on time.

Some excitement was created in America by news dispatches from France, describing the passage of "an airplane armada" over Paris. The French minister of war reviewed a fleet of 72 warplanes. Americans wondered how the French, who had not produced the Wright Brothers, had taken the lead in developing an air force.

Most Americans soon dismissed the French feat—the French were a funny race, nobody should be too surprised by anything they did—and resumed their arguments over Teddy Roosevelt and Woodrow Wilson. The campaign was getting steadily rougher as the contestants entered the closing weeks.

XI. October: Death Reaches Close to T.R. and Wilson

THE COLONEL TAKES A BULLET

With a raw throat that made it difficult for him to lift his voice above a whisper, Theodore Roosevelt arrived in Milwaukee on the 14th of October. He had been forced to cancel several speeches in Indiana and Wisconsin because he could not make himself heard. But the Milwaukee speech was a major one. He felt that he had to give it.

That frosty October evening, wearing his overcoat to keep his chest and body warm, Roosevelt left the Gilpatrick Hotel. He waved to a group of admirers, stepped into an open automobile, and turned to sit down. At that moment he was struck by a bullet from a pistol thrust at him by a man who sprang suddenly from the darkness.

The man, eyes glaring, screamed something that sounded like "No third term!" Later, under police questioning, he said he had tried to kill Roosevelt because he thought the Colonel intended to become a dictator.

Roosevelt slumped back into the car seat. Elbert Martin, one of the Colonel's secretaries, prevented the firing of a second shot by seizing the would-be assassin and shoving him away from the car. Roosevelt's admirers around the automobile then pounded the man on the head and shoulders, and shouts went up: "Lynch him! He shot Roosevelt! Get him, lynch him!"

The Colonel rose immediately and ordered the wild-eyed man brought to him. "Mad," the Colonel said, looking into the man's face. "Don't hurt the poor creature." Policemen seized the man and removed him quickly.

"I've got to make my speech," Roosevelt said, ordering the driver of the car to take him at once to the Milwaukee auditorium. When he reached the hall, physicians there wanted to send him to a hospital. The bullet had ranged four inches into his chest wall. He was bleeding and trembling with shock. The doctors feared that his injury might be fatal.

Roosevelt would not yield to their pleas. His mind was clear and his spirit was unshaken. He had faced death before, in the charge up San Juan Hill. He had preached the doctrine of the strenuous life, and he lived by it. He would not collapse with a single bullet in him.

"I'll make this speech or die; one or the other," he said. He strode to the platform. The audience, not knowing about his injury, gave him a salvo of applause.

The chairman of the meeting banged a gavel, calling for quiet. When the crowd grew still, the chairman said: "I have something to tell you, and I hope you will receive the news with calmness. Colonel Roosevelt has been shot. He is wounded."

Gasps of horror came from people in the auditorium. Men got to their feet. Roosevelt calmed them by moving to the front of the platform and raising one hand. In a low, apologetic tone the Colonel asked: "Please excuse me from making a long speech. I'll do the best I can. You see there is a bullet in my body. But it is nothing. I'm not hurt badly."

He pulled the manuscript of his address from the inner pocket of his overcoat. He saw there was a bullet-hole in the manuscript. The bullet had passed through the coat, the metal spectacles-case in his pocket, and the papers containing the words of his speech. He lifted the bullet-torn manuscript above his head and said: "It takes more than that to kill a Bull Moose!"

The crowd saluted his courage with a roar. Ordinarily an audience might have felt that he was making a display of his bravery. But they did not feel that way about Teddy Roosevelt. They expected him to have endurance far beyond the stamina of most men.

He gathered strength as he spoke. He went on for an hour and a half. Several times he faltered, and men on the platform stepped forward to aid him. He shugged them off. "Let me alone," growled the Colonel. "I'm all right."

Few of his hearers concentrated on what he said; they were fascinated by his pale, determined face. The crowd heeded his plea for quiet until he finished; then the people in the hall gave him a rising ovation.

After he left the platform, he was taken to a nearby hospital and X-rayed. Then he was removed to his private railroad car and taken to Chicago. At the Mercy Hospital there he was joined by his wife, who had rushed to the Middle West from New York.

Governor Wilson announced that he would not speak on national issues until Roosevelt returned to the battle. Wilson and Taft both sent telegrams of admiration and sympathy to the Colonel after learning of his magnificent performance in the Milwaukee auditorium.

Roosevelt insisted that he did not want his opponents to cease their fire. During his six restive days in the hospital, he continued to issue statements and to make plans for his future activities. "The welfare of any one man in this fight is wholly immaterial, compared to the great and fundamental issues involved," he said.

His doctors assured the public that the patient was out of danger and recovering with miraculous speed. The Colonel told his supporters grandiloquently: "It matters little about me, but it matters about the cause we fight for. If one soldier who carries the flag is stricken, another will take it from his hands and carry it on. . . . Tell the people not to worry about me, for if I go down another will take my place. For always, the army is true. Always the cause is there."

Then he called upon his opponents to continue their assaults upon him if they wished to do so.

"Whatever could with truth and propriety have been said against me and my cause before I was shot can, with equal truth and equal propriety, be said against me now," Roosevelt asserted. "The things that cannot be said now are merely the things that ought not to have been said before. This is not a contest about any man; it is a contest concerning principles."

Roosevelt's behavior in this crisis evoked such a wave of popular feeling that the political experts, who had been predicting a landslide for Wilson, began to hedge. It was quite possible that the wounded Roosevelt, pacing in a hospital room, would draw more votes than a healthy Roosevelt, showing his teeth and roaring at antagonists.

To Amos Pinchot and the other passionate liberals in the Progressive Party, however, the attempted assassination of Roosevelt had little bearing on the party's chances. To them, the obvious influence of Wall Street was a handicap the party could not overcome. Perkins was still distributing pro-trust pamphlets and statements. Munsey was still in Roosevelt's confidence, and the liberals were in despair.

The liberals performed many errands for the Colonel, helped with some of his speeches, answered attacks made on him in papers and magazines, sat in scores of conferences, and gave generously of their time and money—but the Colonel was not under their domination, and they knew it. He shared some of their ideas and rejected others. He was closer to Munsey and Perkins than he was to any of them.

At the time, Pinchot and the other dedicated radicals were consumed by rage as well as a mixture of pity and scorn. Roosevelt seemed to be attempting to hoodwink the people. They felt he was posing as a revolutionary when he was actually in the hands of Wall Street manipulators.

Long after the campaign was over, Pinchot admitted that he and his associates had tried to push Roosevelt into a role for which the Colonel was not suited. The Colonel had acted in accordance with his personal qualities and his experience.

No matter how often he said he was a radical and wanted to be a radical, he could not drive himself to be one for very long. In some of his declarations the Colonel expounded his radical ideas. But the conservative businessmen in his camp, knowing him well, regarded these declarations as manifestations of his restless spirit, not as firm outlines of policy.

Roosevelt's vision ranged widely into the future, yet he was an impulsive, moody person, unable to submerge himself in any doctrinaire movement. He showed no desire to plan a long-range program that might some day bring a radical party into power.

His final speech was delivered on October 30 in Madison Square Garden before a crowd of 16,000 devoted followers. Thousands of others packed the streets around the Garden and tried to get inside. He was a wounded hero, and they wanted to salute him.

He had not fully recovered from his wound, and his gestures were rigid and painful. Yet his trumpeting voice had regained its bugle-call tones. He aroused his audience to a high pitch of enthusiasm.

After each sentence he had to wave the crowd into silence. He said that he was crusading for the social and industrial welfare of the country. He expressed the belief that the Progressive Party would have a continuing impact upon the nation in the years to come.

WILSON REACHES NEW HEIGHTS

October was a month of danger and delight for Woodrow Wilson.

He was in danger from overconfidence and from the hazards of travel. He took delight in the wild welcomes given him by the cities he entered in his quest for votes. He was heartened by the evidence of his power in New York, where Tammany had bowed to his will and accepted a liberal Democrat as the right candidate for governor.

On a night journey from Gary, Indiana, where he had received an ovation from a huge crowd of steelworkers, Wilson was aboard a Pullman sleeper which was severely damaged by a runaway freight car. The freight car slammed into the Pullman with crushing force.

The observation platform of the Pullman was smashed. The guard rail was torn off. The windows in the car were broken. Wilson himself was not harmed. His train went on through the night to Omaha, where he arrived safely on October 5.

He was given a roaring reception, and made six speeches in seven hours in the Nebraska city. Crowds followed him from hall to hall. When he left the city auditorium late in the afternoon several thousand persons engulfed his automobile and tried to touch him or shake his hand.

Omaha was warm and friendly, but Lincoln offered him an overwhelming experience. William Jennings Bryan had gathered a mighty army of Democrats, led by nine brass bands and a dozen marching clubs, to greet him at the station. Bryan embraced him when he stepped from the train, and a demonstration of shouting, singing, and cheering lasted for half an hour.

At a banquet given by the Democratic state committee, Wilson declared: "We are free to serve the people of the United States, and in my opinion it was Mr. Bryan who set us free."

Bryan, who had been averaging nearly ten speeches a day for Wilson in the West, urged his friends: "Let me ask you to do twice as much for Wilson as you ever did for Bryan. For I have as much at stake in this fight as he has, and you have as much as I have."

Wilson went to church with Bryan on Sunday, got a day's rest, and then traveled on into Colorado. In Denver he encountered as much exuberance as he had found in Lincoln. Thousands formed a guard of honor for him at the railroad station, thousands more were in the streets to hail him, and 15,000 persons filled the auditorium where he spoke on October 7.

In Colorado Wilson made more attacks on Roosevelt, calling him the director of "the Trust chorus." In Denver's auditorium he discussed the growth of economic classes in the nation; he declared that some groups were getting too much of the national income and others were existing on a bare subsistence level. He promised that he would try to do something to spread the wealth to the poorer classes.

"This is a second struggle for emancipation," Wilson cried. "If America is not to have free enterprise, then she can have freedom of no sort whatever."

He was excited and stimulated by the brass bands, the swarming crowds, the optimism of the Democratic political leaders in the towns of Colorado and Kansas. When he appeared in Kansas City, Missouri, on the evening of October 8, he found the temperature much cooler. Missourians had been disappointed by the defeat of their man, Champ Clark, and their applause for Wilson was limited.

In Kansas City's convention hall Wilson reacted to Roosevelt's public demand for proof or retraction of Wilson's charge that the steel trust was aiding the Progressive ticket. Wilson said he had not intended to indicate that Roosevelt was being financed by the steel corporation.

"What I meant was that they are supporting him with their thought, and their thought is not our thought," Wilson said. "I meant, and I say again, that the kind of control which he proposes is the kind of control that the United States Steel Corporation wants."

After warmer receptions in St. Louis and Chicago than he had received in Kansas City, Wilson finished his swing through the West and Middle West with a train trip through Ohio, speaking to crowds that assembled in Canton, Akron, and other places along the route of the Pennsylvania Railroad. His voice, like Roosevelt's, gave out under the strain.

When he got to Cleveland, where he found an enormous audience, Wilson could not make himself audible to most of his listeners. Those who could hear him, however, listened to another fiery onslaught against the trusts.

"If I did not believe monopoly could be restrained and destroyed I would come to doubt that liberty could be preserved in the United States," Wilson said. "It is a choice of life and death—whether we shall allow this country to be controlled by small groups of men or whether we shall return to the form of government contemplated by the fathers."

Wilson was not really very clear about how monopoly "could be restrained and destroyed" or how Americans could "return to the form of government contemplated by the fathers." But he was obviously in favor of the people and against the rule of "small groups of men." And so the huge audience clapped and shouted for him.

The Cleveland appearance exhausted him. He returned to his home in Princeton, and he spent several days recuperating. His series of triumphs had elated him, but he felt that his election was not yet assured, even though the betting odds were getting longer and longer against Roosevelt and Taft.

The shooting of Roosevelt on October 14 occurred while Wilson was resting at Princeton. It threw his managers into turmoil. No one could now be positive about the reactions of the voters. Wilson decided that in fairness he should stop campaigning. He dropped all of his engagements except those he could not eliminate without subjecting his supporters to serious embarrassment.

When Wilson traveled through Delaware on October 16 and 17 to keep the engagements he could not omit, he talked only about New Jersey questions—the importance of electing state candidates on the Democratic line, and other such topics. At Georgetown he voiced admiration for the personal bravery of Roosevelt: "I came out to fulfill the engagements of this week with very great reluctance, because my thought is constantly of that gallant gentleman lying in the hospital at Chicago."

At this time Wilson's own life was being threatened. Policemen were stationed in the Wilmington Opera House on October 17, after receiving reports that he would be shot. Wilson spoke vigorously, ignoring the threats, and made a graceful acknowledgment of the support he was getting from Senator La Follette, who was now laboring in the Democratic vineyard. La Follette's bitterness against Roosevelt had gradually carried the senator into Wilson's camp, once he became convinced that Taft was out of the running.

Speaking in New York on October 19, Wilson had an unfortunate experience. He was confronted by Maude Malone, a suffragette, who challenged him to give his views on the right of women to vote. He straddled the issue, declaring that women's suffrage was a state matter, "not a question that is dealt with by the National Government at all." Then he talked about "freedom" while Miss Malone was forcibly removed by the police.

In October Wilson clarified his attitude toward Negroes and other colored citizens. Because he had been born in Virginia, because most of his campaigners were southerners, and because he had supposedly drawn the color line against Negro students at Princeton, many Negroes felt that they could not vote for him. So now his advisers, conscious of the importance of the colored vote in the North, pressed him to make known his ideas about the treatment of Negroes.

The opportunity came in mid-October when Bishop Alexander Walters of the African Zion Church, then the head of the National Colored Democratic League, asked Wilson to address members of the League in New York. Wilson wrote Bishop Walters that he would be unable to appear before the League. But he added that he wanted to "assure my colored fellow citizens of my earnest wish to see justice done them in every matter, and not mere grudging justice, but justice executed with liberality and cordial good feeling."

He had already given assurances to a group of representative Negroes that he would "seek to be President of the whole nation and would know no differences of race or creed or section, but [would strive] to act in good conscience and in a Christian spirit through it all."

In his letter to Bishop Walters he went farther than he had ever gone before. He concluded by saying: "My sympathy with them is of long standing, and I want to assure them through you that should I become President of the United States they may count upon me for absolute fair dealing and for everything by which I could assist in advancing the interests of their race in the United States."

Wilson's letter to Bishop Walters satisfied most of the moderate Negro leaders, and even brought over to his side the militant writer and editor, W. E. Burghardt Du Bois, who had earlier opposed him. Du Bois left the Socialist Party to back Wilson, asserting that he wanted "to elect Woodrow Wilson President . . . and prove once for all if the Democratic Party dares to be Democratic when it comes to the black man."

Wilson also had to deal with the charges of pro-Catholicism and anti-Catholicism which plagued Roosevelt and Taft. He was repeatedly criticized because Joseph Tumulty, a Roman Catholic, was his private secretary. He brushed off such attacks as nonsensical. Like Taft and Roosevelt, he hated to see religious prejudice injected into politics.

In a letter to William McAdoo, released to the press on October 22, Wilson tried to settle the question of his religious sympathies. He could not stop the whispering of bigots, but he did make his own position plain to all intelligent observers.

"My attention has been called to the statement that I have become a member of the Knights of Columbus," Wilson wrote. "This is, of course, not true. I have not been asked to join the order either as an active or an honorary member, and am not eligible because I am not a Catholic.

"I must warn my friends everywhere that statements of this kind are all campaign inventions, devised to serve a special purpose. This particular statement has been circulated in selected quarters to create the impression that I am trying to identify myself politically with the great Catholic body. In other quarters all sorts of statements are being set afloat to prove that I am hostile to the Catholics. . . . I am following my own course of thought, playing no favorites."

Bryan thought the anti-Catholic charges were more damaging than the pro-Catholic accusations. So a notable Catholic layman, James Charles Monaghan, was induced to write a pamphlet revealing how many New Jersey Catholics had been appointed to major political jobs by Governor Wilson. The pamphlet, entitled *Is Woodrow Wilson a Bigot?*, also contained Wilson's statements about admirable public services performed by Catholics.

In the middle of October the Hearst newspapers, which had been hammering at Wilson, went over to his support. William Randolph Hearst did not give Wilson personal endorsement, but his editors foresaw a Democratic victory and he permitted them to follow their own desires to back Wilson.

One large Democratic campaign gift became troublesome late in the month. A Senate investigating committee disclosed that Cyrus H. McCormick of the International Harvester Company (called the Harvester Trust) had contributed $12,500. McCormick had gone to Princeton with Wilson and was an old friend. Wilson's enemies pointed out that the governor had never attacked the Harvester Trust in any of his speeches, although he had denounced several of the other trusts by name.

In a statement printed in the Baltimore *Sun* on October 26, Wilson declared that McCormick's money had been returned. Actually, McCormick himself and Cleveland Dodge, another old friend and loyal backer, decided that the McCormick contribution should be withdrawn—to prevent any future embarrassment to Wilson. He acknowledged this in his statement and praised both men for their action.

At the start of the campaign, Wilson had declared: "Nobody owns me. . . ." As the campaign drew near its close, Wilson felt that he could honestly reiterate that declaration. He had drawn upon the assistance of many people, but he was not yoked to any of them.

Toward the end of October, when Roosevelt had recovered from the bullet wound and began issuing appeals to the people again, Wilson took to the road in full cry once more. On October 28 he made a quick swing through parts of Pennsylvania and delivered two major addresses in Philadelphia, one for an audience of liberal Republicans at the Academy of Music and one for a singing throng of 15,000 happy Democrats at the Convention Hall, where he was greeted as "the next President of the United States."

In his talk to the Republicans at the Academy, he declared himself again the champion of the middle class, the candidate who intended to make strenuous efforts to give that class the freedom necessary to create new enterprises.

He was not a disciple of Marx—like Eugene Debs, the Socialist candidate for President—yet he was afraid that Marx's grim prophecies about the fate of capitalism might come true if the monopolists throttled individual initiative.

"We have entered the lists in order to free the average man of enterprise in America, and make ourselves masters of our own fortunes once again," Wilson proclaimed. "The Trusts lie like a great incubus on the productive part of American brains. . . . The sap of manhood may never be allowed to express itself in action in America if we do not see to it that the places where the sap produces the fruit are kept free for its beneficent action."

The progressive Republicans applauded him heartily, perhaps regarding themselves as members of the productive class and sharing Wilson's anxiety that they might be squeezed to death.

In their different ways Taft and Roosevelt—and Debs, too —considered Wilson's approach to the problem of monopolies and the restoration of individual opportunity rather naive and dangerous. Taft thought that during his own administration the government's power to halt or limit the trusts had been effective, and consequently the middle class was now in reasonably good shape. Colonel Roosevelt, as he had trumpeted in a dozen speeches, considered the rise of economic combinations inevitable in modern industrialism; any talk of reversing the trend was poppycock.

All three major candidates were much more affected by

the shadowy presence of Eugene Debs than any of them acknowledged or indeed realized. The vote for Debs in Presidential elections had gone from 94,000 in 1900 to 402,000 four years later and to 420,000 in 1908. The Socialist weekly, *Appeal to Reason,* published in Kansas, had attained a circulation of 500,000. In the 1912 campaign Debs was an associate editor of this publication, contributed many articles to it, and spoke before sizable audiences at lecture engagements arranged by its subscribers.

The Socialists considered that the "progressive" ideas voiced by Wilson sprang in fact from doctrines developed by conservatives. To them, Wilson seemed to echo the views of a McKinley Republican—Judge Peter S. Grosscup of the United States Circuit Court of Appeals—who had declared in an article for *McClure's* magazine in 1905 that "the loss that Republican America now confronts is the loss of the individual hope and prospect—the suppression of the instinct that . . . has made us a nation of individually independent and prosperous people." If most Americans came to feel that their desires to acquire property were futile, the way would be opened for "social and, eventually, political revolution," Grosscup predicted.

And now in 1912 Wilson felt that America was being tempted to take one of two most perilous courses—the course dictated by corporate control, or the course of state socialism. With Brandeis as his guide, Wilson hoped to get the nation on another road—the road of regulated freedom, with individual liberties preserved.

Debs, on the other hand, declared that Wilson and Roosevelt could not face the ultimate realities. Debs felt that the giant corporations would become complete masters of the United States—unless corporate property was seized by the federal government in the name of the people.

Seizure of property was unthinkable to Wilson. He offered no drastic measures to protect the future of the American middle class. Yet his sincerity and his intellectual determination to search for answers made a profound impression on the Philadelphians and on the voters throughout the country who read that speech in their newspapers.

Wilson reached the peak of his campaign in the Madison Square Garden rally on October 31—just one night after the great Roosevelt rally. Both men drew tremendous crowds. Both were engulfed in cheers. Both had great difficulty in making themselves heard.

Yet there was an essential difference between the two rallies. The Bull Moose meeting was a hail-and-farewell for the brave Colonel, for the wounded Rough Rider who was heading for his last political roundup. The Wilson meeting, in contrast, was a feast of optimism. Every Democrat in the Garden seemed to feel that the November voting was a mere formality required by the Constitution. In their eyes Wilson was already President.

Volcanic eruptions of applause had signalled the entry upon the stage of Representative William Sulzer, the liberal Congressman whose nomination for the governorship of New York had been secured with Wilson's help; Augustus Thomas, the noted playwright; Cleveland H. Dodge, Wilson's wealthy friend who had contributed much; and Representative Oscar Underwood, the Alabama congressman who was considered of Presidential timber and who had poured his energies into the Wilson drive.

Thomas had presented Underwood, the crowd had jumped to its feet, and the band was playing "Dixie" when Woodrow Wilson stepped on the platform shortly after nine o'clock. Men and women climbed on their chairs, a rolling roar like the thunder of surf on a beach rose to the ceiling of the Garden, and through the huge hall people waved small American flags.

Wilson's face quivered with emotion. He looked up toward the flag-draped box where his wife watched him with tender pride. He made a gesture toward her, a gesture of thanks for all she had done to help him in his hours of depression, to renew his faith in himself and his destiny under Providence.

While Wilson waved to his wife and bowed to his friends in the Garden that night, the demonstrators paraded and sang. When he tried to quiet them, they yelled louder. The demonstration went on for an hour and four minutes.

Finally, as he began his address, there was absolute silence in the vast hall.

"Fellow citizens, no man could fail to be deeply moved by a demonstration such as we have witnessed tonight," Wilson said. "And yet I am the more thrilled by it because I realize that it is the demonstration for a cause and not for a man. All over this country, from one ocean to the other, men are becoming more aware that in less than a week the common people of America will come into their own again."

In his face and in his address Wilson gave evidence of his consciousness that the struggle to create a more effective government would not end on election day. The struggle would enter a new phase and require new thoughts and new efforts on the part of all those who believed that democracy could be a truly free and truly just form of government.

"What the Democratic Party proposes to do is to go into power and do the things that the Republican Party has been talking about doing for sixteen years," Wilson concluded.

And the crowd roared and the flags waved and the lights blazed down upon the lean man with the scholarly glasses and the angular face, and in the glare of the lights the thin man stood alone there in the Garden. He had traveled a long road from his quiet study in Princeton.

THE INDIAN SUMMER OF MR. TAFT

While Woodrow Wilson experienced the isolation of a victor who must bear the weight of victory, and Colonel Roosevelt suffered the isolation of an old fighter who knew that reinforcements would not reach him in time, William Howard Taft was immersed in the melancholy peace of Indian summer.

He had now abandoned all hope of succeeding himself, but he felt that his administration would stand well in American history. In his talks with friends and supporters, he repeatedly reviewed his achievements. He had extended the civil service. He had established a postal savings system. He had defended the judiciary from partisan attacks. He had introduced more effective methods into the government's operation. He had saved the taxpayers many millions of dollars by creating and strictly conforming to a federal budget.

Taft had tried to protect American rights in Mexico, where a civil war was going on between President Madero and his enemies. Taft had sternly resisted widespread demands for American intervention. He was willing to send small numbers of Marines into Cuba and Nicaragua, but intervention in Mexico might mean a full-scale war.

He declared that "the passing of the border by one regiment of troops would mean war with Mexico, the expenditure of hundreds of millions of dollars, the loss of thousands of lives." Taft felt that America's adventures in other countries had not really been very fruitful. He shuddered at the thought of getting involved in more protracted struggles, such as those which had occurred for years in the Philippines.

He had never bowed to the pressures of oil company executives who wanted him to use the power of the federal government to protect the valuable concessions they had obtained in Mexico. Conservative though he was, respectful though he was to men of wealth and property, Taft placed the interests of his country above those of any private group.

When he spoke proudly of the many suits his attorney general had brought against the trusts, Taft meant what he said. He also was honest in his attempts to remove the worst features of the Payne-Aldrich Tariff Act, the many special clauses designed to protect particular industries supporting powerful lobbies in Washington.

Yet Taft could not get the story of his achievements across to the public. He was inept in his press relations. He lacked keen public-relations advisers. His speeches were turgid, much too long, and were delivered without dramatic force.

He continued to tell visitors to the White House that he expected a Republican victory, although he could not explain how the victory might be achieved. He revealed flashes of anger when he said that members of the Progressive Party could return to the Republican fold if they came in repentance "on their knees."

"A man is a Republican or he is not," said Taft. "Is he going to support the national ticket and is he going to support the state ticket? If he is, he is a Republican. If he is not, he is not a Republican." Taft was tired of hearing about Progressive Republicans and Independent Republicans and all the other varieties of Republicans. He wanted men to take a position and stick by it.

The currents of change were running too fast for him. He did not like what he saw in the new movements, and he did not hesitate to give tongue to his protests, his laments for the old traditions by which his generation had lived.

When Roosevelt was shot, Taft did the gentlemanly thing. He dispatched a message expressing his shock and his sympathy. But two days after the attempted assassination, when it was clear that Roosevelt was out of danger, Taft wrote to his friend, Charles Nagel: "Just what effect Roosevelt's shooting is going to have I don't know. His supporters, and I have no doubt he is willing to profit by it, are making as much of it as they can."

He expressed similar feelings in a note written the next day, October 17, to another friend, Mrs. R. H. Taylor, and added: "Of course, sentiment plays a large part in elections." Taft feared that the would-be assassin had given Roosevelt a chance to win the election.

Generally, however, he maintained the calm which came to him in the autumn days of October—the golden days of Indian summer. The death of Vice-President James Sherman on October 30 disturbed his peace, but he wrote to his brother Horace: "If we survive these blows, we shall indeed show a strength that savors well for the future."

With his essentially stable nature, Taft was sure that he would survive even in defeat—if that came to him.

XII. *November: The People Decide*

THE COLONEL RECEIVES THE VERDICT

As they did every four years, the people went to the polls on the first Tuesday after the first Monday in November, carrying with them their doubts and confusions. After months of charges and countercharges by the candidates, the voters had to rack their brains and make their choice.

How could they know the wisest thing to do? Their former President, Colonel Roosevelt, had bellowed day and night that they could not expect wise or decent government from the two old parties. Their President, Mr. Taft, had warned them that Roosevelt was consumed by the desire for power. Mr. Wilson showed scorn for "T.R." and Taft, and urged them to put their trust in him.

The experts in the newspapers predicted that a large number of their votes would go to Wilson, many votes to Roosevelt, and fewer votes to Taft. No one tried to estimate very closely how many votes would go to Eugene Debs, the tireless Socialist. Even in predicting a Wilson triumph, the experts hedged; no one could calculate how many votes Roosevelt might have gained after he was nearly assassinated.

The polls closed, and the candidates waited.

The Colonel, still walking around with the bullet in his chest because the surgeons had decided it would be dangerous to operate, seemed as buoyant as ever. But there was no gleam of expectation in his eyes. In his cool moments he was a realist.

Well, the fight was the thing. He had made a good one. The weary months of exhorting and gesticulating were finished, and he was glad of that. His sacrifice for the Progressive Party had been delivered with boundless generosity; the value of the sacrifice would be determined by the people in this election and in other elections to come.

As the first tabulations came in, Wilson's strength became obvious. The people wanted a progressive, but they preferred Wilson's brand to his. At 10:45 that night, Wilson's managers claimed victory for the Democratic nominee. Roosevelt waited for another hour, to be certain; then he conceded that Wilson would be the next occupant of the White House.

Shortly before midnight, the Colonel composed and sent off a telegram to Governor Wilson: "The American people by a great plurality have conferred upon you the highest honor in their gift. I congratulate you thereon." This was a routine message; it contained no warmth.

Wilson was not a man of his own breed. He did not understand Wilson very well; he had no personal liking for the Princeton scholar. He understood Taft, and he liked him. On this night when both of them were going down the dark tunnel of defeat, he wondered about Taft and how the old boy might be taking it.

He was not permanently angry at Taft. He could not stay angry at anybody. He struck hard blows, and he was willing to receive hard blows; still he did not hate his opponents. A Roosevelt did not hold a grudge for long.

Still he could not imagine Wilson as President. When he

had been in there himself, he had known how difficult it was to think of any other man occupying the job. Any other man would not fit in; any other man would not know where to find the keys.

Even though he had picked Taft and pushed the big fellow into office as his successor, he had felt uneasy when he had left the Executive Mansion. Yes, he had hurried away with an odd feeling of betrayal—a sense that he had betrayed the people by refusing to serve another term as their Chief Executive, their White Father, their scapegoat, their captive friend. He could have won again, he had enjoyed being President, and he was sure that the people had enjoyed having him there.

Now the image of the White House must be banished from his horizon. Now he must live for his family, for his hunting, for the books he had in mind, for the trips ahead, the voyages he wanted to take, the explorations of unknown jungles. He was still in his fifties, but now he was the Old Man of American politics.

The bullet in his chest reminded him of his mortality, of the sudden death that could strike a man who exposed himself to the fears and hostilities of the millions of frightened people in the world. The bullet itself didn't bother him; he had been ready for sudden death since his cowboy days, since his youth in the Badlands.

Telephone calls and messages came to him from his supporters. He was told that he had fought a magnificent fight; he was told that he had to hold the Progressive battalions together for the elections of 1914 and 1916. He had run second to Wilson and far ahead of Taft. This meant, to his followers, that the Progressive Party would survive and the G.O.P. would die.

He did not think so. He knew how hard it would be to hold a new party together without patronage, without jobs to offer and honors to give. The G.O.P. still had governors and senators, many congressional seats, and local organizations that had weathered many a hurricane. The G.O.P. would not die, but the Progressive Party probably would.

He did not say that publicly. His close associates sensed it in his attitude.

"I accept the result with entire good humor," Roosevelt said to the press. "As for the Progressive cause, I can only repeat . . . the cause in itself must triumph, for this triumph is essential to the well-being of the American people."

He had plenty to do. He had articles to write for *The Outlook*, lectures to prepare, meetings to attend. He had logs to chop for firewood at Sagamore Hill, boats to sail, races to run with the friends of his children. He had ideas to express, missions to fulfill. He could live fully without seeking public office again.

John Schrank, the man who had tried to kill the Colonel in mid-October, was arraigned in Milwaukee on November 12, a week after the election. When the judge asked whether he would plead guilty or not guilty, Schrank answered: "Why, guilty. I did not mean to kill a citizen, Judge; I shot Theodore Roosevelt, because he was a menace to the country. He should not have a third term. I did not want him to have one. I shot him as a warning that men must not try to have more than two terms as President."

Schrank's statements brought Roosevelt letters of friendship from many parts of the world. One came from Sir Edward Grey, the British Foreign Minister, expressing admiration for Roosevelt's coolness in the face of so much danger.

Roosevelt replied on November 15, saying that he was sure that Grey would have behaved better than he had under Schrank's pistol fire in Milwaukee: "You would have shown the absolute courage and coolness and lack of thought of self that your brother showed when mauled by the lions." (Grey's brother, on a hunting trip in Africa, had been severely injured by carnivores.)

He told Grey that he had made the speech with the bullet in his body for two reasons: "It has always seemed to me that the best way to die would be in doing something that ought to be done, whether leading a regiment or doing anything else. Moreover, I felt that under such circumstances it would be very difficult for people to disbelieve in my sincerity, and that therefore they would be apt to accept at face value the speech I wished to make, and which represented my deepest and most earnest convictions."

His courage under fire undoubtedly had drawn many voters to the Bull Moose banner. The Progressive Party had only been in existence for three months when the ballots were cast. Yet Roosevelt carried five states—Michigan, Minnesota, Pennsylvania, South Dakota, and Washington—and got eleven of the thirteen electoral votes from California. In the popular voting, he received 4,126,020, compared with 6,286,214, for Wilson and 3,483,922 for Taft.

The other candidates on the Progressive ticket—candidates for governor, Congress, and seats in state legislatures —ran far behind him. His party did not gain control of a single legislature, and won only a small number of seats in Congress.

To Roosevelt, the failure of the other Progressives was a sign that the party was not deeply rooted in American life. In spite of his declarations that the 1912 struggle was not a struggle to make him President but a battle to overthrow the forces of wealth and privilege, he did not find it difficult to conclude that the voters had been less excited about the Progressive platform than they had been about Theodore Roosevelt.

The Progressive platform had declared: "Behind the ostensible government sits enthroned an invisible government, owing no allegiance and acknowledging no responsibility to the people." Roosevelt believed that this statement was true. He felt that the people, in their confusion or folly, had not understood the significance of the election. He was sure that they would eventually see that a terrible mistake had been made.

Soon after the election, the behind-the-scenes conflict between the Pinchots and the Perkins-Munsey group broke into another savage quarrel. Perkins, as chairman of the Executive Committtee, was unwilling to admit that the Progressive Party was collapsing. Perkins summoned the leaders of the movement to meet in Chicago on December 10, to make plans for the future.

Amos Pinchot and other members of the radical wing welcomed this action because they saw an opportunity to drive Perkins from the chairmanship and to replace him with a man untainted by Wall Street connections. The Pinchots attempted to persuade Roosevelt that this was the only course to follow.

Roosevelt resisted their pressures, and countered by declaring that Perkins was just as good a Progressive as any man in the party. Roosevelt himself indicated plainly that he would not participate in any drastic reorganization. He blamed the party's defeat not on Perkins but on voters who had not responded to the message he and his colleagues had brought them.

MR. TAFT IS SHOCKED

A few days before the election, President Taft gave an exclusive interview to Louis Seibold of the New York *World*. Seibold had begged the President to get the full story of his feud with Roosevelt into the record before it was too late.

W. W. Mischler, Taft's confidential secretary, was present at the interview and prepared a transcript of Seibold's questions and Taft's answers. Seibold said that he would give the whole transcript to the Associated Press and other news agencies, in any form acceptable to Taft.

Some hours later, Seibold was invited to travel with the President by train to New York. Taft was going to the funeral of Vice-President Sherman in Utica and promised Seibold that he would go over the transcript and make it ready for the reporter on the train. But on the trip from Washington to New York, Taft changed his mind; he felt that he had been too harsh in his comments on Roosevelt and he refused to release the interview.

In the closing hours of the campaign Taft did not want to increase the hostility between Roosevelt and himself. Roosevelt had been his closest friend, and he hoped to resume the friendship some day without regard to all the accusations that had been exchanged between them.

He told a reporter: "I am in a philosophical state. I have had to be. The experience I have had in the Presidency has made me so, and what I am very hopeful is that whatever happens the country will go on to ultimate happiness. . . ."

However, the extent of the humiliation inflicted on him by the voters on November 5 shattered the "philosophical state" in which he had faced the election. He accepted the inevitability of his own defeat, but he was shocked by the number of votes given to Roosevelt and the number polled by Debs, the Socialist. He was horrified by the knowledge that there were nearly a million American voters willing to destroy the free-enterprise system.

In a White House memorandum Taft said that the totals for Roosevelt and Debs proved that propaganda for some basic changes in the American type of government had "formidable support." Only Utah and Vermont had remained true to the principles of the Republican Party

Roosevelt and the Bull Moose herd were still the real dangers to the country in Taft's eyes, even though the Colonel would not occupy the White House. The best way to counteract the spread of Progressive propaganda, Taft believed, would be to form a Constitutional Club to educate the people in constitutional principles. He said that the Club should have "money enough to circulate literature and also to employ lecturers and send them over the country, especially into our colleges and universities, to bring the youth and the professors down to earth, instead of allowing them to soar in the blue skies with their heads in the clouds." These ideas appealed to some of the conservative leaders of the nation, but did not lead immediately to the formation of such a club.

Taft received hundreds of letters of sympathy after his crushing repudiation at the polls. Some of these letters suggested that the American people had behaved badly, and were not to be trusted. Taft refused to share this feeling.

"The situation was most peculiar," he wrote to one of his disturbed correspondents. "I have no word of criticism for the people at large. I think a great many of them were misled by the misrepresentations contained in the muckraking press and in the magazines, and I must wait for years if I would be vindicated by the people. . . . I am content to wait."

In many ways Taft showed signs of being immensely relieved by being relieved of the heavy harness of the Presidency. He was sorry that Colonel Roosevelt had obtained more votes than he had; he was sorry to see the Democrats —an incompetent bunch, in his opinion—winning such a triumph; and he was very sorry for his wife, who loved being the First Lady of the land. But he himself felt rather buoyant and happy, once he got over the first shock of the anti-Taft avalanche.

Earlier, he had accepted an invitation to speak at the annual dinner of the Lotos Club in New York on November 16. He kept the engagement, and in his address there he spoke with the gentle humor, the lovable charm, the benign peacefulness that endeared him to many people.

His topic was "The President." He said it was an extremely powerful office, yet he had often been conscious of its frustrations and limitations. He suggested that the President should be elected for one term of six years, and that members of the cabinet should have seats in Congress so that better relations could be maintained between the executive and legislative branches of the government.

He also revealed his own attitude toward the White House: "The position is not a place to be enjoyed by a sensitive man. . . ." Presidents were subjected to so many unfounded accusations, Taft said, that they often fell into despair or became indifferent to "both just and unjust criticism."

"What are we to do with our ex-Presidents?" Taft inquired, smiling at the audience of distinguished guests. "I am not sure Dr. Osler's method of dealing with elderly men would not usefully apply to the treatment of ex-Presidents. The proper and scientific administration of a dose of chloroform or of the fruit of the lotos tree, and the reduction of the flesh of the thus quietly departed to ashes in a funeral pyre to satisfy the wishes of his friends and their families, might make a fitting end to the life of one who has held the highest office. I commend this method for consideration."

Taft declared that he was strongly opposed to a proposal made by William Jennings Bryan, suggesting that former Presidents should be given seats in the Senate. He thought the Senate had enough talkative members, and no more should be added.

Taft closed with a toast to Woodrow Wilson, asking his audience to join him in wishing good health and success to "the able, distinguished, and patriotic gentleman who is to be the next President of the United States." The diners cheered, and Taft sat down in a glow of happiness.

His first inclination, after he had been rejected by the voters, was to go back to Cincinnati and become a lawyer again. He had plenty of friends there, the city was expanding, and he felt that he could develop an excellent practice as a counsellor, choosing cases in which he might participate with propriety.

The multimillionaire steelmaker, Andrew Carnegie, an admirer of Taft because of his labors as President in the cause of international peace, announced that he was prepared to give a pension of $25,000 to ex-Presidents and their widows. Taft believed that Carnegie's intentions were noble, but the President wrote to one of his brothers, Horace Taft: "I can't take the pension for obvious reasons. . . . If you were an ex-president, [there would be] the feeling of embarrassment every time you met old Carnegie."

Taft himself had an annual income from investments of $8,000, and he had saved substantial amounts from his Presidential salary of $75,000 a year, since there was no income tax during his period in the White House. So he was pretty well off, although not wealthy.

The opportunity he really wanted—an offer of a university post—came to him from the place he loved best, the place where he had spent many of his happiest days—Yale. President Hadley asked him to become a professor at the Yale Law School.

"The proposition has some very attractive features about it," Taft declared in a letter to his brother Charles on November 20. "It is a dignified retirement, one which Cleveland had at Princeton, and one which would approve itself to the general sense of propriety of the country. . . . I submitted the matter to the cabinet yesterday, and they all thought it was an admirable suggestion."

The salary was only $5,000 a year—the top for a Yale professor in those days—but Taft was sure that he and Mrs. Taft could get along well financially, considering their private income. He wasn't itching to plunge into the competitive life of a lawyer in Cincinnati, when he came to think of it. He liked the quiet town of New Haven and the leisurely, placid pace of a professor's existence. And his position would give him opportunities to be a persistent advocate of constitutionalism and international peace—the two subjects closest to his heart.

His reaction against the doctrines of the Progressive Party pushed Taft farther and farther toward the conservative side on almost every question. When he had sought the Presidency in 1908, he had described himself as a progressive, determined to continue Roosevelt's policies. His administration had certainly been progressive in many fields, but Taft had now grown afraid of new ideas and "wild notions."

At Yale he planned to be a champion of the established values in American civilization. He would try to combat the radical professors who filled young men's minds with impractical ideas.

Like Roosevelt and Wilson, he was still in his fifties. Despite his excessive weight, he was in good health. As a public-spirited American, anxious to continue to be useful to his fellow men, he wanted to feel that he could serve the oncoming generations.

He had put aside the great dream of his life—his ambition to become Chief Justice of the Supreme Court. The possibility of attaining that place on the high bench seemed extremely remote.

THE HAND OF PROVIDENCE

In the small Cleveland Lane house in Princeton where he lived close to the university he had dominated for so many years, Wilson felt the hand of Providence upon him on the night of November 5. A few hours after the polls had closed, the bell of Old Nassau Hall alerted the campus. Then Wilson heard the tramping feet of students coming toward his house; he saw the red gleam of torches; he heard young voices singing:

> Tune every heart and every voice,
> Bid every care withdraw;

Let all with one accord rejoice,
In praise of Old Nassau.

Joe Tumulty, his round-faced secretary, had come running through the crowd of newspapermen on the porch, shouting: "He's elected, Mrs. Wilson!" And Wilson's wife had clasped the President-elect's hand, and she had offered him her radiant face, lighted with love and faith.

Certainly his mind went back to the time he had stood at his father's gateway as a boy of four, when he had listened to a man saying that Lincoln was elected and there would be war. Providence willing, there would be no war during his Presidency; if any war arose, he would spend his heart's blood to keep America free from it.

Certainly he thought of his father, the beautiful old man who had been proud that day in 1903 when he had been in-augurated as president of Princeton. He had brought his father into his home when the Reverend Dr. Wilson had suf-fered a final illness. He had tried to comfort the old man by singing the hymns his father loved, especially the one called "Crown Him with Many Crowns."

Perhaps his father knew what had happened on this elec-tion night; perhaps his father was aware that Woodrow Wil-son had been elected the next President of the United States. He hoped so; he prayed that his father might know.

The students surrounded the house where Wilson stood in his high moment of election. Tumulty and Dudley Field Malone, one of Wilson's close friends, dragged a rocking chair out onto the porch. While Malone and Tumulty held the arms of the chair, Wilson climbed up on it.

He steadied himself for a second. In the flickering crimson light of the torches everyone saw the tears in his eyes. Then his voice came—and it was clear and calm.

"I have no feeling of triumph tonight, but a feeling of solemn responsibility," Wilson said. "I know the very great task ahead of me and the men associated with me. I look almost with pleading to you, the young men of America, to stand behind me, to support me in the new administration."

The young men huzzaed and waved their torches. The ringing of the Nassau bell filled the air around them with waves of shuddering sound. Some of the newspapermen broke from the porch and rushed toward telephones.

While the students were chanting and marching around the house, a telegram came from William McCombs, the campaign manager: "You have won a splendid and significant victory. At this hour you appear to have received the largest electoral vote ever given to a Presidential candidate. The indications are that your administration will be supported by a Congress, Democratic in both branches." A little later the new Vice-President, Thomas R. Marshall, telegraphed: "I salute you—my chieftain—in all love and loyalty."

Wilson, his wife, and his daughters were inundated by a throng of well-wishers, a tidal wave of telegrams, a constant flow of telephone calls from all parts of the nation. It was long after midnight before Wilson's assistants could clear the house and give the exhausted family a chance to get some sleep.

The next day Wilson read enthusiastic editorials in the papers approving his election—and faced a series of new problems presented by hungry politicians who wanted jobs.

McCombs arrived in Princeton on November 6, carrying a list of suggested cabinet members and a roster of devoted Democrats who must be given, in his opinion, the "immediate and generous consideration" of the President-elect. McCombs acknowledged Wilson's right to appoint his own secretary and "other members of your confidential staff," but he thought Wilson had to consult the National Committee "as to members of the cabinet and heads of other departments and bureaus."

More than 15,000 letters and telegrams descended upon Wilson in the first few days after the voting. Many of these communications asked for jobs, for assistance of varying natures, for charity, for advice, for recognition in one form or another. Politicians hurried to Princeton, to tell Wilson of all the things they had done for him in the campaign.

The President-elect kept his balance. On November 7 he told the press that he would not make any positive decisions for a while. He informed the reporters: "It will be perfectly useless to resort to me for corroboration of any report. No announcement will have the least authority which is not made over my signature."

Correspondents who had found Wilson easily accessible as governor of New Jersey now noted a change in him. He did not go for long walks with reporters on the banks of the Trenton River, as he had done in other months. He withdrew into himself, meditating on his position as the first liberal Democratic President since Thomas Jefferson.

Since the Civil War the federal government had principally represented the economic interests of financiers and industrialists. The Democratic Party under Grover Cleveland had reflected the demands of these groups, and had not attempted to do more than the Republicans had done. Now Wilson faced the prospect of taking office as the spokesman for the "New Freedom"—the program designed to liberate Americans from the rule of big business. All the hopes and yearnings of the Populists and the Bryanities focused on him.

A week after the election, Wilson announced that he would call a special session of Congress to begin around April 15. At this session he would call upon the Democratic majorities in the House and the Senate to carry out the pledges of tariff reform and other promises made in the Democratic platform.

On November 16 Wilson sailed for Bermuda with his

family, a single secretary, and a group of Secret Service men. The secretary, Charles Swem, had won prizes for taking rapid dictation, and Wilson used him to catch up on the thousands of letters he had to write as President-elect. He also had with him a bundle of communications from Colonel House, the wealthy Texan whose sensitivity and intelligence had gained Wilson's respect. House eventually became his closest friend and adviser.

He exchanged letters frequently with Bryan, House, McAdoo, and others who sent him information and suggestions. Many people urged him to put Bryan in his cabinet, in recognition of the Commoner's long service to the Democratic Party. Other leading Democrats, who had opposed the Nebraskan but supported Wilson, vehemently expressed their antagonism whenever Bryan was discussed. Bryan did not attempt to push his own cause; in fact, Bryan said appointments should not be made on the basis of service to the party. Wilson admired the man for that unselfish attitude. He read the letters sent to him, walked on the beach, had quiet evenings with his wife and daughters. The British residents of the island respected his privacy, although they were enormously curious about "the professor" who was about to become the Chief Executive of that unpredictable nation, the United States.

The four weeks in the English atmosphere of the island were described by Wilson as "four weeks of unmixed blessing." He felt that his stay there had "cleared the mind and set the spirit free."

Wilson could not decide what to do about tariff reform, how to improve the banking and currency system to prevent periodic panics, how to regulate the corporations without destroying "free enterprise," how to preserve the laboring man's right to work and right to strike, and how to bring down the costs of living. Those were problems Roosevelt and Taft had failed to solve before him. He did not really know whether he could apply his ideals and his principles to these practical problems—but he meant to try.

Toward the end of his Bermuda visit, a restive attitude toward Wilson appeared in some of the conservative American newspapers. These publications reported that business leaders could see another panic on the horizon if he went too far with his progressive ideas. Veiled warnings were given to the President-elect; he was told that he had to be careful —or a panic might be produced, to show the country the dangers of having a wild-eyed President.

Not shaken by these warnings, Wilson went on writing and thinking, planning and preparing for the day when he would take office. If a crisis came, he would meet it with confidence in his own gifts and the guidance of God.

WAR IN THE BALKANS: CARNEGIE GIVES AWAY A FORTUNE

In addition to Wilson's election, the major events in November were the spreading of a war in the Balkans and Andrew Carnegie's announcement that he was giving away the bulk of his fortune.

The capture of Salonika in Turkey by the Greek army and the fiery destruction rained on Adrianople by bombs hurled from airplanes made large headlines in the leading American newspapers—but most Americans couldn't get deeply interested in the Balkan fighting between the Greeks and Turks.

Carnegie's decision to endow a huge philanthropic foundation with the millions he had obtained from his steel mills stirred editorials and caused a ripple of excitement—and then the excitement quickly faded. The press and the people concentrated on speculations about what Woodrow Wilson would do.

THE COLONEL REFUSES TO BE "TOO RADICAL"

At the Chicago conference of the Progressive Party leaders on December 10, the showdown came on what course the party should pursue in the months and years ahead. The question was: should the party move to the left or the right?

The liberals—the Pinchots, Harold Ickes, Raymond Robins, Joseph Medill McCormick, Charles Merriam, Hiram Johnson, Ben Lindsey, and others—blazed at George Perkins as the symbol of reaction and a block to progress. Despite Roosevelt's stubborn defense of Perkins, they resumed their efforts to get him removed from the chairmanship of the party's Executive Committee.

The men who launched the drive against Perkins were men who stood high in Roosevelt's respect. Gifford Pinchot, head of the Forestry Service during Roosevelt's Presidency, was regarded by the Colonel as the finest public servant in the United States. Amos Pinchot irritated the Colonel, but was known to be a man of rare integrity. Ickes, who later became one of the architects of Franklin D. Roosevelt's New Deal,

279

had served in Illinois as chairman of the Cook County committee of the Progressive Party.

Medill McCormick, publisher of the Chicago *Daily Tribune,* felt that the Pinchots were right in seeking to remove Perkins, but was doubtful about their tactics. McCormick and Robins, a Chicago civic leader, did not favor direct attacks on Perkins. They were willing to let him remain on the Executive Committee, or to permit him to keep the chairmanship if the real executive power could be transferred elsewhere.

Soon after Amos Pinchot arrived in Chicago, a group of Progressives who sought harmony at almost any cost called upon Pinchot in the La Salle Hotel. These Progressives—led by Senator Joseph Dixon of Montana, the head of the 1912 campaign committee, and Oscar Straus, who had served as secretary of commerce and labor under Roosevelt—felt that an open assault on Perkins would tear the party to pieces.

Amos Pinchot said that his principal objective was to get the platform section upholding the Sherman Anti-Trust Act restored to the official records. He insisted that he did not intend to make a public demand for the removal of Perkins, even though he believed that such action might be the only way to establish public confidence in the liberal nature of the Progressive movement. He wanted it to be truly "a party of the people" in the tradition of Lincoln.

The Colonel refused to see Pinchot. But Senator Dixon hurried to the Colonel's room for a private talk before the conference of party leaders got under way in the hotel ballroom. When the meeting began, Dixon stepped to the platform. Dixon announced that a part of the platform containing an endorsement of the Sherman Act had been inadvertently omitted from printed publications. If no one objected, the senator said, he could consider it "the will of the conference that it should be incorporated in future printings."

After that, Amos Pinchot temporarily abandoned his struggle to get Perkins deposed from the chairmanship of the Executive Committee. Amos had found that only his brother Gifford was eager to join him in an all-out fight.

The Colonel persuaded most of the party leaders that the correct course in the future was to be radical, but not "too radical." Roosevelt thought that Perkins would have to get out of the party completely if he were forced from the chairmanship; and the Colonel did not want Perkins to get out. Perkins was an honest man, and he was willing to raise the money needed to keep the party alive.

"The reason that you quote Lincoln with such admiration now is because he succeeded," Roosevelt told Amos. "His success was in large part because he declined to submit for one moment to the constant proposals to rule out the Perkinses, the Munseys, the Flinns, the Wilkinsons of his day and generation who were in the Republican Party."

Roosevelt compared Amos Pinchot and those allied with him to the recalcitrants of Lincoln's time who "did their best to alienate the moderate men without whom the Union could not have been preserved nor slavery abolished." His anger rising, the Colonel declared: "In my judgment every man who now gives any encouragement to our foes by inciting war among ourselves is simply rendering aid to the reactionary elements in this nation. He is acting precisely as the well-meaning extremists acted who in 1864 tried to break up the then Progressive Party, the Lincoln Republican Party. . . .

"I need not say that I feel that the Progressive Party must be the radical party," the Colonel added. "We have no excuse for existing excepting as the radical party; but I want to keep it as the party of sane and tempered radicalism such as that of Abraham Lincoln."

So the Colonel rode off in December of 1912, bestriding two horses—the horse of "tempered radicalism" and the horse of friendship with wealthy corporation owners—and heading in two directions at once: the direction of active leadership and the direction of withdrawal from the company of some of his old associates who had followed him most bravely. He was in great haste to settle the affairs of the Progressive Party.

Perhaps his strange ways, his twists and turns, were accounted for by the speed with which he moved, by the fact that he was so often in such a hurry to push the past behind him.

Then, too, he did not relish the social isolation in which he found himself. The phone seldom rang at Sagamore Hill. His Long Island neighbors were cool to him. Many of them regarded him as a renegade; he was a man who had "turned against his class." They did not wish to take him back into their circles until he had been properly chastened.

When he went to Boston to attend a meeting of the Harvard overseers, his fellow Harvard men bunched together at one end of the room away from him. Only one man spoke cordially to him. He felt unspeakably lonely, rejected by his own kind.

So he sought strenuously to remove the taint of excessive radicalism which kept him from his old companions.

MR. TAFT PREPARES TO BECOME A PROFESSOR

In the last month of the year, in the final phase of his service as President, Taft continued along the smooth White House channel he had worn for himself, unhurried and unwilling to be upset about all the urgent messages concerning the civil war in Mexico, the tariff laws, the civil service, and the other problems that confronted a Chief Executive.

In those days a "lame duck" Congress convened in December. Senators and representatives who had been defeated in the November elections still could make mischief or pass laws unacceptable to the President. Taft sent his regular report to the Congress and several special notes, but did not push the legislators very hard about anything.

He made a swift voyage of inspection to Panama late in December, to see how the construction of the canal was progressing. When he returned to Washington, he resumed his preparations for the transition from his administration to the new one.

Realizing that President-elect Wilson would probably want to know his opinions of the housekeeper, the cooks, the major-domo, and all the staff, Taft made careful notes for future recommendations. He was not a difficult man to please, and he gave generous estimates of all the employees.

As the day of his liberation approached, Taft felt more and more relieved. He was glad to be escaping from the White House with the nation at peace and the government in good order.

When a friend tried to tell him that he might be the Republican candidate again in 1916, Taft brushed the idea aside. "I do not share with you the view that there is any probability of my being selected as a candidate for the Republicans at the end of four years," he wrote.

"I have proven to be a burdensome leader and not one that aroused the multitude, not one that was calculated to lead on to victory in a close contest. I am entirely content to serve in the ranks."

Actually, Taft was suddenly rather popular. He had taken his defeat with savoir-faire. His post-election speeches, mildly humorous and poking fun at himself, had been well received. People thought of him as a good sport, a big man with a generous sense of humor.

His acceptance of the Yale Law School professorship had been greeted with virtually unanimous approval. It was a dignified job at a fine university. A former President could use his talents there and speak freely. And Taft would be completely removed from the commercial atmosphere of a Cincinnati law practice.

Everyone knew that he wouldn't be making much of a salary. Everyone was suddenly conscious of the enormous gap between the cultural prestige of a professor at Yale and the amount of money paid to such a man. Nearly everyone felt that Taft was doing a rather noble thing.

And he himself was delighted to be going back to New Haven. He kept looking over his law books, remembering his days as a federal judge, thinking of the cases he could cite to his students. He loved the buildings and the spacious grounds of Yale. He loved the friends he had made during his years as an undergraduate—friends who had rallied to him a number of times when other people had treated him coldly.

As a student, he had been a Big Man on the Campus. As a professor with the Presidency behind him, he would be a Big Man again—not merely in physical size, but in reputation as well.

The new generation would listen to him, he thought. He might be able to save some of the better students from falling into the traps of radical propaganda. He might be able to communicate to them his own sense of the sacred nature of American institutions, the traditions of the law, the mighty essence of the Constitution into which the Founding Fathers had poured their wisdom.

He made resolutions to work harder than he had ever done before. He knew that he was inclined to procrastinate, to avoid exhausting study and hard thinking, to enjoy dinners and parties more than he should. He was going to turn over a new leaf; he was going to be the most industrious professor on the Yale faculty.

In fact, Taft could scarcely wait for the day when he could relinquish the powers and duties of the Presidential office to Woodrow Wilson.

During December Wilson discovered the painful predicament in which the voters and the Constitution had placed him. The people and the politicians treated him as though he already had power to deal with their problems; the press watched his movements, discussed his visitors, floated rumors about his plans. Businessmen still muttered grimly about an approaching panic.

In those days the change in administrations after a Presidential election did not come until March 4 of the following year. So during the four months after the election the outgoing Chief Executive possessed legal powers which he was reluctant to exercise. And the incoming executive had no actual powers, although everyone's attention was centered upon him.

At times Wilson must have wondered why he had left the academic life Taft was about to enter. He was trying to be both governor of New Jersey and President-elect of the United States, and nobody tried to make things easy for him. He did not make things easy for himself; he set almost impossible standards for Woodrow Wilson. He was determined that he would not compromise in these early weeks of his great opportunity.

McCombs and other advisers had met him at the dock on December 16 when his steamer arrived from Bermuda. He faced trouble in New Jersey and danger from Wall Street. The corporation lobbyists and their political henchmen expected him to resign from the New Jersey governorship without trying to push through anti-trust regulations. Some Wall Street manipulators were planning to depress the stock market, to make it appear that American investors feared the incoming administration.

His advisers, as usual, were divided. Some urged him to be bold, to hit hard at his enemies. Others urged him to go slowly, to move gingerly, to hold his fire until he was in the White House.

Full of new energy after his Bermuda sojourn, Wilson would not heed the counsels of caution. On the night of the 17th, one day after his feet had touched American shores, he hurled some thunderbolts.

He was the guest of honor at a dinner given by the Southern Society at the Waldorf-Astoria. He was saluted happily, and received salvos of cheers. Then, knowing that he had a receptive audience, he departed from the text of the address he had written.

"People make all sorts of sinister predictions as to the trouble we are going to get into down at Washington," Wilson said. "They say that business is going to be disturbed by the changes which are going to be undertaken by the Democratic Party in the economic policy of the country."

Wilson looked around the room. He lifted his head. "Business cannot be disturbed unless the minds of those who conduct it are disturbed. A panic is . . . merely a state of mind, because obviously when a panic occurs there is just as much wealth in the country the day after the panic as the day before. Nothing in material circumstances has changed, but the whole state of mind of the financial community has changed. They dare not part with their money. They call in their loans. They are excited, and they do not always know exactly why."

He glanced quickly at the reporters below him. "That is a natural panic, but you know there are unnatural panics, and sometimes panics are said to occur because certain gentlemen want to create the impression that the wrong thing is going to be done."

His long, lean face grew stern. Then he said grimly: "Frankly I do not believe there is any man living at the present moment who dares use that machinery for that purpose. If he does, I promise him, not for myself but for my countrymen, a gibbet as high as Haman!" (Haman, a Persian courtier, attempted to obtain a massacre of the Jews in Persia, but was hanged on the gallows he had caused to be built for Mordecai.)

Heavy applause came from all parts of the banquet room, but some of the older men and women in the audience shook their heads ruefully. Some of Wilson's timid friends thought he had gone too far. In attempting to avert a panic, he might bring one on.

The next day the New York *Sun*—a conservative paper consistently against Wilson—carried a cartoon depicting the President-elect as "Lord High Executioner Wilson" with a gibbet in the background. The caption read: "The New Gallows-Freedom"—ridiculing Wilson's campaign references to "the New Freedom" he hoped to establish in America. Some other papers were also critical, but the general response to his bold words was favorable; the people felt that he was going to be a President who could not be intimidated.

Four days after his address to the Southern Society, Wilson had to decide what to do with William Jennings Bryan. He knew that Bryan had no experience as a diplomat or as an administrator, and yet Bryan was a former Presidential candidate, a man internationally known, a man who could not be offered a minor position.

At lunch on December 21, after trying to interest Bryan in becoming the U.S. Ambassador to Russia, Wilson took the plunge—he offered Bryan the position of secretary of state. And Bryan accepted with gratitude and joy. The Commoner was passionately dedicated to the maintenance of world peace, and felt that in his new post he might make a contribution to international amity.

Wilson had also decided to appoint William Gibbs Mc-Adoo the secretary of the treasury, and told Bryan of his plan. This was a position William McCombs had coveted, but Wilson felt McCombs was not the kind of man he wanted in his official family. McCombs had labored faithfully to get Wilson to the Presidency, and Wilson appreciated the man's efforts. Still, he could not give a man one of the highest places in the government simply as a reward if the man lacked some essential qualities.

Although he was conscious of Bryan's defects, Wilson was able to convince himself that Bryan had enough talents and strong traits of character to compensate for his lack of experience. He insisted that the appointment was not a political reward, and stressed Bryan's qualifications—natural eloquence, keen interest in foreign affairs, and years of study of the problems the United States faced.

Next came the question of a place for Louis Brandeis, the brilliant lawyer who had helped him so much in thinking out his speeches on competition and federal regulation of giant corporations. Wilson realized that Brandeis was well qualified to be attorney general or secretary of commerce. However, Brandeis had made enemies among wealthy and influential people and among some of the faculty members at Harvard. Brandeis' biting wit and incisive mind, as well as his Jewish faith, had stirred up implacable hostility.

"The best men here, men of affairs as well as lawyers, all of whom voted for you or President Taft will regard the appointment of Mr. Brandeis as a member of your cabinet, should it be made, with profound regret," wrote James Ford Rhodes, the historian, in a letter sent to Wilson from Boston December 19.

Whether or not Wilson gave much weight to this letter or the others he received, the opposition to Brandeis did succeed in making him waver. And he finally passed Brandeis over—to the disappointment and disgust of some of the liberals and intellectuals who had supported him. (Several years later, of course, Wilson placed Brandeis on the Supreme Court and fought for him through a storm of opposition.)

Preparing to enter the Presidency, Wilson was aggressive most of the time and cautious on the few occasions when he listened to his conservative advisers. Colonel House, now his intimate friend, was inclined to recommend appointments and policies to give the Wilson administration a "well-balanced" flavor—and Wilson often paid heed to House. House himself, however, was often shocked by Wilson's sudden displays of daring.

Then, wearied by the conflicts over cabinet jobs and policies being urged upon him, Wilson accepted with pleasure an invitation to celebrate his fifty-sixth birthday on December 28 in his native town—Staunton, Virginia. It opened a path of escape from the fights in which he was engaged. (He had refused to resign from the New Jersey governorship, and was hammering together a series of anti-trust measures which he planned to submit to the legislature when it assembled in January.)

The journey to Staunton was a joyful one. At every railroad station there were cheering crowds. When he crossed the border of Virginia, he was showered with flowers and songs. Students at the University of Virginia in Charlottesville, his law school, gave him a series of salutes.

When Wilson, his wife, and a group of his associates reached Staunton, torchlights were lifted in the air, a military escort surrounded them, and a band played "Home, Sweet Home." As guests of the Reverend Dr. A. M. Fraser, the Presbyterian minister, they were escorted to the Presbyterian manse on the hill—Wilson's birthplace.

Dr. Fraser gave a graceful greeting to the President-elect.

"He went out from us as a very little boy, laden with the prayers and benedictions of a small congregation of Christian people," the minister said. "He comes back to us today, by the favor of an over-ruling Providence, a proven leader of men, wearing the plaudits of the whole civilized world, and chosen to fill the highest civil office ever given to a man by the suffrages of his fellow men."

Wilson responded with humility and deep appreciation for the warm reception he had received. He was in top form when he spoke at the Mary Baldwin Seminary for girls, which had taken over the old church of which his father had been pastor. Wilson had been baptized in this church.

"I stood in the place where I am now standing when I was a student of law in the university at Charlottesville," Wilson said. "I had the very singular good fortune of having five cousins studying at this seminary. I was very fond of those cousins, and I paid them many attentions, and there were numbers of my confreres at the university who accompanied me—out of courtesy—on my visits. And on one occasion when I brought a somewhat numerous company of friends to the spot upon which I am now standing, I remember the great embarrassment with which I submitted to the cross-examination which preceded my entrance at these portals. I have, therefore, not always been welcomed to this spot with open arms."

Then Wilson grew serious. He talked about the new ideals, the new duties of the country. He declared: "My friends, we are clearly entered into a new age. The one thing that the businessmen of the United States are now discovering, some of them for themselves, and some of them by suggestion, is that they are not going to be allowed to make any money except for a *quid pro quo,* that they must render a service or get nothing. . . . 'Are you giving anything to society when you want to take something out of society?' . . . I want to proclaim for my fellow citizens this gospel for the future, that the men who serve will be the men who profit."

His statements made some people wonder whether Wilson had missed his calling. He sounded like a preacher in a pulpit, not like a politician on the verge of becoming President. Cynics across the country scoffed at him.

But his words struck sparks in many places. No one could doubt that he believed in his own gospel. No one could doubt that he meant to apply the principles of Christianity, as he understood those principles, in the struggles ahead.

"This is not a rosewater affair," he warned, referring to the Presidency. "This is an office in which a man must put on his war paint. . . . And there must be some good hard fighting, not only in the next four years, but in the next generation, in order that we may achieve the things that we have set out to achieve."

Over and over, in his campaign and in the weeks after his election, he had told the people what he wanted to achieve with them.

In September in Scranton he had said: "I am fighting, not for the man who has made good, but for the man who is going to make good—the man who is knocking and fighting at the closed doors of opportunity."

In the first week of October in Denver he said: "This is a second struggle for emancipation. If America is not to have free enterprise, then she can have freedom of no sort whatever."

On December 17 in New York he had declared: "A nation is not made of anything physical. A nation is made of its thoughts and its purposes. Nothing can give it dignity except its thoughts. Nothing can give it impulse except its ideals."

For America he wanted not only a rich life, a prosperous life, but a good life—a life of the spirit, reaching upward for full comprehension of man's high destiny.

"We stand in the presence of an awakened nation," Wilson had said in the heat of August, on the day so long ago and far away, on the day when he had accepted his nomination for the Presidency. And the people on the lawn outside the old house at Sea Girt, the men with their straw hats on the backs of their heads and the women with their parasols shading them from the sun, had given him their admiration and their confidence.

"The tonic of such a time is very exhilarating," he had said on that day, with the murmur of the sea behind him. And the faces before him had gleamed with exhilaration. He was their champion. He could not fail. He could not lose.

As he returned from Virginia in the last days of December, in the final days of 1912, Wilson felt the awakened nation behind him. More than ninety million strong, the people were ready to move. He would lead them toward the Promised Land.

XIV. *The Mission of America, Then and Now*

To most of the people in the United States and to most of the observers in other countries who watched and weighed events in America, 1912 was a year of big promises—a year in which millions of Americans looked to a new leader, expecting him to fulfill their desires for quick and rather painless progress.

Theodore Roosevelt, William Howard Taft, and their cohorts passed to the sidelines. Wilson and the New Men—Brandeis and other professors with ideas for expanding the currency, changing the banking system, ripping the tariff laws apart—were expected to transform the economic life of the country.

At the same time the Wilson brand of reform was counted upon to stabilize things—to ward off the really revolutionary threat of Eugene Debs and the Socialists, to keep the familiar institutions of government in steady operation, and to hold the nation on an even keel. Most Americans still held to their belief that everything would work out all right. In 1912 their faith was not severely shaken by strikes and riots or the fiery speeches of radicals.

Most Americans were impatient to do the job Edison had placed before them as the national mission—"to start to make this world over"—yet they wanted the start of the big transformation to be smooth and gradual.

A true American believed that science and industry could achieve limitless progress in the material world—longer life, better working conditions, bigger and better schools, the eventual abolition of poverty.

A true American felt that the growth of giant corporations could be checked without damaging the free-enterprise system.

A true American felt that the United States could continue to develop along its own lines, without being too much affected by what went on in other countries beyond the oceans.

In 1912 millions of Americans lived with these ideas. They heard that the Chinese Empire had crumbled; they knew vaguely that the Turkish Empire was collapsing; they had a notion of the naval race between Britain and Germany because they saw pictures of new British and German battleships in their papers, and they realized that the French had an armada of flying machines and a city in Turkey had been bombed from the air. Yet America was so vast, so strong, so protected on every side, that the turmoil in the world could not come too close.

The possibility of a European war—or at least a war between Germany and England—was talked about occasionally. Yet if such a war occurred, America would keep out. It was preposterous to think that the United States could be drawn into Europe's old quarrels.

There might be fighting in Mexico or Cuba or in the South American countries where the Latins were hot-tempered, as everybody knew. But the Marines and the navy could take care of any difficulties that might arise south of the U.S. borders.

That was the mood of America in 1912. That was the way most Americans looked at things as the year of the Bull Moose and the call for New Freedom became a page in the American record, a part of the American heritage.

AS IT LOOKS NOW

Now in the seventh decade of the twentieth century, as the world spins into the rocketing days of the 1960's, the drums of 1912 are still rolling—and the challenges of that year have led to the harder challenges we face in our time.

Under Wilson's banner the American people set forth bravely to make the world safe for democracy. Wilson could not keep the country out of World War I. After years of blood and bitterness, Wilson failed to make the League of Nations the instrument of peace he had dreamed of creating. In his two terms as President he did much to transform America and the world—but the results were not what he anticipated.

His first election in 1912 was followed by ratification of a constitutional amendment permitting Congress to impose a federal income tax. That tax opened up enormous sources of federal revenue. Responding to the people's demands, the government expanded in a thousand ways. It is still expanding, still seeking to fulfill the big promises made to the people.

Wilson's victory led to the Federal Reserve Act, the establishment of a Federal Trade Commission to regulate business, the Clayton Anti-Trust Act, the spending of millions for agricultural and vocational education, and dozens of other measures. An active leader in the government under Wilson was Franklin D. Roosevelt, who later extended the New Freedom into the New Deal when another crisis struck the nation in 1932.

"America will insist upon recovering in practice those ideals which she has always professed," said Woodrow Wilson.

And America has been trying to do that in a stumbling, half-eager, half-reluctant manner ever since 1912—with detours into blind alleys and side roads, with occasional spasms of revulsion against the whole effort to build a better society and a better world.

The sense of a National Mission has been lost—and we are seeking to recover it.

Yet we know that science and technology have not brought us to the Promised Land the people sought in 1912.

We know that corruption may be exposed again and again —and still continue to thrive with malignant strength.

We know that we have not found the knowledge to control or even to understand the enormous institutions which have developed around us and pulled us into their vortices of power.

Now we have a terrible doubt about what to do with the giant corporations, the giant labor unions, the giant government, the giant pressure groups to which we belong and with which we must deal.

Now we feel the truth of what Wilson said in that tremendous year of political struggle: "Most men are individuals no longer as far as their business, its activities, or its moralities is concerned. They are not units but fractions. . . . They must do what they are told to do, or lose their connection with modern affairs. They are mere cogs in a machine which has men for its parts."

In that same year, seeing the shape of the future in one of his moments of vision, Theodore Roosevelt said: "We, here in America, hold in our hands the hope of the world, the fate of the coming years; and shame and disgrace will be ours if in our eyes the light of high resolve is dimmed, if we trail in the dust the golden hopes of men."

If Roosevelt had won in 1912, the nation would probably have taken a course very similar to the course taken under Wilson. Both men felt that the government had to play a wide and creative role in American life. Roosevelt might have moved faster than Wilson, but the results would have been much the same.

Roosevelt, Wilson, and Taft thought that America's future was clearly certain to be one of vigorous power in the world. Now America has power, but seems uncertain how it should be used.

China has gone Communist—and the sacrifices of ten thousand American missionaries, the gifts of millions of Americans, have gone down into the turbulence of bloody change. Cuba has defied us. Governments in other lands have grown hostile or indifferent to America's voice.

The times call for a leader, as the times called in 1912. The people are still searching, still seeking the fulfillment of the big promises of American life.

Index

Sullivan, Roger, 57, 92, 172–173
Sulzer, William, 162, 258
Sun Yat-Sen, 66
Sweden, 86
Swem, Charles, 277

Taft, Alphonso, 12, 14
Taft, Charles P., 11–12, 14, 120, 272
Taft, Helen (Nellie), 8–11 *passim*, 13, 14–15, 19, 272
Taft, Henry, 241
Taft, Horace, 115–116, 117, 240, 262, 272
Taft, Robert A., 86
Taft, William Howard, 7, 8–21; as Civil Governor in Philippines, 8, 11, 14–15; as federal judge, 11, 13; as Secretary of War, 11, 15, 122; as solicitor general, 11, 13; as assistant Prosecuting Attorney, 13; relationship with T. Roosevelt, 15, 121–125, 264; Roosevelt on, 28–31, 68, 75–76, 95–104, 115–118, 232–234, 238; pre-convention period, 59–64, 84–89, 132; on Mexico, 67; anti-trust activities, 68; on T. Roosevelt, 88–89, 95–96; on primary system, 106–107; in Republican primaries, 115–119, 123–125; attitude toward woman suffrage, 126; at convention, 129–130, 135–144; and Republican National Committee, 130–134; attitudes toward Negroes, 138–139; campaign, 187–194, 239–242, 259–262; nomination acceptance speech, 188; supporters of, 203, 209; reaction to attempted assassination of Roosevelt, 246; reaction to Wilson's election, 268–273; post-election activities, 282–283; professorship at Yale, 283–284

Tammany Hall: and 1912 primary election, 106, 109; and Democratic National Convention, 146, 147, 156, 159, 163, 167; during 1912 elections, 222, 249
Tariff Board, report of, 84
tariffs, question of, 45, 84–85, 101, 184, 211, 226, 261, 277
Taussig, Frank, 84–85
Taylor, R. H., 261
telephone and telegraph companies, 185
Tennessee Coal, Iron & Railroad Company, 228
"Tennis Cabinet," 32
Texas, Democratic convention in, 113
textile workers, 54, 63, 77
Thomas, Augustus, 258
Titanic, 1, 90, 128
trade unions, *see* labor unions
Trevelyan, George Otto, 96
Tribe of Ben Hur, 2
trusts, question of, 18, 31, 45, 68, 71, 127–128, 185, 191, 200–201, 207–208, 214–215, 218–220, 225–226, 228–230, 235–238, 251, 256, 257, 260–261, 277, 285, 289
Tumulty, Joseph, 148, 254, 274
Turkey, 64, 67, 217, 278, 294
25th U.S. Infantry, Colored, 138

Underwood, Oscar, 41, 94, 108, 146, 149, 160, 162, 166, 169, 172, 173, 182, 258
unemployment, 123, 127
unemployment insurance, 127
Union League Clubs, 77
Union Pacific Railroad, 68
United Ancient Druids, 2
United States Steel Corporation, 65, 74, 226, 228, 251
"unit rule," 154–155

Van Hise, Charles, 183
Vardaman, James K., 159–160
Vatican, 241